STAN BREIN

Clinician's

Handbook of

Childhood

Psychopathology

Clinician's
Handbook of
Childhood
Psychopathology

edited by

Martin M. Josephson, M.D.

and

Robert T. Porter, M.D.

𝒜

NEW YORK • JASON ARONSON • LONDON

This book is dedicated with warm affection to Abram Blau, M.D., who served as chief of child psychiatry at the Mount Sinai Hospital for a quarter of a century. Out of his devotion to children he has been a leader in extending services, encouraging scholarly research, and raising standards of training in our field.

PREFACE

This book addresses itself to the principal clinical syndromes and problems encountered in child psychiatry, most of which are not widely met with in the same forms in adult psychiatry. It grew out of a series of presentations for adult psychiatry fellows by the child psychiatry staff at the Mount Sinai School of Medicine. The first year this was undertaken, before these talks were given to the follows they were first presented in the child psychiatry conferences for the reactions and suggestions of the whole staff. The material has undergone continual refinement related to the responses of the fellows, and giving the course each year also occasions updating of the bibliographies on each topic.

Finding and sorting out the better contributions on each topic, and presenting a balanced summary of the intelligent current views became a major goal. Another was to offer useful guides to diagnosis and therapy. At the publisher's suggestion, especially useful references have been annotated in the bibliographies. If brevity is a virtue in a handbook, so is some guidance to good sources for those wishing more in-depth information on given topics. Definition of terms and clarification of concepts have also seemed important. Although we have attempted to indicate most of the responsible approaches to issues (an "eclectic" view), we have had as an organizational principle the developmental approach to the growth of the child—in his family, school, and community—including the special developmental difficulties which may ensue where a child suffers handicaps or traumatic experiences. The classification of disorders in childhood is a fluid one. This represents advances in research and changing historical perspectives on diagnosis and nosology. Naturally there can be no unanimity here, and we have respected the viewpoints of our contributors.

While stemming from instruction of psychiatrists in training, we have sought to address the book to a far larger audience of mental health professionals. We have also tried to have as an overriding concern the ways in which current knowledge may have clinical value in prevention and/or early corrective intervention in behalf of troubled children and their families.

We want to thank International Universities Press and Ray E. Helfer, M.D. for permission to reproduce material published by them.

We also wish to express our appreciation to the following faculty members of the Mount Sinai School of Medicine for the encouragement and support given us in the preparation of this book: Marvin Stein, M.D., Esther and Joseph Klingenstein, Professor of Psychiatry and Chairman of the Department; Mortimer J. Blumenthal, M.D., Associate Clinical Professor of Psychiatry; and George E. Gross, M.D., Associate Clinical Professor of Psychiatry.

In the careful preparation of the manuscripts we are especially grateful to Mary Carter and Louise Chapman. Dr. Jason Aronson and his editors, Michael Farrin and John G. Simmons, have been consistently helpful in our mutual efforts to produce an informative and well-organized book for those with an interest in the mental health of children.

Most of all, we are indebted to our contributors for their scholarly diligence and cooperative spirit.

CONTENTS

Part I
Infantile Psychoses and Early Onset Pathology   1

Part II

Pathologies of Childhood 83

Part III
Neurologically Based and Allied Conditions 261

Part IV
Psychopathology in A Social Frame 349

CONTRIBUTORS

Alan M. Aron, M.D.

Associate Clinical professor of Neurology and Pediatrics, Mount Sinai School of Medicine

Arnold R. Cohen, M.D.

Assistant Clinical Professor of Psychiatry, Mount Sinai School of Medicine

Roberto M. DePaula, M.D.

Clinical Instructor in Psychiatry, Mount Sinai School of Medicine

Alan J. Frisch, M.D.

Senior Clinical Instructor in Psychiatry, Mount Sinai School of Medicine

Ruth R. Fuchs, M.D.

Senior Clinical Instructor in Psychiatry, Mount Sinai School of Medicine

Desmond Heath, M.B.B.Ch.

Senior Clinical Instructor in Psychiatry, Mount Sinai School of Medicine

Richard K. Hill, M.D.

Clinical Assistant Professor of Psychiatry, Cornell University Medical School

Jesse M. Hilsen, M.D.

Senior Clinical Instructor in Psychiatry, Mount Sinai School of Medicine

Leon Hoffman, M.D.
Assistant Clinical Professor of Psychiatry, Mount Sinai School of Medicine

Martin M. Josephson, M.D.
Assistant Clinical Professor of Psychiatry, Mount Sinai School of Medicine

Ruth K. Karush, M.D.
Clinical Instructor in Psychiatry, Mount Sinai School of Medicine

Paul V. Kennedy, M.D.
Assistant in Psychiatry, Mount Sinai School of Medicine

Murray I. Kofkin, M.D.
Assistant Clinical Professor of Psychiatry, Mount Sinai School of Medicine

Ann Z. Korelitz, M.S.W.
Senior Training Supervisor, Ackerman Institute for Family Therapy

William Krakauer, M.D.
Senior Clinical Instructor in Psychiatry, Mount Sinai School of Medicine

Jeremy R. Mack, M.D.
Senior Clinical Instructor in Psychiatry, Mount Sinai School of Medicine

Ildiko Mohacsy, M.D.
Assistant Clinical Professor of Psychiatry, Mount Sinai School of Medicine

Anna J. Munster, M.D.
Assistant Clinical Professor of Psychiatry, Mount Sinai School of Medicine

Joseph M. Nieder, M.D.
Senior Clinical Instructor in Psychiatry, Mount Sinai School of Medicine

Robert T. Porter, M.D.
Associate Clinical Professor of Psychiatry, Mount Sinai School of Medicine

Ronald R. Rawitt, M.D.
Assistant in Psychiatry, Mount Sinai School of Medicine

Robert Reich, M.D.
Assistant Clinical Professor of Psychiatry, Mount Sinai School of Medicine

David Schulman, M.D.
Associate Clinical Professor of Psychiatry, Mount Sinai School of Medicine

Arthur K. Shapiro, M.D.
Clinical Professor of Psychiatry, Mount Sinai School of Medicine

Elaine S. Shapiro, Ph.D.
Associate Clinical Professor of Psychiatry, Mount Sinai School of Medicine

Norman Straker, M.D.
Clinical Assistant Professor of Psychiatry, Cornell University Medical School

Stanley Turecki, M.D.
Assistant Clinical Professor of Pschiatry, Mount Sinai School of Medicine

Anna H. vanderSchraaf, M.D.
Clinical Instructor in Psychiatry, Mount Sinai School of Medicine

Israel Zeifman, M.D.
Senior Clinical Instructor in Psychiatry, Mount Sinai School of Medicine

Clinician's

Handbook of

Childhood

Psychopathology

Part I

Infantile Psychoses and

Early Onset Pathology

Chapter 1

EMOTIONAL DEPRIVATION SYNDROME

Robert Reich, M.D.

DEFINITION, REVIEW OF LITERATURE, AND PREVALENCE

The topics to be covered in this chapter are *maternal deprivation* and its sequelae, *anaclitic depression* and *hospitalism*. The short- and long-term effects of separating a child early in life from its principal caretaking person will be discussed in detail.

The deleterious effects of separating young children from their parents were not fully appreciated until recent times. It is of historical interest that in the twelfth century Frederick II, the German king, experimentally separated a group of children from their parents and had no one speak to them in an effort to learn which was the "original" innate language from which other languages were derived. Most of the children in this early experiment died.

Itard's studies of a feral child, *The Wild Boy of Aveyron*, are well known. Itard attempted unsuccessfully to educate a child about twelve years of age who allegedly grew up without human contact. The boy never learned to speak, never could be socialized, and his behavior remained that of a frightened animal in captivity.

Even into the twentieth century, children were housed in institutions, poorhouses, orphanages, workhouses and the like, with horrendous results. Many died, most failed to develop intellectually, many became psychotic, but there was no systematic study into the etiology of these tragedies.

With the rise of psychoanalytic psychology and the emphasis on the significance of early childhood experience, it would have been expected that consideration would have been given to improved mothering of infants and young children in institutions, but such was not the case. When a child went to the hospital, the parents were sent home and visiting was limited. The sicker the child, the more limited the visiting.

Only when researchers turned from retrospective studies to direct childhood observation was cognizance taken of the effect of emotional deprivation in young children. It was not until World War II, when vast numbers of children were rendered homeless, that the effects of emotional deprivation on children began to be seriously studied and measures taken to remedy a hideous situation. Though it is more than thirty years since the war and the deleterious and long-term effects of maternal deprivation have been established, the problem has not been effectively addressed. In the city of New York alone, there were over 20,000 children reported as seriously abused or neglected in 1975. There seems at present little real appreciation of the dire long-term effects on the individual ego and the social order arising as a consequence of such neglect. In my opinion, parental neglect and its sequelaè (the development of young adults who don't care, the psychopaths and criminals found particularly in our urban centers) constitute the most significant problems which society must face.

The major contributor to the area of *maternal deprivation* has been the British analyst, John Bowlby. In 1948, the

United Nations set up a committee to study the plight of homeless children. A paper was published in the Bulletin of the World Health Organization, "Maternal Care and Mental Health," by Bowlby (1952), which defined maternal deprivation and summarized its short- and long-term effects.

Bowlby stated that the availability and the quality of parental care is a major determinant of the child's mental health. Where a continuous relationship with a warm loving person is unavailable, the child was defined as suffering from maternal deprivation. Individual mothering, Bowlby stated, is essential for human survival, "as essential as vitamins or proteins." Bowlby's definition is so broad and general that it makes scientific precision and comparative studies difficult.

The British psychiatrist Rutter (1972) objects to the term "maternal deprivation." It is his opinion that children who display a reaction to parental absence are really reacting to the lack of basic needs, not to a sense of loss. Moreover, Rutter feels the phrase "maternal" is misleading. He notes the absence is of the basic "caretaking person," which need not be the mother, and so the term for the syndrome is in his opinion a misnomer which tends to obfuscate the real problem.

Pediatricians still tend to describe such afflicted children under the term "failure to thrive," referring in particular to the deficits in height, weight, and head circumference which may be found in grossly deprived young children.

British authors such as O'Connor (1968) have suggested the term "children from restricted environments" while others feel that "mother-child separation in early childhood" best describes the situation.

We suggest the term *emotional deprivation syndrome of early childhood.* This term covers a somewhat wider range and might be an acceptable compromise to the contending viewpoints and lead to the design of studies which might be more easily compared one to the other.

The term *hospitalism* was defined by Spitz as a vitiated condition of the body due to long hospital confinement. It has come to specify the destructive effects on very young infants of being placed in institutional care.

Anaclitic depression, as coined by Spitz, refers to the emotional reaction of infants who lose their good mothering person after the second half of the first year of life.

ETIOLOGY

It is beyond the scope of this article to discuss object relations development in any detail. British researchers speak of difficulties in the development of the bonding process. In this country the work of Mahler on the child's task of developing a sense of object constancy appears to best explain the clinical picture. Mahler's work in this area will be summarized briefly.

The first phase of a child's development is the *autistic phase* —in which there is little self-object differentiation. From the age of three months to three years, the child gradually forms a solid mental representation of the object. For the process of *separation-individuation* to take place and a sense of *object constancy* to be acquired, there must be a loving consistent object present throughout this period.

Separations from the good object before the state of object constancy has been reached (that is, before the age of three years) will be more devastating to a child than after a firm mental representation of the mother has been achieved. Any serious mother-child separation which interferes with the development of object constancy may result in a disturbance in object relations throughout the individual's life, with persistent fears of being abandoned, loneliness, shallow object relations, and a fluidity of object cathexis.

Brief mention should be made here of the work of Harlow (1958) and other animal investigators who showed unequivocally that for rhesus monkeys maternal deprivation resulted in profound disturbances in social, adaptive, and sexual functioning. In particular, the monkeys' subsequent ability to mother was grossly disturbed. It was also demonstrated that this dysfunction was only partially reversible and if the deprivation and isolation lasted long enough, it became irreversible.

These animal researchers tend to confirm Bowlby's ideas about the essentiality of good mothering for normal psychological development.

When discussing long-term sequelae of maternal deprivation, there are those who speak of genetic vulnerability, metabolic abnormalities, inadequate diet, improper prenatal care, the effects of social and cultural deprivation, and poverty as being prime causes of the deprivation syndrome. While problems such as juvenile delinquency are multifactorial in origin, there appears to be sufficient clinical data to underscore the significance of maternal deprivation as an extremely important etiological factor in the development of individuals who have no real feelings for fellow humans. There are no scientific data to support a "biological" etiology for the maternal deprivation syndrome. Its reversibility, if adequate continuing warm care is provided early enough, suggests the psychogenic origin of this condition. It goes without saying that proper warmth, nutrition, and medical care are essential for adequate growth and development. The clinical picture when a child does not have adequate nutrition, for example, due to famine, is quite different from that where a child receives inadequate mothering.

DIAGNOSTIC CONSIDERATIONS

As noted by Bowlby, where a continuous relationship with a warm loving person is unavailable, the child is considered as suffering from maternal deprivation. A minor degree of deprivation may eventually result in acute anxiety, excessive need for love, vengeful feelings and, resulting from this, guilt and depression. These symptoms disrupt the psychic organization, with resulting neuroses and character disorders. More complete deprivation may permanently cripple the capacity to make meaningful relationships.

The first reaction of a child who loses the good mother, for example, after the age of two, is often to reject the substitute mother out of hand. The child becomes acutely and intolerably distressed for a period of days or weeks or more without a break. During much of this time he is in a state of agitated despair, either screaming or daydreaming. Food and comfort are refused. Only exhaustion brings sleep. After some days he becomes quieter and may relapse into apathy, from which he slowly emerges to a more positive response to a strange environment and a substitute mother. There may be regression to enuresis and masturbation. He may give up talking and insist on being carried to the extent that people may consider the child to be retarded. Gradually the child improves, ego functions return, and development continues.

Anna Freud groups the immediate effects of separation in such children as follows:

1. *Psychosomatic conditions*—sleep disturbances, feeding problems, digestive upsets especially constipation, susceptibility to respiratory infections;

2. *Regression in instinctual development*—on the libidinal side this refers to more primitive reactions to need-satisfying objects, clinging, domineering or dependent oral behavior, autoerotic activities such as sucking or rocking; on the aggressive side, biting, spitting, or worse, and domination of aggressive over libidinal impulses;

3. *Regression in ego development*—the ego functions most recently acquired are the first to go—bowel, bladder, speech, social adaptation;

4. *Upsets in libidinal distribution*—in the absence of an acceptable substitute object, the child's object cathexis may be transferred to his own body, resulting in hypochondriasis, or it may be used for cathexis of the self-image, resulting in omnipotency and grandiosity.

In a later paper Bowlby (1960) refined his description of the sequence of response when young children are removed from their mothers and placed with strangers. The first phase was *protest*—loud, angry, tearful behavior, which Bowlby relates to separation anxiety. The next reaction was *despair*—acute pain developing, which Bowlby related to grief and mourning. The final phase was *detachment.*

Bowlby believed that there was an innate instinctual biological seeking for a mother figure and when this tie was breached the above sequence ensued.

Goldfarb compared children who had spent three years of life in an institution which offered little affection but impeccable physical care, with controls who had never been institutionalized.

His conclusion was that the institution children tended to present a history of aggression, distractability and uncontrolled behavior. Normal patterns of anxiety and self-inhibition were not developed. Human identifications were limited and relationships were weak and easily broken.

Goldfarb felt that personality distortions caused by early maternal deprivation were not generally overcome by later community or family experience. If anything, there is a growing inaccessability to change with age.

Among the common long-term disabilities attributed to maternal deprivation are dwarfism, intellectual retardation, chronic depression, inability to feel for others, and a type of affectionless psychopathy leading to delinquency. Among the features noted in the delinquents were superficial relationships, no real feeling, little capacity to care for people or make friends, an inaccessibility exasperating to those who try to help, stealing and pointless deceit and evasion.

In a study of such children admitted to Bellevue Hospital Bender found: "There is an inability to love or feel guilty. There is no conscience. The unconscious fantasy material is shallow. The child shows only a tendency to react to immediate impulses or experiences. Their inability to enter into any relationship makes therapy or even education impossible." Bowlby (1946), in a study of forty-four juvenile thieves, concluded that prolonged separation of a child from his mother in early life stands foremost as a cause of delinquency.

SAMPLE CASES

Peter is an eight-year-old boy originally referred from the school of a wealthy suburban community because of failure to make any kind of scholastic progress, stealing, lying, poor peer relations, and a constant depressed look.

Peter's birth weight was normal. Soon after birth, his mother went back to work in an important executive position. Her husband, a freelance consultant, was unemployed and so was assigned the task of raising Peter, but he was unable to play the maternal role and so adopted the philosophy that the less a child's development is interfered with, the better it will be. At age four, Peter wandered the streets at night as late as eleven o'clock. He was often alone on holidays and weekends. When he entered kindergarten, it was noted that he was considerably shorter than any of his classmates. Pediatric workup was negative except for decreased weight and height for his age. Because of his inability to concentrate, relate, or follow even the most simple instructions, Peter had to repeat both kindergarten and first grade. His academic progress was virtually nil and he became an object of derision among his peers. He currently is in a special class, has no friends, and wanders the streets aimlessly.

In Peter one sees, in association with maternal deprivation, many of the late symptoms associated with this syndrome— dwarfism, intellectual retardation, and depression.

In the inner city areas the cases are more stark. John's parents were both drug addicts. He spent considerable time alone as an infant as his parents were frequently absent. At age two, on a community complaint, he was discovered to have suffered from multiple fractures and cigarette burns and so the court took custody from the family. John was sent to numerous foster homes and schools and succeeded in none. Finally, he was sent to a child caring institution where he did poorly, had few friends, and provoked the staff endlessly. Despite normal intellectual potential, he functioned only minimally academically. Finally, he was arrested for setting fire to an elderly lady whom he had robbed. When he was asked how he could do this, there was no remorse. This case history is typical of the outcome of maternal deprivation suffered by many abused and neglected children.

In 1945, Spitz published a paper entitled "Hospitalism, an inquiry into the genesis of psychiatric conditions in early

Childhood." *Hospitalism* was defined as a vitiated condition of the body due to long hospital confinement. It has come to specify the deleterious effects of the care of infants placed in institutions at an early age. The prototype of such an institution was the foundling home.

Spitz studied a total of 164 infants in four separate groups: one group from a professional background, one in a village population, one in the nursery, and one in a foundling home. We will discuss the nursing and foundling homes.

The nursery was in a penal institution. The babies were those of women who had been pregnant on admission. The children remained in the nursery, cared for part-time by their mothers. The foundling home was a typical well-run orphanage where newborn children who had no one to care for them were placed.

Both institutions were located outside the city on large campuses. Hygienic conditions were carefully maintained. In both institutions infants were transferred from the newborn ward at two to three months of age. In both institutions the children were placed in glass-enclosed cubicles. Food, clothes, and medical care in both institutions were adequate but children in the nursery were almost all breast fed for three months.

In the nursery the children had toys; in the foundling home there were none. In the foundling home the cribs were placed so that children could look only at the ceiling, while in the nursery the children could look out at activities in the corridor. In the foundling home there were a head nurse and five assistants for 45 children. After a few months, the babies were shifted to the general ward where there was one nurse for 8 children. In the nursery, each child was cared for by its own mother or a specially designated mother-substitute.

The results were unbelievable. In the foundling home of 88 children up to the age of two and a half, 23 died; of the surviving children aged eighteen months to two and a half years old, only two spoke a few words. Hardly any could eat alone. All were incontinent.

In contrast, in the nursery, no children died; the children walked, most spoke or made sounds, and they understood the significance of social gestures. The nursery children were significantly advanced in motor activity, adaptive behavior, and personal and social functions as compared to the foundling children.

Spitz's conclusion was that the difference between the fate of the children in the two institutions was due to the mother-child interaction in the nursery and its absence in the foundling home. Individual mothering was essential for human survival.

Spitz's study provoked a revolution in infant care in better quality institutions. The significance of a special mothering figure to care for young children became firmly established.

Unfortunately, Spitz's work was so technically flawed that modern investigators tend to discredit its validity. There was an epidemic of infectious disease at the foundling home which was the cause of many of the deaths. The effects of sensory deprivation on the foundling infants would have to be assessed as well as genetic and other factors.

Another of Spitz's important contributions was that of the concept of *anaclitic depression.* In the second half of the first year of life, a few of the infants observed in the previously described nursery had their loving mother or care-taking person removed from them. The infants soon became weepy and irritable. After a time, a marked withdrawal was noted. The children would lie in their beds refusing to take part in any activity. Any attempt to engage them was futile. Some children lost weight and a gradual decline in the developmental quotient was noted. This behavior lasted about three months and then the weepiness stopped and a frozen rigidity of expression appeared. These children would sit or lie expressionless as if in a trance, not perceiving what went on in the environment. This behavior was accompanied by auto-erotic activity in the oral, anal, and genital zones. Finally contact became impossible. At best, screaming was elicited.

In summary, Spitz described several aspects of this syndrome of anaclitic depression:

1. Apprehension, sadness, crying
2. Lack of contact, rejection of environment, withdrawal
3. Retardation of development, dejection, slowness of movement, stupor
4. Loss of appetite, refusal to eat, weight loss
5. Insomnia
6. A facial expression suggestive of despair

This process, if interrupted by the return of the mother, was reversible, but Spitz felt that if allowed to continue for more than three months the child fell into a condition which he stated resembled a stuporous, deteriorated catatonic state. Spitz felt that this situation in the second half of the first year of life was a special kind of depression and he related it to a mourning process.

TREATMENT AND DISCUSSION

The only treatment for maternal deprivation is not to let it happen. If circumstances result in the loss of a caretaking person there must be an adequate substitute provided as soon as possible. We desperately need more effective services to abused and neglected children. There is a need for child advocacy services. We need a better economic support system so that mothers can stay home and care for their young children. We need a massive educational effort to stress the importance of adequate warm loving care for infants. Hospitals should provide better facilities so parents may remain with their gravely ill children for as long a period as possible. We need a better system of recruiting and training child caring personnel, and they need better reimbursement. Too often parents who will spend great effort and expense choosing a "good school" for their child will accept virtually anyone to look after their infant or toddler—especially if the fee is modest.

Today, throughout the urban United States, juveniles account for an increasing share of the crime rate. As in Bowlby's studies, a majority have suffered severely from parental neglect and deprivation. It might help, until the establishment of some kind of comprehensive preventative program, to provide the best available substitute good mothering for these infants at risk before it is too late. Once certain critical periods in development are past, it is too late for those children suffering from the effects of severe maternal deprivation ever to be able to relate to others in a warm and truly empathic fashion. For the older, adolescent affectionless psychopath already involved in major criminal behavior, the answer appears to be a secure environment where impulses can be controlled by external means while some therapeutic effort is attempted. The prognosis is guarded. Not all children who suffer severe maternal deprivation in early life end up as psychopaths. What distinguishes those who succumb from those who recover awaits further research.

People who are unwilling or unable to spend time looking after children should be discouraged from having them. It is far less costly in human and monetary terms to provide free birth control than to have society care for the child who literally wasn't wanted.

BIBLIOGRAPHY

Beres, D., and Obers, S. (1950). The effects of extreme deprivation in infancy on psychic structure in adolescence. *Psychoanalytic Study of the Child* 5:212–235.

Bowlby, J. (1952). *Maternal Care and Mental Health* (WHO Monograph Series No. 179). Geneva: World Health Organization. (Also available in paperback—New York: Schocken, 1966).

——(1946). *Forty-Four Juvenile Thieves.* London: Bailliere, Tindall and Cox.

——(1960). Grief and mourning in infancy and early childhood (Paper by Bowlby with discussion by A. Freud, M. Schur, et al.). *Psychoanalytic Study of the Child* 15:9–62.

Harlow, H. (1958). The nature of love. *American Psychologist* 13:673–685.

O'Connor, N. (1968). Children in restricted environments. In *Early Experiences and Behavior,* ed. G. Newton and S. Levine. Springfield, Ill.: Charles C Thomas.

Provence, S., and Lipton, R. (1962). *Infants in Institutions.* New York: International Universities Press.

Rutter, M. (1972). *Maternal Deprivation Reassessed.* Baltimore: Penguin Books.

Spitz, R. (1945). Hospitalism: an inquiry into the genesis of psychiatric conditions in early childhood. *Psychoanalytic Study of the Child* 1:53–74.

————(1946). Hospitalism: a follow-up report. *Psychoanalytic Study of the Child* 2:113–117.

Spitz, R., and Wolf, K. (1946). Anaclitic depression: an inquiry into the genesis of psychiatric conditions in early childhood. *Psychoanalytic Study of the Child* 2:313–342.

Chapter 2

PSYCHOTOXIC DISEASES OF INFANCY

Martin M. Josephson, M.D.

DEFINITION

Rene Spitz (1951, 1965) first used the concept of "the psychotoxic diseases of infancy" to describe what he felt were the effects on developing children of various kinds of improper care by their mothers. In contrast to the effects of partial or complete emotional deprivation (described elsewhere in this volume), he felt that in this category specific disturbances of the maternal personality and attitudes would act as "psychological toxins," resulting in corresponding infant diseases. He attempted a detailed examination of these mothers (for the most part, young women confined in a penal institution who were permitted to care for their children under supervision) as well as constructing models of what he felt were the dawning and growing psychological perceptions by their children of these mothers. It would be beyond the scope of this survey to present in great detail his delineations in terms of metapsychology and object relations theory. They do attempt to correlate specific pathology of the mother's mood and perception of the child to discrete infantile conditions. His classification, adapted in a slightly modified way for clarity, is presented in tabular form (Table 1). A brief summary of his views will be given.

TABLE 1
PSYCHOTOXIC DISEASES OF INFANCY (AFTER SPITZ)

Etiological maternal factor	Infant's disease
1. Overt primal rejection	Coma in newborn
2. Primary anxious overpermissiveness	Three months' colic
3. Hostility in the guise of anxiety	Infantile eczema
4. Oscillations between pampering and hostility	Hypermotility
5. Cyclical mood swings	Fecal play
6. Hostility consciously compensated	Aggressive hyperactive

Overt primal rejection by the mother was described by Spitz as including rejection of the child, pregnancy, and motherhood. The child may die "accidentally" or through infanticide or may be given up for adoption. If kept, the infant may sink into a stuporous, semicomatose state on efforts to feed, sometimes requiring tube feeding or clysis. By instructing the mother in the details of nursing, the infant could recover as nursing became possible. Spitz's conclusion was that "in this archaic period, the infant's contacts with his surround have only just been transferred from the umbilical cord to the mouth and have changed from transfusion to incorporation" and that the manifest symptoms in such cases "will be expressed through oral symptoms as a paralysis of incorporation during the first days of life."

The next picture linked primary anxious overpermissiveness in the mother with three months' colic in the infant (between about three to six months of age). He hypothesized

that it required an infant that is hypertonic both in muscula-
ture and peristalsis. Excess food produces excess intestinal
activity. The mothers were felt to show anxious overconcern.
Spitz viewed the two functions of nursing to be the ingestion
of food and the discharge of tension through the oral
mucosa. He felt a vicious cycle developed in which the hypertonic infant was unable to get rid of his tension normally in
the nursing process. "Instead he discharges it through post-
prandial screaming and motor agitation . . . the oversolicitous
mother immediately feeds the child again . . . for a brief
period the child becomes quiet . . . however the food again
overloads the digestive system, increasing tension . . . leading
to renewed colic and screaming" with the mother again responding by feeding. Methods to deal with tension without
the irritant of unnecessary food would include use of the
pacifier, cradle-rocking or carrying the infant.

The third condition described tied infantile eczema (between six and eighteen months) to an attitude of hostility in
the guise of manifest anxiety in the mothering figure. Such
mothers are viewed as infantile, concerned about the fragility
of their children and disinclined to touch them. Affective
physical contact was avoided. Spitz felt this interfered with
the infant's development of early forms of identification with
his mother, leading to subsequent impairment in forming
relationships with others. Spitz speculated whether the infant's cutaneous response of eczema might be a demand to
incite more touching or else a withdrawal in which the infant
would give himself stimuli in the somatic sphere not forthcoming from the mother. With increasing locomotion in the
second year of life, the child could seek stimuli for himself
and the condition could subside.

The next group, from six months of age on, linked rapid
oscillations between pampering and hostile attitudes in the

mother to hypermotility (rocking) in the infant. The child is alternately the object of fondling and rage. Spitz viewed this self-contradictory and inconsistent maternal behavior as impeding the child's ability to form a unified mental representation of her to which he could relate. The rocking of the child was described as his investing emotionally in his own body rather than in the beginning of a relationship with the mother.

The fifth category related longer range cyclical mood swings of the mother to fecal play and coprophagia in the child (between nine and fifteen months of age). These long-term mood swings of the mother (depression, extreme hostility, oversolicitousness) might be two to six months in duration. Such a child is hypothesized to have formed a relation to his mother in one phase of her mood and then to have "lost" this rudimentary mental representation of her as her mood altered. This was seen as leading to manipulation of concrete things, like feces, as a substitute for the "loss" experienced. Spitz also felt the child might identify with the depressive and incorporative tendencies of the mother, expressing this in coprophagia.

The last grouping, appearing by two years of age, tied a mother who consciously compensates for her hostility to her child to a picture of hyperactivity in the child. This was the only category not derived from the study of the mothers in the penal institution. The mothers in this picture, often from intellectual or professional circles, were described as showing a "syrupy sweetness" to their children. These women were felt to be basically narcissistic and to use their children for their own exhibitionistic satisfaction. This is the only group where fathers are mentioned and they are described as "successful, aggressive, hearty, loud, exhibitionistic, frightening the child through rough play." The children are given masses of toys, becoming quite good at their use but by the second year they lag in social development and are apt to become hyperactive and destructive.

Subsequent investigators have not confirmed the specificity of maternal personality to the discrete conditions described by Spitz. His term "psychotoxic diseases of infancy" has been retained in practice, however, to describe a heterogeneous group of manifestations in young children to which various authors have described different causations and meanings. Among these conditions are: various early feeding disturbances; infantile eczema and dermatitis; and disturbances in activity levels and patterns (including hypermotility, rocking, body swaying, head rolling, head banging, teeth grinding, and hair pulling).

REVIEW OF LITERATURE

From an extensive literature of over seventy references bearing on the subject, only a limited number will be cited. Spitz himself made reference to the work of Ribble (1938) on "coma in the newborn" in which nursing infants who were unable to grasp the nipple were described as becoming listless, sleepy or even stuporous. Richmond, Eddy, and Green (1958) reported on disturbed autonomic functioning manifested by colic, regurgitation, rumination, and diarrhea in infants who had undergone disordered emotional availability of their mothers. Williams (1951) related dermatitis to maternal behavior causing anxiety and hostility in infants and children. In a study of rhythmic motor patterns with onset in the first two years of life, Lourie (1949) viewed such movements as expressing and relieving tension connected with apprehension, dissatisfaction, anger, boredom, pain, frustration, or physical restraint. Provence and Lipton (1962) in their classic study of institutionalized foundling infants delineated four forms of rocking: (1) transient rocking in transitional periods between stages of motor mastery; (2) rocking as an autoerotic gratification in a disturbed mother-infant relationship; (3) rocking in infantile psychosis where it is extremely preoccupying and difficult to interrupt; and (4) rocking in the institutionalized infants which served discharge of a primitive and global sort yielding only minimal self-comforting and gratification and easily interrupted by the approach of an adult. Brody (1960) classified rocking in three categories: *normative,* communicating direct pleasure or reassurance, often at times of new motor mastery; *repetitious,* with no social function and monotonously often leading to sleep; and *agitated,* rapid and fatiguing in quality and often found in autistic children, where it may persist in preference to the mother when she is present.

In a study of private pediatric practices, Kravitz, Rosenthal, et al. (1960) collected a series of 135 infant and child head bangers. They viewed it as a maturational pattern emerging in transition from sitting to crawling and at the time of eruption of the incisor teeth. Mean age of onset was eight months with an average duration of seventeen months. Global assessment of the mother-child relation was good in two-thirds of the cases. In a review of head rolling (Spasmus nutans), Fineman, Kuniholm, and Sheridan (1971) felt that such children experienced disturbed relationships with their mothers. These children accordingly formed such tenuous attachments to their mothers that states of inner tension would be relieved by self-initiated, compensatory autoarousal, the head rolling seeming to express a scanning or searching function rather than a gratification. Mannino and Delgado (1969) reported on trichotillomania (hair twirling and pulling) as a form of tension relief and gratification present in a variety of psychiatric pictures but with pathological family functioning at the expense of the child.

INCIDENCE

Spitz did not address general incidence since he was studying a particular and somewhat atypical population of delinquent mothers. He did give age ranges for the conditions he described:

TABLE 2
AGE RANGES FOR PSYCHOTOXIC
DISEASES OF INFANCY (AFTER SPITZ)

Infant's disease	Age range
coma in the newborn	immediate postnatal period
three months' colic	three to six months
infantile eczema	six to eighteen months
hypermotility (rocking)	six months on
fecal play	nine to fifteen months
aggressive, hyperactive	by second year

Lourie found the incidence of rhythmic patterns to be 10 percent in private practice and 15 to 20 percent in an unselected clinic population. Onset was between one month and two years of age.

Kravitz, Rosenthal, et al. (1960) found an incidence for head banging of 3.6 percent in private pediatric practice. The male-female ratio was 3.5:1. Mean onset was eight months with an average duration of seventeen months. It occurred at bed or nap time in the group studied in 78 percent of the children. Half did it less than fifteen minutes at a time, a quarter for an hour or longer. Two thirds also had body rocking but 18 percent were without other motor rhythm patterns. Among head bangers, 53 percent were first-born and 32 percent second-born. Only 20 percent of their siblings had head banging too. A history of separation from their mothers was present in a fourth of the cases. While the majority ended by twenty-five months, 30 percent went on for durations as long as ten years.

Mannino and Delgado (1969) reported on prior studies of trichotillomania which showed incidences of between 0.0005 and 0.006. A Japanese study of teeth grinding in children found a frequency of 11.6 percent.

Fecal play and coprophagia seem not to have been addressed since Spitz's description.

ETIOLOGY AND DYNAMICS

In addition to Spitz's attempt to correlate these disorders to particular personality characteristics of mothers, as mentioned above, many other authors have tended to implicate the mother in less specific ways. Often the mother-child relation is depicted as disturbed with the mother viewed as rejecting, emotionally unavailable, depressed, distracted, tense, overwhelmed, or anxious. She is seen as inadequately or incorrectly responding to the infant's need for consistent, concerned physical and emotional comforting. Sometimes the frame of reference is enlarged to include the whole family as a collectively stressed and distressed unit. Occasionally, worry over a physically ill older sibling is felt to preoccupy the mother and compromise her former ability to deal adequately with her younger infant.

Several investigators refer in a general way to possible predisposing familial and constitutional factors, e.g., that teeth grinding is influenced by hereditary factors at a statistically significant level. Immaturity of the gut is held by some to underlie the disorders presenting as colic.

Repetitive motor patterns as a not infrequent manifestation at points of transition in development are frequently mentioned (e.g., eruption of teeth or shift from sitting to standing). Sensory deprivation as an etiology has some adherents. Many animal studies have investigated restrictions of movement which seem to correlate with stereotyped motor behavior, though findings in humans are less clear-cut. Head banging has also been found to be more frequent in the rapid eye movement periods of sleep than in the non-REM periods.

Attempts to see some of these categories as related to particular psychiatric diagnoses seem nonspecific at best. Some writers have connected some repetitive motor patterns to autism or, more broadly, to psychosis but not in a way that can be deemed pathognomonic. Occasionally, physical illnesses have been suggested as playing a part, including rickets, otitis media, and unspecified viral diseases. One author noted the concurrence of head rolling and nystagmus. Pediatric authors have elaborated on the role of allergy in colic and eczema. The last of Spitz's categories, which is most sketchy in description, of aggressive, hyperactive children might require in older children a differentiation from hyperkinesis or minimal brain dysfunction.

TREATMENT

Authors who have addressed treatment are largely those who believe in the etiological role of the mother's quality of relating to her child. Some investigators have favored brief hospitalization of the child with his care being given over to a single nurse, adept at providing comfort and appropriate stimulation to the child. Concurrently, work is done with the family and support given to the mother. Sometimes she is taught the successful ways of handling the child by the experienced nurse who forms a benign, noncritical model for identification. Rehospitalization for the problem proves not to be required. Often, the same approach is attempted on an outpatient basis. No extensive character transformation of the mother is attempted but rather an effort is made to enlarge her awareness of her infant's emotional needs. Efforts are also made to ease family tensions and to provide some time each day when the mother may be relieved by someone else in her care of the infant.

In addition, in the repetitive motor pattern pictures, there have been some attempts to replace the rhythmic movement with rhythmic auditory stimuli like a metronome or a loud-ticking clock. Efforts to make the movements purposeful have also been tried utilizing swings and seesaws, though these seem to have passed their vogue. In head rolling, attempts have been made to offer a visual focus, followed by efforts to maintain it. However, even with these particular suggestions, an effort to work with the family is usually included.

When allergy is felt to underlie the colic or eczema, pediatric management has been to seek the offending dietary or local allergen and eliminate it. Antispasmodics for the gut and topical lotions for the skin are utilized.

DIAGNOSIS AND DISCUSSION

In practice, most of these conditions only come to the attention of the child psychiatrist after pediatric investigation and management have not produced an etiology or effective treatment. As always, a psychiatric diagnosis should not be made by exclusion. Rather, emotional factors should be demonstrated to play a critical role, even along the somewhat loosely drawn lines that have been described. Certainly in any failure to thrive or with persistent colic or eczema, the various anatomical, genetic, physiological, dietary and allergic bases must be ruled out by appropriate means. The purely developmental nature of some of the repetitive motor patterns can be assessed in part by their diminution in the presence of an available emotionally significant figure.

If indeed there is a deficiency or distortion in the emotional caretaking process afforded the infant, this is to be determined by a careful evaluation of the family. Various factors may have come to affect the capacities of the caretaker (usually the mother) to sufficiently emotionally nurture the infant in satisfactory ways. The mother may come from a similarly emotionally deficient background herself. Sometimes it may be a function of her own immaturity at that point in her life. The absence of prior models of good mothering may play a part, often amenable to improvement with the surrogate mother-nurse's demonstrations. Family intercurrent circumstances may play a role. A death in the family (particularly of a maternal grandparent) may lead to depression in the mother and compromise her abilities to optimally interact with her child. Family stresses like a sick sibling, marital difficulties or the absence of a spouse may all contribute to the picture. More severe pathology in the mother (such as inadequate personality, narcissistic character disorder, or psychosis) augment the possibilities of such disorders.

From the side of the infant or child, the range of responses might be viewed as limited to the avenues of expression available to him at various points in his development. The earlier in time, the less complete and more fragile his achievement of a stable internal psychological representation of the mother would be; correspondingly, the more likelihood there is of his responses being mediated in terms of a rudimentary body ego and his physical functioning. These would appear diffuse in nature, perhaps constitutionally determined (in terms of physically vulnerable areas) and lacking in specific psychological meaning. That such an early disorder might remain a nidus for later psychophysiological reactions has been warned of by some authors.

Certainly, to address familial difficulties, relieve tensions in the mother, provide her with support after a stressful, frustrating, sometimes frightening experience with her child, can work to relieve the situation. By the way the involved professionals manifest their concern for and response to the emotional needs of the child, models are provided for more adaptive responses. In some cases, the mother herself may require some form of ongoing psychiatric treatment. When children have to be apart from families, as in foundling institutions, the critical importance of maintaining one central mothering figure has been demonstrated to forestall many of these symptom pictures.

Whether parent education curricula, which include sufficient awareness of the emotional needs of the infant and how these are to be met, can exercise a preventive role will become clearer as such programs may be more widely adopted.

SUMMARY

A heterogeneous group of disorders in the infant and young child were described by Spitz with an attempt to link each disorder to a specific distorting, "psychotoxic" effect of the mother's emotional interaction with her child. Later authors have broadened the term to include many physical, motor, or habit disturbances of young children, often attributed to an emotional etiology but without agreement on the specific maternal patterns postulated by Spitz. Nonetheless, the feeling of many investigators is that the presence of inadequate or distorted mothering may lead the infant to respond with the limited, largely physical means within his still relatively primitive repertoire which form the symptom pictures described above. Appropriate intervention to remedy the quality of the mother-child emotional relationship and relieve family stress has been widely reported to be the effective means to deal with these disorders.

BIBLIOGRAPHY

Brody, S. (1960). Self-rocking in infancy. *Journal of the American Academy of Child Psychiatry* 6(4):615–643. An examination of this pattern in clinical and psychoanalytic terms.

Fineman, J., Kuniholm, P., and Sheridan, S. (1971). Spasmus nutans: a syndrome of auto-arousal. *Journal of the American Academy of Child Psychiatry* 10(1):136–155. A review of head rolling and a presentation of this picture in a set of twins.

Kravitz, H., Rosenthal, V., et al. (1960). A study of head banging in infants and children. *Diseases of the Nervous*

System 21:203–208. A study of incidence and duration in pediatric practice.

Lourie, R. (1949). Studies on bed rocking, head-banging, and related rhythm patterns. *Clinical Proceedings of the Children's Hospital (Washington)* 5:295–302. A study of rhythm patterns in 130 children.

Mannino, F., and Delgado, R. (1969). Trichotillomania in children: a review. *American Journal of Psychiatry* 126(4):-505–511. A review of hair pulling and hair twirling with clinical illustrations.

Provence, S., and Lipton, R. (1962). *Infants in Institutions.* New York: International Universities Press. A classic, quantified description of the deleterious effects of maternal deprivation on foundling infants.

Ribble, M. (1938). Clinical studies of instinctive reactions in newborn babies. *American Journal of Psychiatry* 95:149–160. Observation on sucking behavior in neonates.

Richmond, J., Eddy, E., and Green, M. (1958). Rumination: a psychosomatic syndrome of infancy. *Pediatrics* 22A:49–55. An effective treatment approach in ruminating infants through brief hospitalization.

Spitz, R. (1951). The psychogenic diseases in infancy: an attempt at their etiologic classification. *Psychoanalytic Study of the Child* 6:255–275. Spitz's early description of the effects of disordered mothering on infants.

Spitz, R. (1965). *The First Year of Life.* New York: International Universities Press, pp. 199–266. Spitz's later extensive elaboration of the psychotoxic diseases.

Williams, D. (1951). Management of atopic dermatitis in children. *Archives of Dermatology and Syphilology* 65(5):545–560. An examination of the mother-child relationship in global terms in fifty-three children with dermatitis.

Chapter 3

EARLY ONSET PSYCHOSIS—AUTISTIC

Robert Reich, M.D.

DEFINITION, REVIEW OF LITERATURE, AND PREVALENCE

It was only in the 1930s that childhood schizophrenia began to emerge as a distinct clinical entity. Kanner (1943) published a paper on a syndrome he named "infantile autism." He postulated a distinct psychiatric disorder revealing itself to the perceptive observer in the first two years of life, characterized by extreme aloofness, avoidance of human contact, severe speech disturbance or mutism, an insistence on sameness and a fascination with material objects in preference to human contact. While the term autism has a number of different meanings in psychiatry, referring to a type of thinking or a type of behavior characterized by avoidance of human contact, we feel the name infantile autism should be reserved for the specific syndrome first described by Kanner.

Beyond the matter of nosology are many unanswered questions. What is the relationship between autism, childhood schizophrenia, and adult schizophrenia? What is the distinction between mental retardation and some of the manifestations of early childhood psychosis? Is infantile autism a form of childhood schizophrenia or another disease entity entirely? Is infantile autism a functional illness or an organic illness of undetermined etiology?

We would suggest the following classification for *childhood psychoses:*

I. *Organic psychoses of childhood*
   1. Infectious, neoplastic, degenerative, toxic, metabolic (onset any age)
   2. Psychosis with mental retardation (onset any age)
II. *Childhood psychoses of undetermined origin*
   1. Infantile autism (onset 0–3 years)
   2. Developmental child psychosis—includes symbiotic psychosis (onset 3–7 years)
   3. Childhood schizophrenia (onset 7–13 years)
   4. Schizophrenia adult type (onset 13+ years)

It should be noted that the majority of authors today classify infantile autism as being of organic etiology. Ornitz (1976), for example, speaks of an underlying neurophysiological disorder and authors such as Chess have stressed that a significant number of patients diagnosed as suffering from infantile autism were shown to have had congenital rubella.

While onset of the condition would appear to be a poor method of classification of the childhood psychoses of undetermined etiology, the clinical picture coincides to a considerable extent with the age of onset. While there may be profound regression making a psychosis beginning at a later age similar in appearance to one developing earlier, it is our impression that close clinical observation will reveal differences between the two conditions.

Rutter (1972) suggested the abandonment of the term "childhood schizophrenia" and links all manifestations of psychosis in children under the term "childhood psychosis," although he does make special allowance for infantile autism and "degenerative psychosis" with onset between ages three and five.

The prevalence of early onset childhood psychosis ranges in various studies from two to six per 10,000 in the general population. Lotter (1966) found a prevalence of autism of 4.5 per 10,000 in an English population. Infantile autism occurs more frequently in males than females in ranges varying in different studies from 2:1 to 4.2:1. Between 50 percent and 70 percent of cases of childhood psychosis are noted to have symptoms from birth onwards and fit the picture of infantile autism.

ETIOLOGY

As previously stated, most authors today regard infantile autism as an organic illness akin to mental retardation. Despite this, there have been few consistent findings pinpointing organic pathology. While there are striking dynamic factors in some cases, many authors find it difficult to accept the idea that dynamic factors would play such a major role as to cause developmental deviations this profound so soon after birth.

FAMILY CHARACTERISTICS

Kanner's old notion that the parents of autistic children were intelligent and successful but cold, noncommunicative, hostile and rejecting of their child from birth is not supported by clinical studies. The parents of autistic children do not appear to be statistically of unusual intelligence nor do there appear to be, in most cases, clearly definable dynamic factors which could account for the extensive psychopathology of the child. The concept of the schizophrenogenic mother has over the years not proved to be helpful.

CONSTITUTIONAL FACTORS

Most authors agree that there is no increased incidence of autism, schizophrenia, or affective disorders in the parents or siblings of the autistic child. While twin studies have suggested that monozygotic pairs are more likely to be concordant for and dizygotic twins discordant for autism, the number of monozygotic twins discordant for autism suggests factors other than genetic in operation. Attempts to find chromosomal abnormalities or dermatographic patterns in autistic children have been largely unsuccessful.

NEUROLOGICAL STUDIES

The neurological examination of the autistic child is essentially unremarkable. Some authors report "soft" neurological signs (such as poor muscle tone, hyperreflexia, hypo- or hyperkinesis) in as many as 50% of cases, but these findings are debatable. There have been no consistent electroencephalographic patterns noted.

Autistic children are felt to have problems in visual and auditory discrimination skills and in cross modal information processing (i.e., auditory to vocal, auditory to visual, etc.). It is believed by some that the autistic children can only process one sensory cue at a time and are overwhelmed by multiple sensory cues. Because of the above, some autistic children were treated by sensory deprivation but the results have not been encouraging.

There appears to be a consistent supression of vestibular nystagmus in autistic children and this is a finding replicated by a number of investigators. The significance of this finding remains unclear but it is utilized by some authors to emphasize their certainty about the "organic" nature of this condition.

BIOLOGICAL STUDIES

Studies of indoleamine metabolism in autistic children remain inconclusive. One study suggested a decreased urinary excretion of 5-hydroxyindoleacetic acid in response to a tryptophane load. Findings in this area could not be replicated. Similarly some researchers reported an increased level of serotonin in peripheral blood of autistic children but findings in this area as well could not be replicated.

Still other studies focused on plasma cholinesterase activity, serum magnesium, copper and ceruloplasmin activity but the results did not clearly show abnormalities in these areas specific to autistic children.

It has been reported by several authors that autistic children show evidence of hypopituitarism and an abnormal peripheral white blood cell pattern but these findings too remain largely unproven.

It appears at this time that there is no clear evidence of any specific biochemical abnormality in autistic children.

DIAGNOSTIC COORDINATES

The signs and symptoms of infantile autism have not been better catalogued by anyone than by Kanner (1943), the investigator who first described the syndrome.

There has been remarkable unanimity among various authors as to the clinical picture. For convenience we will divide

the symptom complex into four different categories: I—
problems with relatedness, II—disturbances in speech and
language, III—disturbances in sensorimotor behavior, IV—
disturbances in intellectual functioning.

I. *Problems with relatedness*

1. *Extreme self-isolation, aloofness, or withdrawal.* Very early in
infancy perceptive mothers will note something is wrong
with their child. He does not "mold" in their arms but remains stiff. Some parents describe their children as "good"
babies, self-sufficient, happiest when alone, acting as if people weren't there, etc. Anything from the outside which attempts to interfere is treated as a noxious stimulus by the
infant.

2. *Unresponsiveness.* Unlike normal children, the child does
not anticipate being picked up. This is noted from about four
months onward.

3. *Lack of eye contact.* The child appears to be looking
through or past people. In our experience this is a much
quoted but unreliable sign.

4. *Displays more attention to objects than people.* A child entering
the office seeks out toys and ignores people and conversation
as if they did not exist. If a child is stuck with a pin, he will
focus attention on the pin and not the person causing the
pain.

5. *Difficulty in playing with other children.* Autistic children
relate minimally if at all to other children. Even after they
improve, they often are awkward and have difficulty in empa-
thizing with others.

6. *Uses person as an object or tool.* To the autistic child a person
may be viewed as a ladder to get things from high places. An
arm may be viewed as a hook to get things down from a shelf
without regard to the person whose arm is being employed.

II. *Problems with language*
  1. *Failure to develop speech or mutism.*
  2. *Limited speech or echolalia which may be immediate or delayed.* The speech is noncommunicative and words lose their flexibility. A child may say refrigerator but only in a specific context.
  Often the echolalia takes on a personal quality resembling the neologisms of adult psychoses.
  3. *Pronominal reversal.* The child calls himself "you" in response to the mother's command "I want you to do this." This is really similar to the echolalia described above.

III. *Sensorimotor disturbance*
  1. *Attempt to maintain sameness.* The child attempts to maintain sameness in objects and their placements and in behavior patterns. Furniture movement by anyone but the child may cause considerable rage or panic. The child may not be able to go to sleep unless a certain ritualized format is undertaken. Deviation from the pattern may produce overwhelming anxiety which may be alleviated only by starting from the beginning. These symptoms resemble those found in very severe obsessive-compulsive neurosis.
  2. *Repeated manipulation of objects.* The child may repeatedly manipulate objects without regard to function. Toys may be just turned over and over again, instead of played with in the usual manner.
  3. *Unusual body movement.* The autistic child often shows repetitive body movements such as rocking back and forth. There is a winglike flailing of the hands when excited which may be quite characteristic of such children. Often there is unusual body posturing. A serious or sad facial expression is often noted.

4. *Abnormal response to stimuli.* The child may show avoidance, hypo- or hypersensitivity, especially to sound. The autistic child may or may not be afraid of noise. He may make noise himself but outside noises may startle him. Very loud noises may be totally ignored. There may be abnormal fears or lack of appropriate sense of fear.

IV. *Intelligence*

1. *Impression of normal intelligence.* Initially the child may appear of normal intelligence. Further scrutiny may reveal retardation with islets of intelligent functioning. Specialized intelligence testing shows that 40% of autistic children have IQs less than 50 and 70% of all autistic children have IQs in the retarded range.

2. *Unusual abilities.* Some autistic children have amazingly good rote memory. Parents may feel their children are unusually gifted. In some cases these aptitudes are so highly developed as to warrant the term "idiot savant."

For cases fulfilling the diagnostic criteria of early infantile autism, the prognosis is poor overall. The ability to acquire communicative speech by age six is a significant prognostic indicator. Perhaps the most reliable prognostic indicator is measurable intelligence, with those having the highest IQs the most likely to "recover"—recovery being the ability to function independently outside the home or institutional setting. A recovery rate of 20 percent is found in most series and is generally accepted as the recovery rate in appropriately diagnosed cases. Recent studies, suggesting that cases which have not improved significantly after intensive residential treatment may show slow improvement over many years, remain to be verified.

TREATMENT

The results of psychotherapy or psychotherapy plus milieu therapy have been disappointing overall as well as technically difficult and time consuming. The chief proponent of a psychotherapeutic approach is Bettelheim (1967) who hospitalizes autistic children and provides them with an intense one-to-one relationship.

Others have tried using sensory modalities such as tactile stimulation to help these children. In this approach, the therapist does not wait for the child but actively tries to stimulate him with tactile, kinesthetic, and proprioceptive stimuli gratifying to the child. Music and other rhythmic stimuli have been utilized. Parents are often enlisted to assist in these treatment modalities.

Much of the current treatment of infantile autism is educational in nature with these children viewed as suffering from perceptual and intellectual handicaps rather than difficulties in object relations per se.

Such treatment consists of structured training, particularly in speech and visual discrimination. The importance of speech training is stressed, with numerous techniques including operant conditioning, other reinforcement techniques and even the use of sign language in an attempt to improve communicative skills.

Operant conditioning techniques have been used to reinforce socially acceptable behavior in these children by helping them respond to environmental cues.

Sensory deprivation techniques, aversive conditioning techniques and other such measures have been tried but have been of little value in most studies. Hormones, trace metals and vitamins do not in themselves help.

Psychotropic medications of all kinds, including LSD, have

been tried but have been of little assistance in ameliorating the underlying disorder. Psychotropic medication can be of assistance in some cases on a symptomatic basis. Often the doses required for effectiveness put the patient to sleep or otherwise interfere with the educational training which forms the cornerstone of current therapeutic efforts.

Overall, we do not have a definitive treatment for infantile autism. The therapeutic approach currently in vogue is to utilize educational conditioning methods with emphasis on the development of communicative speech, the acquisition of behavior which would make the child more self-sufficient, and the elimination of behavioral problems which make the above difficult. A flexible approach utilizing the parents as paraprofessionals to continue working with the child at home, combined with educational and conditioning techniques, speech training, plus psychotherapy, family counseling and pharmacological therapy as indicated, appears to be the treatment of choice. The issue of institutional vs. noninstitutional treatment depends in large measure on the degree of disability the child presents plus the availability of adequate funding to support several years of residential treatment. In the most severe cases permanent institutional care may be required.

BIBLIOGRAPHY

(See end of next chapter on symbiotic psychosis).

Chapter 4

EARLY ONSET PSYCHOSIS—SYMBIOTIC

Robert Reich, M.D.

DEFINITION AND PREVALENCE

The term symbiotic psychosis, defined by Mahler (1952), refers to a psychotic condition characterized by affective states of panic when the child is separated from the mother and is often accompanied by profound regression and delusional states. With onset typically between ages 3 and 5, extreme developmental regression is a characteristic feature and may be severe enough to make distinction between autism and symbiotic psychosis difficult except by history. Although the term symbiotic psychosis is widely accepted by child analysts it is not listed in standard nomenclature but is categorized under childhood schizophrenia or other psychoses of childhood. In our classification it is listed under developmental childhood psychoses.

No reliable prevalence figures could be found for this condition but it occurs much less frequently than infantile autism and must fall within the range of two to six per 10,000 population, previously cited for all psychotic disorders of childhood.

ETIOLOGY

In order to fully understand symbiotic psychosis we must review normal child development. For the first three or four months of life, the infant passes through what is now known as the *autistic stage;* i.e., there is little self/object differentiation. From three months to three years, the child passes through the subphases of *separation-individuation.*

From the age of three to ten months the infant passes through the substage of *differentiation* in which he becomes aware that his needs cannot be satisfied by hallucinatory wish fulfillment and that he is dependent on an object outside himself—the mother or caretaking person.

From about ten to fifteen months, the infant passes through the *practicing period*—he plays peek-a-boo, in which he gradually becomes used to not seeing the mother. With the increase in motor skills, the infant gradually attains the ability to be away from his mother physically.

The next phase of development from fifteen months to two years is called *rapprochment* where the infant shadows the mother like a duckling. It is as if he is frightened by his own capacity to separate from his mother.

The final substage, two to three years of age, represents the consolidation of the process and the beginning of *emotional object constancy.* The child gradually begins to form a differentiated persistent mental representation of the mothering person even in her absence and can thereby better master feelings of loneliness and fear.

In children who develop a symbiotic psychosis, the mother-infant symbiotic relationship does not proceed to the stage of object constancy. The mental representation of the mother remains fused with that of the self. Such a child sees the mother as omnipotent, and in not clearly distinguishing himself from her, he retains his posture in this imagined shared omnipotence.

Profound developmental difficulties occurring during the process of separation-individuation are the underlying cause of symbiotic psychosis.

The above represents the psychoanalytic point of view. There are those who argue that this psychosis is organic in nature and may be genetically determined. The regression in development is seen as a response to underlying organic pathology. The results of the biological studies cited under autism are generally representative of the outcome of biological research on all of the early childhood psychoses. No definite organic cause for this syndrome has been found although many observers feel such a cause will be found in time and current therapeutic efforts are largely palliative in nature.

DIAGNOSTIC CONSIDERATIONS

Symbiotic children seem quite normal during the first year or two of life except for sleep disturbance. These children are usually described as fussy or oversensitive infants. With the maturation of the motor apparatus the trouble starts. Symbiotic psychosis generally manifests itself between the ages of three and five years. Generally it is ushered in by a separation from the mother, i.e., via sickness, the birth of a sibling, or placement in a nursery school. The child reacts to this separation with intense anxiety of such a severe nature as to resemble the distress of early infancy. These children are literally in a panic, acutely agitated, and exhibit almost catatoniclike behavior. The child's ability to tolerate even minor frustrations decreases markedly.

In an effort to cope with these panics, there are hallucinations, and the child often hypercathects and becomes preoccupied with one part of his body. For example, one child went around saying compulsively, "These hands, are they my hands, could these hands kill?" There are often hallucinatory soliloquies in which the ambivalently cathected object can be heard fighting with the person himself. These children crave body contact but often this degenerates into a biting and hitting at the object in order to capture and devour it, to literally incorporate the object into the self.

If the process continues such children may deteriorate further and present an autisticlike picture as described in the previous chapter. Mixed pictures showing symbiotic and autistic features are fairly common. These children generally do not show the same picture of severe intellectual retardation as found in autistic children.

TREATMENT

Psychoanalytically oriented treatment of such children, often with added psychotropic medication, can be effective. What one tries to do is form a symbiotic tie between the child and the therapist and then gradually rework with the child the process of separation-individuation until object constancy is reached. In some cases this may be effectively done in a hospital or residential treatment center which facilitates the child's development of the symbiotic relationship to the therapist.

Many therapists do not clearly separate the symbiotic child psychosis from the autistic psychosis and thus the symbiotic children do not get adequate psychotherapy to alleviate this distressing condition. To be effective psychotherapy must probably be more frequent than once a week and must be correctly conceptualized.

Many of the mothers of children with symbiotic psychosis demonstrate significant problems in separating from the children. Disturbances in the mothering process, where the mother may be unable to distinguish the child from herself, require intense work with the mother for successful treatment. Such mothers, if untreated, cannot permit separation from the child and may withdraw the child from treatment or sabotage therapy in other ways.

Twenty years ago all cases of early childhood psychosis were regarded as functional in origin and psychotherapy was prescribed with enthusiasm. The blame for the condition was placed on the mother.

Today the pendulum has swung the other way and a strictly biological approach with Pavlovian conditioning and perceptual retraining rules the day. The nondynamically oriented ocular therapist, the behavior conditioner, the orthomolecular biologist today provide much of the therapy of early childhood psychosis. What must be done is a better process of screening out those children who would benefit more from psychotherapeutic techniques and those who need a behavioral approach. Perhaps both are needed.

Unfortunately, there are few treatment facilities providing adequate care for children with early onset child psychosis. Treatment tends to take a long time, is very costly, and the results are uncertain. In today's climate, where even mental health care must show a significant cost-benefit ratio, the outlook for the development of more specialized centers to treat these conditions is poor. Many children with early onset child psychosis will have to continue to go without or receive inadequate care, with the burden falling on concerned parents.

BIBLIOGRAPHY

Bettelheim, B. (1967). *The Empty Fortress.* New York: Free Press.

Hingtgen, J., and Brysen, C. (1972). Recent developments in the study of early childhood psychosis: infantile autism, childhood schizophrenia, and related disorders. *Schizophrenia Bulletin* 5:8–54. Good summary of research.

Kanner, L. (1943). Autistic disturbance of affective content. *Nervous Child* 2:217–250.

————(1973). *Childhood Psychosis: Initial Studies and New Insights.* Washington: V. H. Winston. Complete clinical survey of infantile autism—excellent book.

Lotter, V. (1966). Epidemiology of autistic conditions in young children. *Social Psychiatry* 1:124–137.

Mahler, M. (1952). On child psychosis and schizophrenia: autistic and symbiotic infantile psychoses. *Psychoanalytic Study of the Child* 7:286–305.

Ornitz, E., and Ritvo, E. (1976). The syndrome of autism: a critical review. *American Journal of Psychiatry* 133:610–622. An excellent survey article. A good presentation of organic factors.

Rimland, B. (1964). *Infantile Autism.* New York: Appleton-Century-Crofts.

Rutter, M. (1972). Childhood schizophrenia reconsidered. *Journal of Autism and Childhood Schizophrenia* 20:315–337.

Chapter 5

CHILDHOOD PSYCHOSIS (CHILDHOOD

SCHIZOPHRENIA)

Jeremy R. Mack, M.D.

DEFINITION OF SYNDROME

Any consideration of childhood schizophrenia must start by dealing with one fundamental question: can such an entity be defined? While there is basic agreement on some essential aspects of this condition, there are contradictory findings by many investigators, *all* of whom believe they are working with a psychotic or schizophrenic population of children. In this review, I will attempt to respond to this question of definition and to this confusion. In this chapter the term "childhood schizophrenia" will be used with the understanding that its onset may be in the infantile period prior to thirty months.

Different descriptive terminology has been applied to the same or similar groups of children: for example, childhood schizophrenia (Bender 1947), infantile autism (Kanner 1942), atypical development (Rank 1949), organic psychosis or chronic brain damage (Knobloch and Pasamanick 1962), or borderline psychosis (Ekstein and Wallerstein 1957). Usually the term childhood psychosis is used to apply to the entire range of severe childhood aberrations.

The presence of opposing findings by different workers on the same question is not unusual in studies of infantile psychosis. Psychotic children are sometimes seen as totally detached, poor in adaptive skills and language ability, and subnormal in intelligence. Other studies find such children to have complicated defensive structures: phobic, obsessional, paranoid, and depressive. With regard to the prevalence of mental disease in the families of psychotic children, a number of authors found adult schizophrenia in the relatives. Other studies find very little schizophrenia in parents and relatives.

REVIEW OF LITERATURE

Differences among present-day workers may be elucidated by a review of the development of the concept of childhood psychosis. Originally this entity was thought of as related to adult psychosis, especially with regard to diagnosis, prognosis, and treatment. In the late nineteenth century for example, workers described infantile manias, dementias, and insanity. Reference was made to constitutional, psychological, and organic bases for these conditions. Workers attempted to differentiate the "manias" from mental deficiency. Changes in classification and criteria for diagnosis of adult disorders in the early twentieth century gave rise, when applied to children, to such categories as dementia precocissima of De Sanctis in 1925 and Hulse's dementia infantilis in 1954. Both terms sound as if derived from Kraepelin's dementia praecox of 1919.

Kraepelin's influence tended to reduce attention to social and psychological factors in the origin and outcome of serious childhood disorders, as well as those of adults. During the time of his preeminence, studies found the clinical outcome of psychotic children to be consistently poor, as "dementia" was inevitable.

Bleuler placed greater stress on adaptational and intrapsychic features of psychosis. The early child clinicians, Bradley (1941) and Potter (1933), applied Bleuler's criteria of psychosis in their diagnostic work with children. His emphasis on diversity of outcome and clinical course probably influenced the development of a more hopeful attitude in those attempting to treat psychotic children. In addition, the diagnostic entity, childhood schizophrenia, may well have been derivative of Bleuler's distinction between adult and adolescent schizophrenia.

In the third decade of this century, the diagnosis of childhood psychosis was increasingly accepted. Potter (1933) set out a diagnostic scheme which took into account the immaturity and developmental aspects of childhood. His criteria included: (1) a general retraction of interest from the environment; (2) unrealistic thinking, feeling, and acting; (3) thought disturbance; (4) defect in emotional rapport; (5) diminution, rigidity, and distortion of affect. In 1941, Bradley and Bowen attempted to distinguish between children having schizophrenic psychosis and schizoid personalities. They noted that apathy and blunting, characteristics of adult schizophrenics, were *not* present in their sample of children. They recommended that the course of the child's development must be considered in the diagnosis as well as the symptomatology. Despert (1938) defined schizophrenia as a "disease process in which the loss of affective contact with reality is coincident with or determined by the appearance of autistic thinking and accompanied by specific phenomena of regression and dissociation." Her diagnostic criteria seem not as sharply defined as Potter's, but she stressed the child's failure to achieve normal emotional responsiveness to reality. In addition, she made reference to the aberrant speech function of her study group. She stressed her observation that words were *not* used for their function in communication and that there was a dissociation between "language sign" and "language function."

Since 1940 the field of childhood psychosis has been dominated by a relatively small number of investigators who have made increasingly precise definitions of this entity. Included in this group are Bender, Eisenberg, Goldfarb, Kanner, Mahler, Rank, Rimland, and Rutter. Of these workers, it is probably Bender whose monumental study primarily established childhood psychosis as an entity.

In Bender's view, the disorders that she observed were a form of schizophrenia which she termed childhood schizophrenia. This point is deserving of mention I think, because so much has been made recently of the distinction between the forms of pathology seen in children of this group and those of adult schizophrenics. Rutter has argued that there are such extreme differences in the symptoms and epidemiological features of childhood and adult schizophrenias as to indicate that they are two distinct disease states. Therefore, the similarity of label is misleading, he feels. Fish (1977) on the other hand has recently presented evidence favoring the concept of a continuity between the two states.

The term *childhood schizophrenia* however is still in use and was defined by Bender as "a total psychobiological disorder in the regulation of maturation of all the basic behavior functions seen clinically in childhood. Thus it is a maturational lag with embryonic features as characterized by primitive, (embryonic) plasticity in all patterned behavior in the autonomic, or vegetative, perceptual, motor, intellectual, emotional, and social areas." Bender feels that other conditions such as encephalopathies or defective interpersonal relationships may produce reactions with schizophrenic features. However, in childhood schizophrenia there is an *essential* quality of psychosis. Further, in every case one may find disturbance of vasomotor function, either deficient, or excessive, reflected in excessive flushing or pallor, perspiration, or blueness of the extremities. Response to infection is either a shocklike state with excessive fever or unusually quick recovery. Physiologic responses are aberrant: sleeping, eating, and elimination rhythms are out of order. Pubertal changes in boys and girls are either pre- or post-mature. Growth abnormalities are frequent and result in excessive thinness or obesity, tallness or shortness.

"Nearly specific" for childhood schizophrenia, in Bender's view, are certain postural responses. The whirling response, normally not seen after age six, is frequently seen in schizophrenic children above this age and corresponds, she contends, to their intrinsic impulse to rotate and whirl in outward motility and even in their fantasies. Many of the psychological problems of these children—body fears, poor engagement with the real environment, and disorganized awareness of time, space, and person—derive in her view from this intrinsic tendency to whirl. Perhaps reactive to this phenomenon and these fears are what Bender sees as characteristic behaviors in these children of bodily dependence and physical compliance—their ways of leaning on the adult and melting into the shape of any body with which they are in contact. Her concept is that the schizophrenic child is searching for a source of stability—a center of gravity—with which to defend himself against his inner disorganization.

With regard to physical impulsivity and lack of coordination, Bender's group of children demonstrated darting behaviors and facial grimacing. Their lack of concern with body secretion, body extensions, and clothing, represented, in her view, their poor perceptions of their bodies. She noted further aberrations of perception and poor visuomotor ability as reflected in their tendency to turn horizontal figures to vertical, their poor reproduction of visual images, motor impulsivity, and vague differentiation of figure and ground. Finally, the most common age of onset of this condition in her sample was the period between three and four and a half years.

Other investigators have not been able to confirm the universality and "near specific" quality of symptoms she describes as such, and other institutions dealing with schizophrenic children have found the most common age of onset to be younger. Among the children at the Henry Ittleson Center, for example, the most common age of onset is the first year.

Bender feels that the tendency to childhood schizophrenia is genetically determined. However, the clinical onset derives from a physiological crisis producing decompensation resulting in the symptom picture described. Usually, the crisis occurs around the birth process, and produces one of six clinical expressions of childhood schizophrenia: (1) pseudo-defective (retarded with autistic withdrawal); (2) pseudo-neurotic (serious disturbance but good intelligence and active ideation); (3) psychosomatic (visceral, respiratory, and allergic symptoms); (4) pseudo-psychopathic (impulsivity and antisocial symptoms); (5) frank psychotic; (6) latent schizophrenic (symptoms may never manifest themselves or the patients may be spontaneously symptom-free, especially in latency in girls or puberty in boys). The assumed link between childhood and adult schizophrenia is substantiated by follow-up reports (Bender 1953) indicating that approximately two thirds of her original group were also diagnosed as schizophrenic in adolescence or adulthood. Therefore, childhood schizophrenia and adult schizophrenia are linked presumably by the same genetic determination.

The second dominating force in the field of childhood psychosis since 1940 has been Kanner who in 1942 described early infantile autism. He contended that infantile autism was a distinct diagnostic grouping differentiated from other entities in the larger group of infantile psychosis on the basis of early onset, course of disease, and familial background (see Early Onset Psychosis—Autistic).

Mention should be made of Rank (1949) and Putnam (1955), both representative of a group of workers in Boston who have introduced the use of the term "atypical" to describe deviant children. Employment of this term, they felt, would have the advantage of avoiding the question of the relationship of childhood to adult schizophrenia.

In a review of the apparently confusing and contradictory findings by different workers describing different study populations, some outstanding and common trends can be separated out: (1) all observers have noted serious alterations in biological and psychological development, either in the form of regressions or arrests; (2) all workers are aware of the disordering of the total personality of the psychotic child; (3) all observers note a serious disturbance of emotional engagement with object, human or nonhuman (related to this is the perception that these children are unable to appreciate the essential living character of people); (4) many authors have presumed that the schizophrenic child was genetically or constitutionally vulnerable in the face of emotional stress; (5) there is a tendency towards the relinquishing of "single cause" explanations.

INCIDENCE

Probably because of lack of uniformity and acceptance of classification, data on incidence and prevalence of childhood psychosis is meager. However, the condition seems relatively rare. Lotter in 1967 reported a prevalence of four in ten thousand children in a survey of 76,000 children. Treffert in 1970 found a prevalence of 3.1 per ten thousand children. Of these he separated out 25 percent infantile autists, 57 percent later onset childhood schizophrenics, and 18 percent organic infantile psychotics.

All studies show a higher ratio of boys to girls. The ratio varies from 2 to 1 to 2.7 to 1.

ETIOLOGY

The etiology of childhood psychosis is not established. Theories fall into three main classes: (1) atypism, referring to a primary and intrinsic deficiency in the child; (2) psychosocial causality; (3) a transactional or adaptational position, in which each of the atypical traits is seen as an outcome of the interplay between the child's adaptive potentials and the specific restricting or enhancing qualities of the psychosocial environment.

Theories of atypism involve three bodies of evidence: genetic, biochemical, and neurological. With regard to the genetic question, Bender felt that one gene was responsible for both childhood and adulthood schizophrenia. She based this on finding that a majority of her study population became schizophrenic in adult life, and that there was a high family incidence of mental illness among the relatives of her patients (43 percent of the fathers and 40 percent of the mothers were so afflicted). Prevalence of schizophrenia in families has been surveyed by other workers. Meyers and Goldfarb (1962), in studying the parents of the Ittleson group, found schizophrenia in 28 percent of the mothers, 13 percent of the fathers, and 8 percent of the sibs.

Turning to another area of study bearing on the atypism concept, biochemical studies have been mainly negative and, in addition, suffer from the limitation that it is impossible to determine direction of cause. A list of substances whose effect has been studied includes ceruloplasmin, lactate, pyruvate, serotonin, hair amino acids, L-dopa, sialic acid, creatinine phosphokinase, plasma and erythrocyte cholinesterase, free fatty acids, dopamine beta-hydroxylase, and catechol-o-methyl transferase.

With regard to central nervous system impairment, many studies have documented an increase in prenatal and perinatal difficulties in childhood schizophrenia. Minor anatomic abnormalities—so-called "stigmata"—often associated with abnormal biological states such as Down's syndrome, are found with increased frequency in psychotic children. The same findings apply to "soft signs," neurological signs whose anatomic pathological correlates have not been demonstrated. Kennard in 1949 found a higher incidence of electroencephalographic abnormalities in hospitalized schizophrenic children than in normal members of their families. Other workers have found convulsive manifestations in high number among their groups of schizophrenic children and in follow-up studies.

Recently Hanson and Gottesman (1976) have argued that there is no good evidence to substantiate the concept of genetic determination in the development of childhood psychoses beginning before age five. They feel that biological factors are more likely as determinants for this condition. In addition, they point out that the extreme rareness of autism and childhood psychosis makes analysis of data very difficult.

Theories of psychosocial influence may be ranged along a spectrum from "no influence" (Rutter, Bender) to Szurek who feels that infantile psychosis is the result of emotional conflict.

The transactional viewpoint is probably best represented by Anthony and by Goldfarb who feel that the symptoms of childhood psychosis represent the end result of interaction of deficient substrate with an environment which then may or may not be further altered by the symptom picture itself. Goldfarb, for example, has developed the concept of "parental perplexity" which may exacerbate responses of an essentially psychotic child.

DIAGNOSTIC CONSIDERATIONS (INCLUDING CLASSIFICATION OF CHILDHOOD PSYCHOSIS)

There are four major schemes proposed for classifying childhood psychosis, namely those proposed by: (1) Eisenberg, (2) Rutter, (3) the Group For The Advancement of Psychiatry, and (4) Diagnostic and Statistical Manual III, American Psychiatric Association, (DSM-III).

Eisenberg (1966) proposed two divisions of psychotic disorders: (1) those caused by or associated with impairment of brain tissue, where tissue pathology is demonstrable; and (2) those disorders in which clearly defined structural changes have not as *yet* been demonstrated. In the first division would be included toxic, metabolic, degenerative, dysrhythmic, traumatic, and neoplastic psychoses. Of the remaining functional psychoses, Eisenberg proposed two major subgroups: the infantile autistic psychoses, with onset in the first year and the schizophrenias, which start after eight years of age and satisfy the criteria for adult schizophrenia. He would also include in the functional group *folie à deux,* manic-depressive disease, and finally a group which he terms "psychoses associated with maturation failure." This last group, which he considers of doubtful necessity, contains most of what is ordinarily regarded as childhood schizophrenia. Therefore, the largest group of childhood psychotics are virtually unclassified, according to his arrangement.

The classification of child psychosis proposed by Rutter comprises schizophrenia, disintegrative psychosis, infantile autism, and other psychoses of childhood. However, nowhere in Rutter's scheme is a category specifically for those psychotic children—usually designated as childhood schizophrenic—with onset of profound relational and other disorders prior to thirty months but without the clearly defined autistic symptom picture as described by Kanner. Disintegrative psychosis is regarded as a profound regression appearing after age four in children who have developed normally. Childhood schizophrenia is meant as a state resembling that condition as seen in adults but occurring in older children. "Other psychoses" in Rutter's system includes Gilles de la Tourette, acute confusional states, and ". . . a larger number of non-specific disorders of psychotic intensity which do not exactly fit the criteria for autism, schizophrenia, or disintegrative psychosis. . . ." Most children usually designated by the term childhood schizophrenic would therefore fall into this class, in Rutter's view.

The GAP report of 1966 has suggested a further classifying scheme which again leaves childhood schizophrenia to fend for itself between the two distinct entities of infantile autism and adultlike schizophrenia occurring in later childhood.

As this is written, the latest draft of DSM-III has attempted to remedy the situation of a clinical population without an identity. This scheme of classification recognizes, within the class of childhood psychosis, two entities with onset prior to thirty months. Atypical childhood psychosis, in addition to infantile autism, may begin in this age span and is distinguished from autism mainly by the use of the Creak (1961) criteria, rather than the symptom picture described by Kanner for autists.

The Creak British Working Group (1961) made an effort to establish criteria for what they preferred to call the "schizophrenic syndrome in children." Preference for this term was on the basis that "psychosis" includes many disturbances in addition to the range of disorders described by the functional psychoses. This group defined nine diagnostic points. Some involved interpretation of behavior; others referred to developmental and historical data. Almost all reports of schizophrenic children describe symptoms which can be found in this set of criteria. The nine points are as follows:

1. Gross and sustained impairment of emotional relationships with people.

2. Apparent unawareness of his own personal identity to a degree inappropriate to his age.

3. Pathological preoccupation with particular objects or certain characteristics of them, without regard to their accepted functions.

4. Sustained resistance to change in the environment and a striving to maintain sameness.

5. Abnormal perceptual experience (in the absence of discernible organic abnormality) is implied by excessive, diminished, or unpredictable response to sensory stimuli—for example, visual and auditory avoidance, insensitivity to pain and temperature.

6. Acute, excessive, and seemingly illogical anxiety is a frequent phenomenon.

7. Speech may have been lost or never acquired, or may have never developed beyond an earlier stage level.

8. Distortion in motility patterns—for example, *(a)* excess, as in hyperkinesis; *(b)* immobility, as in catatonia; *(c)* bizarre postures, or ritualistic mannerisms, such as rocking and spinning (themselves or objects).

9. A background of serious retardation in which islets of normal, near-normal, or exceptional intellectual function or skill may appear.

Since the diagnosis of childhood psychosis is a symptom diagnosis, it is of no meaning to attempt to differentiate it from mental deficiency, epilepsy, brain damage, etc. These conditions can coexist with childhood psychosis.

A broad range of adaptive functions—including sensory functioning, cognition, speech, motility, and relational behavior—has been studied. In reviewing these studies, Goldfarb (1970) notes the demonstrated failures in all areas of adaptive behavior, although the findings vary according to level and pattern of impairment.

Frequently the histories of psychotic children arouse suspicion of impaired sensory functions. The possibility of deafness is frequently raised. In addition, many of these children seem to manifest hypo- or hypersensitivity to sensory stimulation. However, these children do not differ in visual, auditory, and tactile acuity from normals (Goldfarb 1961). They do show higher threshold for perception of speech than for pure tones. Therefore, the phenomenon of "not hearing" is not a primary defect of sensory acuity. Rather it may reflect altered attention to or poor integration of human speech by the children.

With regard to their capacity to perceive form and pattern, the psychotic children are inferior to normals. This was shown experimentally by the following four tests: two-point discrimination, finger location, figure-group discrimination, and configurational closure.

In studies of directional orientation, as manifested by a tendency to rotation in the reproduction of design, Fuller found schizophrenic children show a higher rotation effect than both normals and non-schizophrenic emotionally disturbed children. Perhaps the schizophrenic child is less able to use the visual cues for purposes of orientation. Witkin showed that, in the normal child, ability to distinguish figure from ground parallels ability to perceive his own body as discrete from the total surrounding field. Similarly, one might expect that a schizophrenic child who can't distinguish right from left within himself would have difficulty in making such distinction with regard to objects in the outer world. Therefore, his deficiencies in body awareness might exacerbate his problems in spatial orientation.

Impairments in the *conceptual organization* of experience have been noted by all clinical observers of psychotic children (Bender, Goldfarb, Kanner). These impairments are shown in deficiencies of concept of self, body, outer world, time, space, and other persons. They may account for the schizophrenic child's use of "language sign" as opposed to "language function" mentioned by Despert.

These children are bound in a concrete way to the immediacy of a situation and have difficulty in moving to an abstract attitude. This concrete orientation has been confirmed by Norman who noted that psychotic children, as compared to normals, paid more attention to the surface attributes of test objects than the function of these objects.

Perhaps because it measures overall adaptative qualities

such as attention, concentration, and persistence, the intelligence test has been seen as an excellent measure of ego competence as well as the best single measure of integrative functioning. Psychotic children are generally inferior to normals in verbal, performance, and full scale IQ. In the Goldfarb (1961) study, 54 percent had full IQs less than 75 and only 23 percent had full scale IQs of over 90. A majority of schizophrenic children are therefore seriously retarded and only a small proportion show average functioning. However, significant shifts in IQ have been reported in children undergoing treatment.

Conceptual difficulties have, furthermore, been implicated in impairments in the reception and integration of incoming stimuli. This defect was stressed by several workers including Hermelin and O'Connor who proposed a normal developmental sequence of receptive preferences starting with enteroceptive and visceral sensation as dominant in infants, progressing to tactile, kinesthetic, and olfactory senses, and culminating with maturation in the primary use of the distance receptors—hearing and vision. Observation of the psychotic children reveals an obvious preference for proximal receptors—touch, smell, and taste. This tendency contributes to the detached, isolated, and bizarre appearance of the children. It also aids in understanding their lack of eye contact and meaningful use of vocal contact, and would seem to be involved in their impairment of conceptualization and abstraction, which of course require distance and perspective.

From the beginning of the modern concept of childhood psychosis, the diagnostic criteria for this condition have always included *speech and language difficulty.* The concepts of Bender, Despert, and Kanner in this connection have already been mentioned. Systematic investigation has confirmed the correlation between retardation of language and severity of clinical impairment. Anthony (1958) has correlated language level and level of autistic withdrawal. Eisenberg observed that when language was totally impaired at age five, adolescent adjustment was consistently poor.

Schizophrenic children often do not include the normal nonverbal aspects of speech which contribute so much to the communication of meaning and mood. Their vocal quality is often loud, high pitched, and without intonation. Connotative expressions, formed by appropriate alterations of phrasing, phonation, rhythm, articulation, stress and volume are often not employed. All of the behaviors previously described involve neurological functioning. In addition, the findings of so-called soft signs in many schizophrenic children should be noted. As noted above, soft signs are *neurological signs* whose anatomic pathological correlates have not been demonstrated. They include gait disturbances, overflow, whirling, toe walking, deviant vestibular reactions, deviant postural and righting reactions, extinction of double simultaneous sensation, and "stigmata."

By definition, psychotic children manifest disorders in their *relational behavior* to others and the expression of their attachments. They have generally been judged low in human responsiveness. In a 1962 study comparing childhood schizophrenics with normals and retardates, Schachter found the psychotic children were severely impaired in relating to persons and things. Retardates were like schizophrenics in their relations with things, but were like normals in their relations with persons.

TREATMENT AND OUTCOME

Treatment approaches have included psychotherapeutic, conditioning, and biological approaches. Most workers would agree that the preferred treatment for children with this condition consists of a combination of a special milieu and psychotherapy. Important choices—depending on the severity of the child's condition and the family's contribution to it—will need to be made between day vs. residential treatment programs, and the manner and extent of parental involvement in the treatment process. Therapeutic centers should be organized in such a clear and formal way as to help these children make sense and pattern out of themselves and their environment. In this connection speech therapy is frequently of great help. Psychotherapy with the child should be formulated in large part on the basis of the ratio of organic to psychosocial contribution to the child's current difficulty. Some patients will require more analytic approaches; others will benefit more from focus on formal aspects of behavior (appropriate self-care, speech, use of pronouns, etc.). A central problem shared by psychotic children of whatever etiology is grandiosity, the persistence of an early infantile state, which usually needs to be identified and dealt with vigorously.

Recently Engelhart and his group (1973) have reported improvement in the total population of psychotic children placed on antipsychotic medication. With regard to outcome, DeMyer (1973) found, in a seven year longitudinal study, that most infantile autists remained educationally retarded, and 42 percent were institutionalized. In a higher IQ group, 1–2 percent recovered to normal, 5–15 percent reached a borderline status, 16–25 percent had a fair prognosis and 60–75 percent had a poor prognosis. She found that the best predictor of functional capacity was the rating at intake. The next best indicators were performance IQ and severity of illness. Treffert (1973) studied fifty-seven psychotic subjects over an eleven-year treatment period. One third of these children ultimately were discharged to home. The rate of discharge was positively correlated with late onset, development of speech by age five, and completion of toilet training by the time of admission. The balance were those who had psychosis of earlier onset, and these children remained in hospital.

SUMMARY

The field of childhood psychosis is in an early state, with much effort still being spent on issues of taxonomy. The search for variables—like enzymes or performance/verbal IQ ratios—which will aid in making distinctions between disorders is hindered by diagnostic unclarity in that one population of infantile psychotics may be quite different from another. Techniques for making distinctions have reflected the historical movement of psychiatric trends through phenomenology, psychoanalysis, learning theory, and biochemical and physiological approaches. Two factors with regard to infantile psychosis seem to have held constant: the incidence is quite small and the outcome is generally poor.

BIBLIOGRAPHY

Anthony, E.J. (1958). An experimental approach to the psychopathology of childhood. *British Journal of Medical Psychology* 31:211–223.

Bender, L. (1947). Childhood schizophrenia: clinical study of one hundred schizophrenic children. *American Journal of Orthopsychiatry* 17:40–56.

———(1953). Childhood schizophrenia. *Psychiatric Quarterly* 27:663–681.

Bradley, C. (1941). *Schizophrenia in Childhood.* New York: Macmillan.

Creak, M. (1961). Schizophrenic syndrome in children. Progress report of a working party. *Cerebral Palsy Bulletin* 3:-501–504.

DeMyer, M. (1973). Prognosis in autism—a follow-up study. *Journal of Autism and Childhood Schizophrenia* 3:199–246.

Despert, J. (1938). Schizophrenia in childhood. *Psychiatric Quarterly* 12:366–371.

Eisenberg, L. (1966). Psychotic disorders in childhood. In *Biological Basis of Pediatric Practice,* ed. R. Cook. New York: McGraw-Hill.

Ekstein, R., and Wallerstein, J. (1957). Choice of interpretation in the treatment of borderline and psychotic children. *Bulletin of the Menninger Clinic* 21:199–207.

Engelhardt, D., Polizos, P., Waizer, J., and Hoffman, S. (1973). A double-blind comparison of fluphenazine and haloperidol in outpatient schizophrenic children. *Journal of Autism and Childhood Schizophrenia* 3:128–137.

Fish, B. (1977). Neurobiological antecedants of schizophrenia in children. *Archives of General Psychiatry* 34:1297–1313.

Goldfarb, W. (1961). *Childhood Schizophrenia.* Cambridge, Mass.: Harvard University Press.

———(1970). Childhood psychosis. In *Carmichael's Manual of Child Psychology,* ed. P. Mussen, 3rd ed. pp. 765–830. New York: Wiley.

Hanson, D., and Gottesman, I. (1976). The genetics, if any, of infantile autism and childhood schizophrenia. *Journal of Autism and Childhood Schizophrenia* 6:209–234.

Kanner, L. (1942). Autistic disturbances of affective contact. *Nervous Child* 2:217–250.

Knobloch, H., and Pasamanick, B. (1962). Etiologic factors in early infantile autism and childhood schizophrenia. Address at Tenth International Congress of Pediatrics, Lisbon, September.

Meyers, D., and Goldfarb, W. (1962). Psychiatric appraisal of parents and siblings of schizophrenic children. *American Journal of Psychiatry* 118:902–915.

Potter, H. (1933). Schizophrenia in children. *American Journal of Psychiatry* 12:1253–1270.

Rank, B. (1949). Adaptation of the psychoanalytic technique for the treatment of young children with atypical development. *American Journal of Orthopsychiatry* 19:130–139.

Rutter, M. (1972). Childhood schizophrenia reconsidered. *Journal of Autism and Childhood Schizophrenia* 2:315–337.

Treffert, D., McAndrew, J., and Dreifurst, P. (1973). An inpatient treatment program and outcome for 57 autistic and schizophrenic children. *Journal of Autism and Childhood Schizophrenia* 3:138–153.

Chapter 6

BORDERLINE CONDITIONS

Ruth R. Fuchs, M.D.

Anna H. vanderSchraaf, M.D.

DEFINITION

Freedman and Kaplan define borderline state (borderline psychosis) as a "state in which the symptoms are so unclear or transient, that it is difficult to classify the patient as psychotic or non-psychotic." According to these authors, "the term borderline or borderland was first used by Hughes in 1884 to designate conditions lying between schizophrenia and neurosis."

The authors of this chapter define borderline conditions (or states) of childhood as those characterized by diverse symptomatology with underlying deviant, abnormal, and/or uneven development of psychic structure and function, especially pertaining to perceptions and feelings toward self- and object representations. By *self-representation* is meant an enduring schema constructed by the ego out of the multitude of realistic and distorted self-images which the individual has had at different times. *Object representations* refer to enduring schemas of particular persons other than the self modeled by the ego from a multitude of impressions, images, and experiences.

REVIEW OF LITERATURE

The early literature deals with the subject in descriptive terms. Freud in 1913 spoke of "incipient schizophrenia, masked by a neurotic facade." The earlier trend appeared to be to regard the condition as one of "latent, potential or a transitional stage of psychosis." The terminology used by the following authors attest to this notion: Fliess, as well as Zilboorg—"ambulatory schizophrenia"; Hoch and Polatin—"pseudo-neurotic schizophrenia."

The question whether it represented a continuum between or a coexistence of neurosis and psychosis was another issue. Rangel and Arieti seemed to favor, while Fenichel rejected, the idea of a spectrum based on severity of illness.

Knight in 1954 delineated the condition, described recognizable symptoms, and recommended a specific therapeutic technique. An attempt at formulating structural characteristics was made the same year by Bychowski. J. Frosch in 1961 described the "psychotic character"—a clinical entity with specific diagnostic criteria much like those now assigned to the borderline group of patients. He emphasized features useful to distinguish the psychotic character from the psychotic. He spoke of the intact capacity for reality testing. Even when having hallucinations, the patient recognizes these as such. Diffusion of ego boundaries is said to be reversible. Object relations are on a need-gratifying level.

In the early child literature Mahler (1949) reported on sixteen cases of childhood psychosis, and defined three types according to onset and severity. One of these, with benign pathology, more ego development, and an ability to use neurotic defense mechanisms, may correspond to the present-day borderline category.

Weil (1953) cited cases with severe disturbances in ego development and she pointed to a constitutional element which she called "deviant anlage."

Geleerd (1946) described children with behavior disorders and deviation in almost all phases of development and the need for the presence of an adult to maintain their hold on reality. She spoke of a short "reality span." In a later paper (1958) she attempted to define etiology and symptomatology in order to differentiate this entity from neurosis.

Rosenfeld and Sprince (1963) emphasized that the degree of deviation of ego development does not distinguish borderline from schizophrenia. The capacity for internalization and inner representation of self and object based upon object cathexis is the crucial area for assessment and prediction.

O. Kernberg (1967) outlined the basic personality structure and disturbance in object relations in adolescent and adult borderline conditions. He enumerated presumptive and definitive factors for diagnosis, and reviewed the key contributions of others in the literature.

Ekstein and Wallerstein (1954) focused on ego organization in borderline and psychotic children. Pine (1974) discussed the "borders" with neurosis and psychosis and conceptualized the borderline child as showing an "arrest or aberrant development of ego functions and object relations." He distinguished six types: *(a)* chronic ego deviance (Weil's "deviant children"); *(b)* shifting levels of overall ego organization; *(c)* internal disorganization depending on external factors, e.g., children who integrate when hospitalized; and *(d)* incomplete internalization of psychosis, e.g., disturbance in a child living with a psychotic parent. The first two groups are based on the internal structure, the last two are related to external factors. He adds the categories *(e)* ego limitations, and *(f)* schizoid personality, as two groups with more fixed defensive and coping mechanisms.

Beres (1956) and Geleerd (1958) stress the differences in clinical presentation due to the stage of the developing child. (A. Freud's listing of chronological defense operations may be referred to in this regard).

Special therapeutic techniques are found in articles by Ekstein and Wallerstein (1956), Rosenfeld and Sprince (1965), Chethik and Fast (1970), Wax (1973), Tooley (1973), and P. Kernberg (1977 unpublished).

INCIDENCE

A survey of the literature reveals only two references, those of Aarkrog, in *Acta Scandinavia* in 1973 and 1975, regarding incidence of borderline admissions to the adolescent unit of Bispebjerg Hospital. In this study for the period of 1968–1975, one third of one hundred admissions were psychotic and borderline in equal numbers. Therefore the incidence of borderlines among admitted adolescents is approximately 15 percent.

It is our opinion that the diverse clinical manifestations and the absence of the condition as an entity in the *Diagnostic and Statistical Manual II* handicap statistical studies.

ETIOLOGY AND DYNAMICS

Normal development is based on favorable constitutional and environmental factors. Constitutional factors such as the "strength of the drives and the biologically provided sub-

strate of the ego apparatus enter importantly into the determination of the outcome of potentially traumatic experiences
not only as to mastery versus fixation, but also to the nature
of the acquired ego defenses and adaptive techniques" (Settlage). O. Kernberg noted the importance of oral aggression,
coupled with a history of severe frustration. Blindness, deafness, and defect in the motor apparatus could equally alter
the course of development.

The importance of the human object for early psychic development has been well established. The loss of or separation from the mother can occur not only because of physical
separation, but also because of libidinal decathexis of the
child by her. In terms of family contributions, Settlage states
"symptoms and defenses can be gained through identification with a parent." Commenting on the role of the father,
he points to the help the father can offer the child in resisting
the powerful attraction to the symbiotic partner in his move
towards autonomy. Pathological communications between
family members have been mentioned by P. Kernberg, such
as "family secrets, narcissistic use of the child, dominant
intrusive behavior, depersonification of the child, who is
treated as an object to soothe a mother's anxiety rather than
as a person in his own right."

The timing of the traumatic experience leading to the borderline state is accepted to be in (or during) the *rapprochement*
subphase of Mahler's separation-individuation; P. Kernberg
(1977) places it several months earlier in the *differentiation* or
practicing subphases.

Settlage emphasizes that in the formation of psychopathology, the correlation of the psychic trauma with the
newly delineated phases and emerging attainments of primary psychic development "are pivotal." Thus, the age specific tasks in the *rapprochement* subphase also constitute the

areas of vulnerability in the *rapprochement crisis:* the timing of the trauma, degree of impact and severity of defensive response, and area of personality involved are all important. He describes the age specific tasks of the *rapprochement* subphase: (1) mastery of cognitively intensified separation anxiety; (2) affirmation of the sense of basic trust; (3) gradual deflation and relinquishment of the sense of omnipotence experienced in the symbiotic dual unity with the mother; (4) gradual compensation for the deflated sense of omnipotence through development of the child's burgeoning ego capacities and sense of autonomy; (5) firming up of a core-sense of self; (6) establishment of sense of capability for ego control and modulation of strong libidinal and aggressive urges and affects (infantile rage); (7) healing of the developmentally normal tendency to maintain the relation with the love object by splitting it into a "good" and "bad" object, thus also healing the corresponding intrapsychic split; (8) supplanting the splitting defense with repression as the later defensive means of curbing unacceptable affects and impulses toward the love objects.

Settlage believes that in the narcissistic personality the lack of ego deficit and good functioning suggest a good mother-child relationship in the first year of life. Difficulty during the *rapprochement* subphase may account for the deficit in self-esteem and sense of self, and the longing for but fear of intimacy in object relationships. He points out that some mothers can capably minister to a totally dependent infant but not to an individuating assertive toddler, who normally resists control and discipline. Such a mother can defensively temporarily withdraw emotional support from the child, abandoning him to his impulses and affects or she can respond with "abrupt, excessive anger and assertion of control. In either case, the mother's not being libidinally and helpfully available to the child poses the threat of intrapsychic loss, potentially engendering a severe 'rapprochement' crisis."

The child, deprived of needed external regulatory help, resorts to stringent defenses that not only impair self-object differentiation but cause faulty ego development. Central among the defensive operations is "splitting" which with the other early forms of denial, idealization, devaluation and projection make up the primitive yet structured forms of defense.

DIAGNOSTIC CONSIDERATIONS

The infinite range of clinical presentation of the borderline conditions in children calls for careful history taking and a prolonged diagnostic evaluation extending into the initial therapeutic work.

The presenting complaint in the preschooler might be disordered speech, extreme aggression, or unrelatedness. The latency child can come with behavior problems, underachievement, daydreaming, or multiple neurotic symptoms such as obsessions, compulsions, and phobias lasting beyond their age appropriate phases. An adolescent might present with hysterical traits and symptoms, a schizoid personality, or behavior disorders beyond the expected turmoil of this period.

Poor impulse control and a low frustration tolerance lead to numerous behavioral disturbances. Frustration might not only lead to aggressive behavior but can cause withdrawal or retreat into a fantasy world.

Lack of sublimatory channels might show in the exclusive choice of one area of interest, mostly pursued in isolation.

Joyless play in young children and underachievement in academic work are common.

Anxiety has a specific quality. Signal anxiety leading to defensive operations is unknown. Often a minimal stimulus evokes extreme anxiety, bordering on panic, experienced as annihilation or disintegration.

An assessment of libidinal development finds appropriate phase dominance in psychosexual development has not been achieved. Aggression seems absent or uncontrolled and excessive. Prominent bisexual conflict can exist and is based on identification problems.

Object relationships are on a need-satisfying level. There is a difficulty in maintaining object cathexis and these children are constantly on the border between object cathexis and identification. The sense of self is disturbed. The sense of time is impaired, the future is of scant consequence.

Superego functioning and reality testing remain overly dependent on the external object and are therefore relatively unstable. The capacity for feelings of concern, guilt, and empathy is reduced and superego functioning is on a punitive level. Reality adaptation is compromised, the pleasure principle prevails, and when frustration occurs an illusory world is created to provide gratification.

In another area of specific ego function, that of the motor apparatus, deviance or fluctuating levels have been reported, e.g., peculiar gait, bizarre posture, rigidity, hyperactivity, and lack of modulation in speech.

Disturbed speech, which is often reversible, occurs. There are shifts into primary process thinking with condensation, substitution of a part for the whole, ease of displacement and symbolization. Magical thought is possibly based on a faulty barrier between conscious and preconscious thinking.

Perceptual disturbances such as hallucinations have been

observed. The incapacity to inhibit and select stimuli (especially emotionally-laden ones) might lead to distractibility.

Defense mechanisms are primitive, with splitting, faulty repression, denial, projection, idealization, and devaluation prominent.

TREATMENT

Treatment of borderline states in children has been of great interest to clinicians and theoreticians. Ekstein and Wallerstein (1956) describe the difficulties in treatment engendered by the "autistic and symbiotic cast" of the therapeutic relationship at the beginning of treatment (the precipitous fluctuations in role of defense mechanisms, the rapid changes in ego states). They note "ego regression was directly preceded by an inadvertent rebuke or lack of comprehension by the therapist of the child's message, and the return into the secondary process followed directly upon the therapist's retrieving the error and demonstrating his sympathy and understanding." The maintenance of the therapeutic relationship, often made possible by interpreting within the regression, lays a foundation for the new development of identificatory processes rather than the superimposition of an unstable facade. They comment on the difficult necessity for the therapist of "living oneself into" the world of the borderline child.

Rosenfeld and Sprince (1965) compare the therapist's meeting of the child's need for symbiosis to the mother's offering herself as a symbiotic object to the child. This implies—on the part of the mother and the therapist—permitting the "blurring of ego boundaries" with that of the child as well as "stepping back into a protective position in case of need." The authors recommend "ego supportive handling" of borderline children, and aim to help the child become aware that tension can be at least temporarily contained and acting out controlled. On the other hand, they concede that the borderline child might need to "relive early traumata through a type of treatment offering opportunities for regressively experiencing developmental processes." The authors feel such treatment might require an institutional setting.

Several points of view about interpretation of aggressive conflict are presented. Such an interpretation was deemed important in the development of therapeutic attachment. However, such interpretations can be taken by the child as the therapist siding with the aggressive drive, leading to an increase in aggressive behavior. On the other hand, the child may take the words of the therapist literally, and think of himself as "bad" thus reinforcing an already existing bad self-image. They conclude that what matters is "not the kind of approach" but rather the question of balance, timing and the personality of the therapist.

Chethik and Fast (1970) describe the use of fantasy. Rather than viewing fantasy as an obstacle to therapy to be gotten rid of, they advocate helping the child grow out of it. They recognize fantasy as an integral part of development; in borderline children, the illusory world contributes the firm libidinal base from which the child explores the possibilities of achieving an "identity in a benign external world." They suggest that the therapist, rather than avoiding fantasies, actively participate in and encourage their elaboration. He can then delineate the underlying fears and anxieties, including any possible reality elements, and help the child to work them through. "His presence is the representation of the external world in contact with the illusory one . . . as the child begins to trust the therapist he can be allowed to function more independently within the fantasy and in relating elements to reality." Thus, they regard the therapist as a major vehicle for the child's very gradual integration of the illusory world with the real one.

Tooley (1973) views "playing crazy" as the borderline child's tendency to make controlled excursions into psychosis to reassure himself that he is not caught up in a terrifying process outside of his control. Tooley suggests that borderline children enjoy the introduction of reality rules into their play because these rules are experienced as minute threats swiftly mastered. "It functions, I believe as the mother-child dyad is theorized to function in the transitional object phase in which the mother judiciously introduces minimal and manageable doses of frustration and separation along with gratification in her weaning of the child to the reality principle." Tooley recommends "playing it right" as a way to make the child's play more complex and satisfying by adding one element of unpredictability—a surprise that is pleasant because it proves to be manageable. "To the borderline child sameness means love and unity; difference means separateness and loss." The central fantasy may be regarded as a transitional phenomenon, a help in mastering the trauma of separation, a comfort when the outer world is too remote and unsatisfying and the inner world too chaotic and formless. The therapist, in play with the borderline child, can increase reality connections gradually as the patient's tolerance increases, and make interventions "by means of arguments" which allow the patient to consider them in disguised form.

P. Kernberg (1977) emphasizes the importance of individuation and separation from parents as a goal in treatment. This may be done through joint work with the mother-child dyad or through family therapy, since multiple projective identifications* and mutual distortions need to be unraveled. Anxieties concerning the process of individuation, with either fear of abandonment or annihilation, must be worked through and the separation-individuation phase thus recapitulated.

Settlage proposes the concept of the analytic process as being both a therapeutic and developmental process. He feels the analyst can function as a temporary auxiliary ego while adhering at the same time to the precept of abstention from gratification of the patient's libidinal as opposed to ego needs.

DISCUSSION

The interest in "borderline" adults has existed for about a century and in the latter third of this period many contributions toward understanding the borderline child have been added.

However, only with recent advances in infant and child observation, theories of child development, and therapeutic innovations has this condition emerged as a discrete entity.

Consequently the recognition of the "borderline condition" underlying the variegated symptomatology is of great clinical importance in regard to more effective therapy and thus more hopeful prognosis.

---

*Projective identification is characterized by lack of differentiation between self and object, especially as pertains to aggressive impulses, by continuing to experience the impulse as well as the fear of that impulse while the projection is active and by the need to control the external object.

SUMMARY

A historical review and current concepts of the borderline child have been provided. Diagnostic criteria and therapeutic technique based on the specific psychopathology are presented. The need for recognition of the condition beneath the numerous surface manifestations has been emphasized to insure correct therapeutic approaches.

BIBLIOGRAPHY

Beres, D. (1956). Ego deviation and the concept of schizophrenia. *Psychoanalytic Study of the Child* 11:164–235.

Chethik, M., and Fast, I. (1970). A function of fantasy in the borderline child. *American Journal of Orthopsychiatry* 40:-756–765.

Ekstein, R., and Wallerstein, J. (1954). Observations on the psychology of borderline and psychotic children: report from a current psychotherapy research project at Southard School. *Psychoanalytic Study of the Child* 9:344–369.

———(1956). Observations on the psychotherapy of borderline and psychotic children. *Psychoanalytic Study of the Child* 11:303–311.

Geleerd, E. (1946). A contribution to the problem of psychoses in childhood. *Psychoanalytic Study of the Child.* 2:-271–291.

———(1958). Borderline states in childhood and adolescence. *Psychoanalytic Study of the Child* 13:279–295.

Kernberg, O. (1967). Borderline personality organization. *Journal of American Psychoanalytic Association.* 15:641–685.

Kernberg, P. (1977). Borderline conditions: childhood and adolescent aspects. Paper presented at the Second An-

nual Combined meeting of the Society for Adolescent
Psychiatry and the New York Council on Child Psychiatry. New York, April 1977.

Mahler, M., Ross, J., and DeFries, Z. (1949). Clinical studies
in benign and malignant cases of childhood psychosis.
American Journal of Orthopsychiatry 19:295–305.

Pine, F. (1974). On the concept "borderline" in children.
Psychoanalytic Study of the Child 19:341–368.

Rosenfeld, S., and Sprince, M. (1963). An attempt to formulate the meaning of the concept "borderline." *Psychoanalytic Study of the Child* 18:603–635.

———(1965). Some thoughts on the technical handling of
borderline children. *Psychoanalytic Study of the Child* 20:-
495–517.

Settlage, C. (1977). The psychoanalytic understanding of
narcissistic and borderline personality disorders—advances in developmental theory. *Journal of the American
Psychoanalytic Association* 4:805–833.

Tooley, K. (1973). Playing it right—a technique for the treatment of borderline children. *Journal of the American Academy of Child Psychiatry* 12:615–631.

Wax, D. (1973). Learning how to pretend: a distinction between intent and pretence observed in the treatment of
a borderline psychotic boy. *British Journal of Medical Psychology* 64:297–302.

Weil, A. (1953). Certain severe disturbances of ego development in childhood. *Psychoanalytic Study of the Child* 8:-
271–286.

Part II

Pathologies of Childhood

Section A

The Common Neuroses

and Affective Disorders

Chapter 7

OBSESSIVE-COMPULSIVE SYNDROMES

Ruth K. Karush, M. D.

DEFINITION

Classical obsessive-compulsive illness has three basic components:

1. Unwanted repetitive ideas, images, affects or impulses which we call obsessions and which neither reason, logic nor conscious effort are able to influence.

2. Repetitive, stereotyped, and usually trivial acts which we call compulsions. For the patient, the failure to perform the act results in an increase in anxiety. Once performed, however, there is usually a temporary reduction in tension.

3. The obsessions and compulsions are recognized as unreasonable and alien to the personality and the patient feels that they must be combatted and resisted.

Anxiety that has been aroused by an unconscious conflict is dealt with by the occurrence of thoughts (obsessions), acts (compulsions), or a mixture of both, which are defensively isolated from the unacceptable wish. The overt behavior of the child is often the opposite of the unconscious wish. For example, excessive cleanliness and washing counteract

wishes to soil and mess. These children usually appear unhappy. They are humorless and serious-looking, with a gross
deficit of spontaneity. While their verbal communications are
frequently felt to be their forte, children suffering from
obsessive-compulsive disease often use their linguistic
competency to confuse and mystify rather than to communicate meaningfully. They are not good mixers and usually
prefer solitary play.

Obsessive-compulsive illness of children represents a significant exaggeration of the normal behavior of all children.
Compulsive ritualization is inherent in normal development.
Piaget identified this behavior in infants. Gesell mentioned
the ages of two and three years as being an especially prominent period for the development of complicated ritualistic
behavior. The young "anal stage" child must do everything
"just so" in eating, toileting, dressing and play. According to
Gesell, "ritualization is a method of defining and perhaps
improving new abilities, but it is itself a general ability and
product of growth." The normal play of children is filled with
ritualistic and compulsive behavior. Adams (1973, p. 6)
speaks of ritualized collective play as the form of play in
which peer group norms and group influences are at the
forefront. Jacks, hopscotch, jump rope that school children
play for hours, have a compulsive quality. Their overdoing of
the rules leads one to suspect that, according to their inner
wishes, the children are a group of young lawbreakers.

Ritualized solitary play that is not in the second or third
year of life might be viewed as a possible precursor to obsessional illness. Adams (1973, p. 6) points out the emotional
isolation and withdrawal of a child engaged in a solitary,
repetitive activity. Sometimes, because of its driven quality,
obsessive collecting can look like a neurotic symptom. Usually, however, it is short-lived. Finally, circumscribed inter-

ests, or impulsions as Bender called them, may look even more serious. Children with circumscribed interests are those who become immersed in very specialized subjects, such as short-wave radio or stereo recordings, to the exclusion of everything else. Their development is one-sided. Even impulsions can be dropped or overcome as the child grows and development proceeds.

It remains for us to differentiate the obsessive-compulsive character from the obsessional neurotic. Those children who suffer from the character disorder are those who have a generally obsessive-compulsive style but few overt symptoms. They are rigid, overinhibited, overconscientious, overdutiful, and unable to relax easily. They usually do not utilize rituals. Children with an obsessive-compulsive neurosis are ill with definite symptoms. They suffer distress when prevented from completing a ritual or when concerned about being unable to control it themselves. Finally, it must be noted that obsessive-compulsive symptomatology can be seen in other illnesses such as depression, schizophrenia, and brain damage.

REVIEW OF THE LITERATURE

In the literature there is some disagreement as to whether the obsessive-compulsive neurosis can even be seen in children. As early as 1875, Legrand du Saulle concluded that the obsessive malady began only at puberty or later. General textbooks of child psychiatry indicate that the onset before puberty is rare. Kanner points out that children are infrequently brought for the treatment of this neurosis before the age of fourteen. He comments on the many analytic authors who in reporting adult analyses have traced obsessive symptoms to childhood. Kanner makes the interesting point that while the obsessive adolescent or adult limits his rumination to himself, the obsessive child forces others to participate in his defensive activities. For example, his mother must dress him in a certain way and she must answer his repetitious questions. Benjamin as well as Bakwin and Bakwin agree that while obsessive ideas and compulsive actions are common in children, they are relatively innocuous and not neurotic.

Other authors, usually reporting from specific clinical data, give evidence that this illness does occur in childhood. One of the earliest references to disabling compulsive symptoms in a child was recorded by Freud in 1895. He mentioned an eleven-year-old girl who already showed obsessions. In 1903, Janet cited a case of a five-year-old obsessive child. But Freud in *The Predisposition to Obsessional Neurosis,* published in 1913, assigned age six to eight as the usual time of onset, an idea that has remained extremely influential. Muriel Hall, in 1935, reported two cases of obsessive-compulsive neurosis in twelve-year-old children and gave an optimistic view of the prognosis of the disease in children.

Five years later, Bender and Schilder described a syndrome called *impulsions* where, as described earlier, the children, usually male, were preoccupied with very specific interests to the exclusion of other activities. These authors felt that a significant percentage of the cases of obsessive-compulsive neuroses formerly reported fell into the impulsion category and the neurosis was rare before age ten. In 1942, Leo Berman reviewed 3,050 cases admitted to Bellevue Hospital and the Bradley Home during a four-year period. Sixty-two of these cases had been diagnosed as having obsessive-compulsive neurosis. More careful examination eliminated all but six. The average age of these cases was eleven and a half.

In the early 1950s Bonnard, Freiberg, and Bornstein each published an account of successful psychoanalytic treatment of young obsessive children. Regner, in 1959, in the Scandinavian literature, indicated that the diagnosis in children is not uncommon but that most of the cases were resistant to psychotherapy. Then, Anna Freud's *Normality and Pathology in Childhood,* published in 1965, presented the view that obsessions in all childhood stages are very likely to be fluid and may be indistinct from hysteria, antisocial reactions, or phobias. Judd (1965) published his detailed study of five obsessive children. He listed eight traits which all five children had in common. Traumatic bowel training had not been present in four of the five cases. Adams (1973) published forty-nine case histories in a book devoted to obsessive behavior in children.

INCIDENCE

It appears that obsessive illness is a relative rarity among children. The condition, in general, is felt to occur in the upper brackets of social class, intelligence, and education, but cases among the less privileged are extremely difficult to identify because these children cannot afford and consequently do not receive treatment. We can find figures concerning the number of children who are labeled as obsessive neurotics and who are treated in outpatient or inpatient facilities, but the reliability of these statistics is doubtful. Generally, there is a reluctance to hospitalize children and outpatient records tend to be poor. Nagera reported in 1965 that the percentage of patients diagnosed as obsessional neurotics at the Hampstead Clinic in London was less than 3 percent. Judd (1965), in California, found an incidence of 1.2 percent.

About 20 percent of obsessional neuroses began before the age of fifteen; 50 to 60 percent began earlier than age twenty. The maximal prevalence of obsessional neurosis in the U.S. was estimated by Woodruff and Pitts in 1964 to be 5 persons of all ages in every 10,000 of the general population (0.05 percent). The actual prevalence could be as low as one-tenth of this, or 0.005 percent. Thus, obsessive neurosis is a rare form of mental illness, occurring in fewer than 2 percent of large groups of emotionally disturbed children. The sex distribution of obsessive illness is, in general, identical to that of the more general psychiatric caseload carried by a given hospital or clinic. Anthony found a slight preponderance of females, whereas Adams reported just the opposite.

About 10 percent of the parents of obsessional children also suffer from obsessional illness and between 40 and 60 percent of them show obsessional traits. This is not offered as proof of heredity since the effect may be the result of social conditioning.

ETIOLOGY AND DYNAMICS

In discussing the etiology of obsessive-compulsive disease it is important to keep in mind the fact that the same mental illness may emerge from different circumstances. Also, in the field of child psychiatry there are no one-cause explanations, but rather there are general principles to aid us in making dynamic assessments.

According to psychoanalytic theory, obsessions are the consequence of the emergence of repressed instinctual impulses from the unconscious. The released elements are then transferred to the sphere of consciousness in conjunction with some idea or set of ideas that has no conscious relation to the unconscious impulse—the child is unable to understand why he is obsessed in this way. The reaction is interpreted as a defense against aggressive and sexual impulses, particularly in relation to the oedipus complex. There is a regression to the anal phase, but the impulses at this level are also intolerable and are warded off by reaction-formation, isolation and undoing. Because repression is now superfluous, the offensive impulses can exist in consciousness but when they do they are divorced from their affective significance and remain meaningless to the child. Anna Freud contended that obsessional neurosis can be traced back to the anal stage, but sees a causal role in anality only if there were fixations such as those arising from undue interference by the environment with the child's anal impulses. In other words, oedipal conflicts may emerge and promote regression to anality in "a child with constitutionally strong anal component instincts" (Nagera 1966, p. 66) but the ego will object to the regression and an obsessional neurosis could develop. There is hardly ever a complete and simple regression to the anal phase, but rather a regressive analization of oedipal conflicts.

Because of the familial tendency, several investigators have assumed a specific constitutional predisposition and terms such as ideo-obsessive constitution and obsessive psychopathic constitution have arisen. The child-rearing of obsessional parents is rigidly scheduled and the child learns early that what he is taught is right and that to do otherwise is wrong. The child's world is clean, neat, and orderly and it is probable that a child of such an environment will develop the same attitudes. It is unclear to what extent obsessional neurotics and personality disorders can be related to difficulties in toilet training. An investigation of five-year-olds showed no behavioral difference in those who had been trained early and punitively as compared with those trained late and permissively. It is possible that the cause lies not in the toilet training itself but in the child's total inflexible environment. In the terms of Rado and other neo-Freudians, the interpersonal setting is what counts. For them, it is not anality per se, but the mode of enraged defiance alternating with guilty fear which stamps the obsessive's neurotic style.

The basic personality has been investigated from different points of view. Psychoanalysts elaborating on the original triad of Freud—orderliness, frugality, and obstinancy—have emphasized the stubbornness, egocentricity and inflexibility of the obsessive person. Whether obsessional traits are viewed in positive or negative terms seems to depend on the adjustment of the child. For example, if he is doing well in school, his ambitious and intellectual parents are inclined to treat his obsessional traits with respect, whereas the traits of the child with a school problem may be viewed as objectionable. There is a tendency for some children to have leakage symptoms, so that they show dirtiness, disorderliness and compliance in the setting of a perfect obsessional personality. This is characteristic in certain cases of encopresis.

As in Freud's case of the Rat Man, the child begins his obsessional illness with eruption of unacceptable thoughts—sometimes blasphemous, sometimes sexual, and sometimes aggressive. He tries hard to think of something else and shake off the disturbing thought, sometimes even literally with a ticlike movement. Unlike adults, he forces his parents to participate in his rituals, answer his questions and cater to his obsessional wants. The mother's compulsions may not fit those of the child and she tends to become increasingly impatient so that the mother and child are soon locked in a battle. The child is caught between two wrongs—his unconscious wishes are wrong and his conscious defenses are wrong.

Case Example. A six-and-a-half-year-old boy developed compulsive hand-washing rituals not long after his parents' divorce. Other symptoms included temper tantrums and a fear that he might be poisoned if his hands touched something that he would ultimately eat. In general, he was quite sloppy about his personal habits. It was learned in his treatment that his fears of being poisoned developed soon after his father told him about the dangers of eating wild mushrooms. Later his hand washing rituals were connected to masturbation. He experienced guilt that his erotic fantasies regarding his mother were responsible for his parents' divorce and he feared retaliation by poisoning.

DIAGNOSTIC CONSIDERATIONS

These disorders must be distinguished from the normal compulsive rituals of the toddler. There is no obsessional neurosis in which reaction-formation and intellectualization do not play a large part. This is useful in differentiating between obsessions proper and some other manifestations which appear similar on the surface—repetitive tendencies which are found in very young normal children and also in mental defectives. These are preconflictual patterns which arise from the repetition compulsion and have only their monotony in common with obsessions (A. Freud 1966). Also, the driven behavior of addicts is due to the full force of the id drives and not to the ego mechanisms behind them.

An unresolved controversy is the relationship of obsessive-compulsive neurosis to schizophrenia. Bleuler and others have indicated an intimate relationship between these illnesses and imply that obsessive-compulsive neurosis is a latent schizophrenic process. Aubrey Lewis stated that obsessive-compulsive neurotic adults rarely become schizophrenic, but that schizophrenia in adolescents may be ushered in by obsessional symptoms. Despert (1955) reported a definite difference between obsessive-compulsive neurosis and childhood schizophrenia. She stated that while the anxiety, panic, and fantasies of the neurotic child may temporarily distract his attention from the environment, his reality testing remains intact. There is no interference with his ability to abstract and no other thought disorder present. Also, the neurotic child experiences his pathological mental contents as alien, which is not characteristic of the psychotic child.

Depression occurring in childhood is not easy to recognize, nor is it easy to differentiate from obsessive neurosis. The depressed child often misbehaves and is antisocial rather than saddened or detached. Usually, when a child presents with obsessions and an affect of sadness, he is more likely to be suffering from an obsessional illness rather than from a depressive one. Tics, phobic reactions, and psychophysiologic disorders are less easily differentiated from obsessive neurosis and each of them might occur as accessory symptoms in an obsessive child.

TREATMENT

The treatment for obsessional neurosis in childhood is psychotherapy or psychoanalysis. One expects the treatment to last one and one-half to three years. In general, the duration of treatment may be shortened by increasing the frequency of the sessions. Also, older children seem to require a longer span of time in treatment. Drugs do not have a place in the treatment of these children. Also, behavior modification is not advocated—the child is the expert in obsession and he should be trying out nonobsessive modes.

According to Anthony, therapy with these children takes place in a series of stages. In the first one, the child is relieved to talk about his peculiar symptoms without being laughed at, punished, or criticized. Also, he can express his anger at the repercussions that his illness brings. In the second stage, the child attempts to use the therapist as he uses his mother, as a participant in his compulsions. When the therapist balks at this role, a stormy situation follows. In the third stage, the child's defenses are less inflexible and a greater amount of leakage enters the treatment. Messiness and aggression follow with the child seemingly wallowing in his regressions. As this state disminishes, oedipal wishes and thoughts emerge and the remaining treatment resembles that of other neurotic children.

DISCUSSION

In discussing obsessional neurosis one's attention is usually turned to the anal phase which in psychoanalytic theory is considered to be the fixation point. A condition which seems to favor an obsessional outcome at a later stage is precocious ego development of the child. In other words, this type of child has an increased awareness of environmental demands. Also, when there is precocious ego development, there is an incompatibility between high aesthetic and moral demands and early instinctual activity (the ego and superego are too advanced to tolerate the anal-sadistic drives). In each case it is difficult to ascertain whether the child's objection to anal sadism has been taken from environmental attitudes or whether it represents an internal attitude (Nagera 1976). Children going through the anal-sadistic stage of development tend to react to this situation of conflict with specific obsessional symptom formation though they do not have an obsessional neurosis. Frequently, the early obsessional symptomatology is only transitory, disappearing when development advances. Before a final assessment can be made as to the factors predisposing an individual to obsessional neurosis, it is necessary to examine, not only the anal stage, but the previous as well as the later ones. Thus, there is no direct correlation between preoedipal manifestations of obsessional symptoms and later obsessional developments.

Although Freud and others indicated that obsessional neurosis can develop at any time during latency or adolescence, surprisingly few cases are diagnosed during those periods. Experience with adults seems to contradict the lack of cases. The discrepancy can be partially accounted for by the developmental tendency to keep conflicts flexible for as long as possible in childhood. Disturbances seen in childhood show conflict and symptom formation at different levels. The tendency to an early settlement of a situation of conflict in the form of an obsessional neurosis is rare and might be viewed as a poor prognostic sign (Nagera 1976).

SUMMARY

Obsessive-compulsive behaviors run the gamut from normality to severe psychopathology. Obsessive-compulsive neurosis, however, is a rarity in outpatient child psychiatry clinics. The obsessive child is forced, constrained, unhappy, and lacks the spontaneity of childhood. He must think certain thoughts or carry out certain rituals which may seem silly or trivial, even to the child, but felt by him to be a life and death matter. Obsessive-compulsive parents beget obsessive-compulsive children and there seems to be a basic lack of empathy of the parents for the child and the condition of childhood. According to psychoanalytic theory there is a libidinal regression from the phallic-oedipal stage to the anal-sadistic level. Thus, there can be no obsessive-compulsive neurosis before the phallic-oedipal level has been achieved. Long and intensive treatment is required to help these children become more spontaneous and symptom-free.

BIBLIOGRAPHY

Adams, P. (1973). *Obsessive Children: A Socio-psychiatric Study.* New York: Brunner/Mazel. A complete survey of obsessive behavior in children, including a review of the range of behavior, an account of the psychoanalytic approaches to it, a study of its social roots as well as forty-nine case histories.

Despert, J. (1955). Differential diagnosis between obsessive-compulsive neurosis and schizophrenia in children. *Proceedings of the American Psychopathological Association* 44:-240–253.

Freud, A. (1966). Obsessional neurosis: a summary of psychoanalytic views as presented at the Congress. *International Journal of Psycho-analysis* 47:116–122.

Judd, L. (1965). Obsessive-compulsive neurosis in children. *Archives of General Psychiatry* 12:136–143. A clinical study of six obsessive children as well as a review of literature.

Laughlin, H. (1967). *The Neuroses.* Washington: Butterworths. A comprehensive textbook of neurotic disorders with an eclectic approach including an understanding of intrafamilial relations and sociocultural milieu.

Nágera, H. (1966). *Early Childhood Disturbances, the Infantile*

Neurosis and the Adulthood Disturbances: Problems of a Developmental Psychoanalytic Psychology. New York: International Universities Press.

————(1976). *Obsessional Neuroses: Developmental Psychopathology.* New York: Jason Aronson. A detailed study of the obsessional neuroses, which includes Freud's formulations as well as those of Freud's co-workers and followers. A developmental approach to the etiology of the obsessional neuroses is advocated.

Chapter 8

PHOBIAS

Joseph M. Nieder, M.D.

DEFINITION

A phobia in childhood may be defined as a specific recurring fear which does not yield to reassurance on the part of the parent or other adult. A phobia would have to be distinguished from a simple anxiety state of childhood in that the phobia is of a more specific, focused nature and may be of longer duration. For example, in an anxiety state of childhood the child might be generally fearful, tense and anxious, but without a specific focus, target, or explanation for the anxiety. However, in a phobia, the child relates his anxiety to one or more specific objects, events, or circumstances, such as going in an elevator, riding through a tunnel, seeing or being approached by a large dog, going to sleep alone in a dark room, or going to school.

Kessler, in her book *Psychopathology of Childhood* (1966), uses the terms "morbid fear," "irrational" and "persistent" to define a phobia. She tries to differentiate fears from phobias stating that the "hallmark of phobia is the child's preoccupation with the object or situation he fears."

REVIEW OF LITERATURE

The classic and landmark article on phobias in children is Freud's case history and discussion of a horse phobia in a five-year-old boy, Hans, published in 1909. In this case Freud showed that little Hans' fear of horses resulted from his own hostile and aggressive impulses which were projected first onto his father and then displaced from his father onto a horse. Freud first described the psychodynamics and unconscious conflicts and processes that led to the development of a phobia. In 1926, Freud further elaborated the psychodynamics of phobias, anxieties, and symptoms in *Inhibitions, Symptoms, and Anxiety.*

Since that time there has been much written in the psychoanalytic literature on phobias, with Bornstein's (1949) analysis of Frankie being an excellent example of an analysis of a phobia in a child. Fraiberg (1959) in her book *The Magic Years* describes the early foundations of children's fears and phobias.

Another frequently discussed topic is school phobia: an elucidation of the psychodynamics and interactions between mother and child has been given by Eisenberg (1958). More recently, there have been a number of excellent articles on learning and behavioral theories of anxiety states and phobias, describing the ways in which phobias may be seen as conditioned or learned responses, as opposed to being simply intrapsychic conflicts (Wolpe and Lazarus 1966). The treatment of anxiety states and phobias employing behavioral techniques and biofeedback is a recent development worthy of attention. General survey articles on phobias in children can be found in Kessler (1966), as well as Freedman and Kaplan (1975), and Harrison and McDermott (1972).

INCIDENCE

Fears in children would have to be considered universal. It would indeed be difficult to imagine a child passing through his or her childhood years without at least the transient development at some point of what are often called phobias. Certainly no child could escape the common anxieties and fears of childhood: separation from parents, being lost, abandoned, being in the dark, going to sleep alone at night, bad dreams, animals, monsters, injury, or death.

The major criterion of incidence would be the separation of those universal fears and anxieties from the more fixed definitive syndromes which would deserve the title "phobias." These phobias lack a transient nature and do not respond to parental reassurance as would the anxieties and fears of everyday childhood experience. Actual fixed phobic states would be much less common than the transient fears of childhood.

ETIOLOGY AND DYNAMICS

The pathogenesis of phobias in children is based on the earliest of the child's fears and anxieties, dating back to concerns about separation, abandonment, or the loss of the mother or caring person. Prior to separation anxiety the child experiences tension states and is aware of physiological states such as being wet, in pain, hungry, or cold. Separation anxiety follows upon the establishment of the first object relationship, that with the mother, and the loss of this relationship has been correlated with depression in the child as described by Spitz (1965). If one observes the child in the midst of separation anxiety one sees a look of dread on the child's face, with an affect state best described as stark terror, as if abandoned. The child seems to experience total anxiety and seems overwhelmed by this affect. This separation anxiety is then carried over into stranger anxiety several months later, usually beginning about eight or nine months of age. Here, too, the child is inconsolable and at times will scream uncontrollably.

The next great fear seems to involve bedtime with issues of the dark and of going to sleep. Once again the underlying theme seems that of being alone, of being abandoned with no one to help, and no one to meet the child's needs. This commonly leads into a sleep disturbance, again an almost universal phenomenon somewhere between fifteen and thirty months of age. Also common around this age are the disturbances around toilet training, with fear of falling in the toilet and concerns about losing one's bowel movements. These fears are frequently followed by concerns about the loss of body parts, which various authors have related to the fear of castration. The fears at this stage are commonly related to bodily injury, and children at this age frequently have Band-aids all over their bodies as if to repair the imagined damage. Fears of water, of bathing, of going down the bathtub drain, and of loud noises are also very common at this stage. About this time children often experience nightmares, bad dreams and, occasionally, night terrors.

At ages four and five phobias are very common but take on a more symbolic expression, with the introduction of monsters: Dracula, Frankenstein, giants, dangerous animals, big dogs or, as in the case of Little Hans, a horse. This is the stage of symbolic thinking and parallels the content of the dream activity of a child of this age. These fears are also correlated with fairy tales and with children's stories such as the giant in Jack and the Beanstalk, the witches in Hansel and Gretel, and the Wizard of Oz, or the bad fairy in Sleeping Beauty.

One sees a major crystallization of phobic organization in the school phobia, which actually represents a type of separation anxiety. Again one sees the look and sense of dread, the overwhelming panic and the stark terror that one saw in the child of six or eight months of age. It is as if there is a terrible, unknown, uncontrollable fate. This anxiety is usually related more to the preverbal dread of the period from six to nine months than to the real danger that school represents. The key issue is a separation fear concerning the mother or a mother substitute and is generally relieved by her presence.

For a phobia to become firmly established requires some resonant response in the mother, based on her own fears, anxieties, and even her own phobias. The mother then reacts as if a real danger exists and thus reinforces the fear of the child. Another possible genesis would be where the mother transmits a phobia of her own to the child. The first situation described derives from the child's own fears but is reinforced by the mother, whereas the second derives from the mother's own concerns which are then transmitted to the child.

The phobias of childhood may now take on a more elaborate symbolic quality. Examples would include means of travel (airplanes, elevators, subways and buses), heights (acrophobia), closed spaces (claustrophobia), or open spaces (agoraphobia). These all involve a sense of helplessness and a fear of being overwhelmed. There is often a sexualized anxiety related to conflicts over erotic arousal with mounting excitement and tension frequently related to masturbatory fantasies or urges. Earlier phobic states described revolved around outside or external danger whereas this sexualized anxiety revolves around loss of control over internal drives, wishes or fantasies.

In the early (preoedipal) phase of development, anxiety and phobic antecedents seem to center around the feared loss of the mother. In the next phase (early phallic-oedipal), phobic concerns often concern danger or harm to one's self. Phobias of animals or monsters may relate to a fear of being attacked or overwhelmed by a larger or more powerful animal, creature, etc. This often arises at a time of aggressive or hostile feelings, wishes or fantasies towards one or both parents. A typical precipitating event might be a reprimand by a parent followed by an angry reaction either verbally or in thought on the part of the child. There may be dreams of a lion, a monster, a dragon or whatever, coming to attack the defenseless child. In this classic formulation the phobic object is the displacement of the fear of the parent toward whom the child has aggressive wishes.

Later symbolic elaboration of the phobia may involve internalized superego conflicts with exaggerated fears of death, illness, cancer, germs, etc. These represent unconscious self-punishment for unacceptable wishes and fantasies.

DIAGNOSTIC CONSIDERATIONS

Phobias in children as a diagnostic category must be separated from the common anxiety states of childhood as well as from the child's concern with nightmares, bad dreams and frightening experiences that they witness in reality or on television. School phobia as a distinct symptom or diagnostic category must also be separated and distinguished from the common anxiety of children about to begin school. One must look for a state of phobic avoidance which can be differentiated from a general inhibition of activity. Whereas a phobic adult can often avoid those aspects of his life which are frightening, the child is not as capable of doing so since so much of his activity is structured and determined by parents, school, and society.

Diagnostically one must also consider the ego and personality structure of the child since a phobia may exist within a well-organized and functioning child or in one who is in a totally disorganized psychotic state. Other areas needing assessment include the relationship with parents and peers, the child's ability to learn and function at school, and other manifestations of general ego functions. One must evaluate the extent to which the phobia invades and disrupts the child's life. For example, in a panphobic state the entire personality might be at the mercy of the phobic concerns.

One should also ascertain the extent to which the child recognizes the phobia as unreal, within age-appropriate capacities for reality-testing. When a phobia is active, a child has a greatly reduced capacity to assess reality clearly. However, in some children invasion of reality functioning and testing is so great and the child's life so distorted that one would be forced to consider childhood psychosis or childhood schizophrenia in one's differential diagnosis. One must exercise caution in making this more severe diagnosis because severe panic and anxiety in phobic states might appear abruptly but then disappear just as quickly without any intervention or treatment.

TREATMENT

Consideration of treatment for phobias in children must be related to a variety of factors. Among these are the intensity and the duration of the phobia, the age of the child, the involvement of parental psychopathology, whether the child's symptoms can be considered a normal response (that is, one that most children at that age might have) or an indication of other, more severe psychopathology. To expand this idea, although the anxiety of separation from the mother at six months of age or stranger anxiety at eight months of age may be very intense, these are normal developmental steps and an indication of increasing perceptual differentiation on the part of the child. Certainly one would not think of treating the transient separation or stranger anxiety one sees in most children. In the same vein, most "normal" children develop a resistance to going to sleep at about eighteen to twenty-four months of age with anxiety about being alone or in the dark that approaches phobic intensity. Also most children at some later phase develop fears of monsters, animals, or of being hurt or injured. These are usually transient anxiety and phobic states and not necessarily an indication of either psychopathology or of the need for psychotherapy.

However in some children the fears and phobias of childhood are not transient but become progressively worse and increasingly incorporate more aspects of daily life, leading to restrictions in relationships, play, and learning. They become an impediment to further emotional and intellectual growth. It is here that professional evaluation and perhaps therapeutic intervention would be appropriate. In attempting to decide if psychotherapy is indicated for the child's phobia, an important determination revolves around the meaning of the symptom to the parents and their ability to deal with the symptom in a realistic, nondistorted way. If the parent, especially the mother, by remaining objective can realistically reassure the young child, the child should be able to master a simple transient phobic disturbance. However, if the anxiety or phobia of the child recreates in the parent feelings of great fear and anxiety from his or her own past, or if it occurs in an area of distorted reality testing based on the parent's neurosis, the parent cannot reassure the child but instead conveys the feeling that the fear is realistic thus reinforcing the phobia.

For the young child with an acute anxiety or phobia, intervention may only need to involve work with the parents. By offering the mother simple guidelines and reassurance, most transient phobias are shortlived. An example would be the child who has fear of the dark or a fear of being alone in his room before going to sleep. Many parents tend to allow such a child to come into their room or share their bed. The symptom thereby provides a large secondary gain, and this tends to strongly reinforce it. One explains to the parents the need for the child to sleep in his own room and offers ways of reassuring the child so that he can master the conflict. For example, to reassure the child in his room one might suggest that the mother go into the child's room briefly, or if necessary even sit in the child's room for a few moments, but then leave with the reassurance that all will be well and that now it is time for the child to go to sleep.

In those cases where the mother or parents are deeply involved in the child's phobia, as is seen in school phobia for example, one often works with both parents and child. This is especially the case where the child's symptoms touch an area of unresolved conflict in the mother or parents or the parents are strongly identified with the child's problem. At times because of the identification, they might even deny that it is a problem at all. Such cases go on for years before coming to the attention of the pediatrician or child psychiatrist.

In some situations a phobia is an expression of a neurotic conflict within the child, a struggle between inner wishes and drives and internalized prohibitions or inhibitions. In such a case the conflict leads to a phobia as an outgrowth of anxiety without distorted parental involvement. In such a case the major focus of treatment would be with the child, with guidance to the parents playing an ancillary role.

Depending on the theoretical orientation of the therapist and resources available, treatment may range from advice on making the child face his fears directly, to dynamically based therapy, or even to classic psychoanalysis. It is difficult to generalize on the treatment required without studying each particular case, but a few general patterns may be elaborated. If the child has a newly acquired fear, whether based on a reality event, a dream, or fantasy, a direct approach to help the child deal with the phobic situation would be simplest. Such a situation might exist for example where a child had a bad experience while swimming and then developed a fear of going into the water. A similar experience would be a child who had an unpleasant experience at school and then was reluctant to return to school. Direct reassurance as well as definite pressure to face the fear could prevent the development of a chronic phobia.

On the opposite end of the scale is a situation wherein a phobia has existed for years and has led to an impoverishment of general personality development with a child's entire life organized around his fear. Often the whole family is at the mercy of the phobia, with a great deal of secondary gain accruing to the child as he or she can manipulate the family at will. Usually in such instances the phobia is one which one or both parents had as children or with which they can strongly identify. In such a situation anything less than intensive psychotherapy for the child with guidance of the parents would probably not be successful.

In recent years many therapists have begun to employ behavioral techniques to deal with either acute or chronic phobias in children. A full discussion of such techniques is not possible here but they include generalized relaxation, desensitization with the use of a hierarchy of fears, as well as facing the phobic situation directly with a therapist present. For example, the child afraid of elevators might picture the following hierarchy in order: first walking toward an elevator, next standing in front of an elevator, pressing the elevator button, having the elevator arrive at his floor, having the door open, getting in, pressing a floor button, having the elevator move, and finally getting stuck between floors with no one else present and the alarm button out of order. The child would learn to deal with each mental picture within the context of a relaxed body and mind. As a further step one might actually accompany the child to the elevator and help him in dealing with the feared situation directly, being able to talk about the fear as it actually occurs.

DISCUSSION

I have found it useful to employ a number of techniques, including counseling, behavioral approaches and psychotherapy to deal with a wide variety of phobias in children. In limited phobias such as a fear of elevators, swimming pools, bridges, and even school, such treatment techniques can be very successful within a short period of time. In general, unless one is beginning a classical psychoanalysis with a child, or is confronted by a child frankly psychotic or bordering on the psychotic, it usually is prudent to begin with the simplest and most directive techniques. These include counseling the parents, parental counseling of the child, and direct confrontation within the limits of the child's anxiety. The more time-consuming psychoanalytic and exploratory techniques would then be used only when the symptom is an expression of greater personality involvement and distortion. As a word of caution, however, regarding treatment: one must not overlook the fact that the symptom per se might disappear but the phobic picture go on as a general phobic personality structure. In such a case, which happens quite often, the child is symptom-free but generally timid, fearful, cautious, reluctant to try anything new, and generally inhibited and constricted in thought, fantasy, and action. Therefore one must consider the meaning of the symptom within the context of the child's total development to avoid major personality distortions in adult life.

SUMMARY

A brief description was given of a variety of phobias in children. Phobias were presented as symptoms rather than as a specific disease entity. Some would be considered essentially "normal stages of development" through which almost all children proceed. Others might be considered an indication of clear psychopathology with distortions of the child's personality, intellectual development, and object relationships. Work with parents may suffice for common fears which may be transient, while more intensive therapeutic measures should be considered if the fixity and duration of the symptoms threaten the child's healthy development.

BIBLIOGRAPHY

Bornstein, B. (1949). An analysis of a phobic child. *Psychoanalytic Study of the Child* 3/4:181–226. New York: International Universities Press.

Eisenberg, L. (1958). School phobia: a study in the communication of anxiety. *American Journal of Psychiatry* 114:712–718.

Fraiberg, S. (1959). *The Magic Years.* New York: Scribner.

Freedman, A., Kaplan, H., and Sadock, B. (1975). *Comprehensive Textbook of Psychiatry II.* Baltimore: Williams and Wilkins.

Freud, S. (1909). The analysis of a phobia in a five-year-old boy. *Standard Edition* 10.

———(1926). Inhibitions, symptoms and anxiety. *Standard Edition* 20.

Harrison, S., and McDermott, J. (1972). *Childhood Psychopathology.* New York: International Universities Press.

Kessler, J. (1966). *Psychopathology of Childhood.* Englewood Cliffs, N.J.: Prentice-Hall.

Spitz, R. (1965). *The First Year of Life.* New York: International Universities Press.

Wolpe, J., and Lazarus, A. (1966). *Behavior Therapy Techniques.* New York: Pergamon Press.

Chapter 9

DEPRESSIONS

Alan J. Frisch, M.D.

DEFINITION

A depressed child is one who is characteristically sad, unhappy, often without interest in the outside world. He feels rejected and unloved, is not easily comforted, nor can his interest be readily engaged. He frequently suffers from insomnia or other sleep disturbance. He prefers autoerotic or other self-comforting activities to play. If he has any complaint at all, it may be of a stomach-ache or headache, rarely of depression per se.

After saying this, we must add that depressions can be short or long, mild or severe, in children of any age and in a variety of situations. After this much assurance we enter many areas of doubt, disagreement, and semantic confusion. Our discussion must mention *anaclitic depression* (Spitz 1946) a specific reaction of the first year of life and the *depressive position* (Melanie Klein 1948). It must take into account depressive reactions to stress, illness or hospitalization, to separations from the loved objects, and to death, especially the death of a parent or sibling. Sleep disturbances must also be mentioned because of their connections with depression, and with ego development during the second year of life.

We should ask several questions, among them:

When is depressive affect a normal response and when is it pathological?

When do developmental deviations become fixed maladaptations?

At what age can one see a full-blown depressive neurosis?

How do we diagnose depression in children when they rarely complain as adults do, nor do their parents usually see them as depressed?

We must also wrestle with certain problems special to a discussion of children, such as the subtle interplay between developmental progress, fixation, and regression and the maturation of psychic structure.

REVIEW OF LITERATURE AND DYNAMICS

The psychiatric literature, with a few notable exceptions (Mahler 1961, Joffe and Sandler 1965, and the Kleinians with their special use of "depressive position") has been quite meager. This surely reflects lack of awareness in the community at large, though recently this has begun to change. There is no category "Depression, childhood type" in DSM II, nor do depressed children fit readily into any of the categories offered. In Freedman and Kaplan's *Comprehensive Textbook of Psychiatry* we find two references to childhood depression. Under adjustment reactions in late childhood there is a report of a twelve-year-old, depressed over an impending divorce. The second reference is to a depressive reaction to an acute illness.

The psychoanalytic literature offers us more. Spitz, in two classic papers (1945, 1946) described the syndrome which he named *anaclitic depression.* He observed children in a foundling home, deprived of their mothers. At ages 6–12 months the symptoms of weepiness, withdrawal, retarded development, loss of appetite, insomnia and a facial expression which looked much like that of an adult depressive were described. Spitz concluded that all this was a reaction to the loss of the loved one. If the mother returned, the symptoms were reversible up to a point, but after some months became irreversible. This is a special syndrome of the first year of life. It is a failure to thrive in the face of profound psychological neglect. It is a psychosis, but different from later psychoses because of the immaturity of the psychic apparatus. Spitz takes pains to delineate this situation from what Melanie Klein calls the *depressive position.*

Kleinian theory (1948) postulates a *depressive position* which each child experiences during his first six months, in response to the many anxieties he suffers in the postnatal world. According to Klein, in the earliest months, when only parts of objects can be distinguished, the infant splits these objects into good and bad, according to whether they are need-satisfying or frustrating. He also splits his ego into loving and hating parts. Projection and introjection then take place and the child then establishes what Klein calls the *paranoid-schizoid* position during his first three months. He is now threatened by his own projected hostility. In the second three months mother is perceived as a whole object, and the child establishes his *depressive position.* Both good and bad feelings seem now to emanate from the same object (mother) and the child feels ambivalence. The threat now is that he will destroy his beloved. His task is to work through this ambivalence. He develops feelings of longing for the good object and he develops manic defenses against the feelings of longing.

What can we use from all this? Let us say that early in life the child who has poorly integrated coping mechanisms, has to develop the ability to tolerate painful feelings. How he does so may be the prototype for later methods of coping.

Klein is not popular in North America (she did most of her work in England). She seems to ascribe to the earliest periods in life complex aspects of development for which the psychic apparatus is not yet ready.

E. Bibring (1953) defines depression as the emotional expression of a state of helplessness. Frequent frustration of a child's needs results first in anxiety and then in anger. When his distress signals meet no ameliorative response his initial anger will be replaced by exhaustion, feelings of helplessness and eventually by depression.

Mahler (1961) notes the large gap between the disorders depicted by Spitz and the depressions in later childhood. Depression relates to the *symbiotic phase* of normal development. [See chapter 4, Early Onset Psychosis—Symbiotic]. "This stage of development is characterized by the specific smiling response which the symbiotic object elicits, and the discriminatory anxiety and fear of strangers which the infant exhibits at or around 8 months." She states that during normal symbiosis the infant behaves as though he and mother were a dual unity with a common external membrane. As he begins to walk the toddler begins to achieve physical autonomy while his emotional development lags behind. In infantile autistic psychosis the central disturbance is the child's inability to perceive the mother and her functioning on his behalf. In symbiotic psychosis there is regression to a secondary undifferentiated stage of mother-child unity and a psychotic fusion with the need-satisfying object.

Mahler continues on affective disorders: "It has been conclusively established that the immature personality

structure of the infant or older child is not capable of producing a state of depression such as that seen in the adult.
But grief as a basic ego reaction does prevail . . . The
child's grief is remarkably short-lived because his ego cannot sustain itself without taking prompt defensive actions
against object loss. It cannot survive in an objectless state
for any length of time." Instead one sees other ego reactions such as denial and repression.

Mahler defines grief as "the reaction specific to object loss,
and anxiety as the reaction specific to the danger which this
loss entails." The child appears depressed, helpless, appre-
hensive that she will not be rescued by her libidinal object.
What is required is sufficient ego maturation to experience
the affect of longing, which is the precursor of sadness and
grief. "Grief is dependent on that measure of human object
cathexis which prevails from the second half of the first year
on; it is dependent upon the cathexis of the living Gestalt of
the need-satisfying mother."

Mahler then speaks of grief reactions and longings, precursors of depression in normal children under stress and in
symbiotic-psychotic children. It is these reactions which
bridge the gap between anaclitic depression and the adultlike
depressions of older children.

Freud, in his classic *Mourning and Melancholia* (1917) com-
pares melancholia (depression) with its normal prototype
(mourning). Both are reactions to a loss. Mourning is a self-
limited state. Melancholia may persist without relief. What
distinguishes them is that in melancholia the loss has been
"withdrawn from consciousness." The feelings of lowered
self-esteem are understood by Freud as reproaches against
the lost one turned around onto the self.

Bowlby (1960) addresses himself to the reactions of children when removed from their mothers to the care of stran-

gers. The sequence "protest, despair, detachment" seem to represent in order: separation anxiety, grief and mourning, and defensive adaptation. Bowlby feels that, despite Freud and Melanie Klein's work, our literature pays too little attention to the terms "grief and mourning" in early childhood. Loss of the breast, he states, really means loss of mother, or her love. What Klein calls the *depressive position,* Bowlby sees in children after six months of age and continuing beyond four years. Both Spitz and Anna Freud, he feels, fail to call a child's apathetic withdrawal after mother leaves a mourning reaction. Bowlby maintains that young children respond to maternal loss quite like adults.

Bowlby's work has drawn much criticism. Most specific is that of Joffe and Sandler (1965). Bowlby calls "mourning" the set of psychological processes initiated by the loss of the love object. Joffe and Sandler would differentiate pain, psychic pain, from the depressive response and from mourning. "In the depressive response the yearning for the lost state is suppressed through a generalized inhibition of function. . . . Mourning can be regarded as involving a continual facing of the painful situation, a gradual acceptance of the fact of the unattainability of the lost ideal state . . ."

Joffe and Sandler go on to describe the effects of psychic pain and depression on the process of individuation. They point to the role of ambivalence. "If the object were only loved, regaining of the lost object would equally restore a sense of well being." As he develops, the child constantly is made aware of discrepancies between his actual state and his ideal state. These states are at first magical and omnipotent. Their investment must be withdrawn as the child faces new realities. The authors define mental pain as the response to this discrepancy. From the side of the drives, the response to this is aggression. What is lost, especially after object constancy has been established, is a state of the self. Depression will follow only if there has been inadequate aggressive response to reduce the longing. From the ego's point of view, a prominent response is individuation, with its own working through. Individuation, then, is spurred by psychic pain and by the need to defend against object loss, and the loss of the ideal state of the self. The results can range from growth on the one hand to depression and cessation of development on the other.

INCIDENCE

It is hard to quote incidence figures for a syndrome whose diagnostic criteria are not universally agreed upon. Here we seem to be speaking of several interlocking diagnostic entities.

In the Isle of Wight Study, Rutter and his colleagues (1970) found an incidence of two per thousand of children utterly anhedonic; these were older children.

DIAGNOSTIC CONSIDERATIONS

One difficulty in diagnosing depressions in children stems from the problem that what looks like the clinical picture in an adult, may not signify depression in a child. For example, let us follow Anna Freud's (1965) discussion of sleep disturbances in children. Miss Freud notes that however successfully a child sleeps during the first year, he will have sleep difficulties during his second. "With the strengthening of the child's object ties and his involvement in the happenings of the external world, withdrawal of libido and of ego interests to the self becomes a prerequisite for sleep. . . . The anxiety aroused by the process makes the toddler cling all the more tenaciously to his wakefulness." This only improves, she states, when the child's development progresses to more secure object relations so that the necessary regression (to sleep) can take place without fear. Though this looks like adult melancholia, it is not. It is, in fact, age adequate behavior for the second year.

How, then, to diagnose? It is popular today to draw up diagnostic profiles. If we do not experience depression directly, what are the masking symptoms or depressive equivalents? Several authors (Glaser, Toolan, Cytryn and McKnew, Bakwin and Renshaw) have addressed themselves to this. Symptoms common to most of these studies are aggresiveness, angry outbursts, temper tantrums, poor school performance or avoidance, running away, physical complaints and psychosomatic symptoms.

What are the symptoms of depression when it is expressed overtly? One or all of the following may be seen: dysphoria, withdrawal, sleep disturbance, poor school performance, sadness, helplessness, loss of self-esteem; also feelings of being bad, of inability to do things, of not being liked, weepiness, moodiness, excessive self-criticism, suicidal ideation, headache, nausea, hypochondriasis. Beck (1972) has developed a depressive inventory for adults and has modified it for use with children (see in Schulterbrand, 1977). His children were between ten and fifteen and would represent the upper limits of our group. Depressive equivalents were eliminated because of difficulty in agreeing on symptoms. It was difficult to evaluate change of function without collecting data from parents. Validation has not yet been published.

In 1977, the Subcommittee on Clinical Criteria for Diagnosis of Depression in Children recommended the following criteria: (1) dysphoria must be present and (2) there must be impairment in response, with reduction in self-initiated activities in many areas of behavior. Formerly pleasurable activities no longer afford pleasure nor do they regulate behavior. If both criteria are met, one can diagnose childhood depression. Secondary symptoms will vary with age. This state of affairs must persist for at least four weeks.

In light of the difficulties in agreeing on the symptoms of depression, a multibattery approach to assessment has been proposed. One should measure facial expression and motor behavior. Social response and social adjustment in response to parents, peers, and teachers should be evaluated. Age related task performance and problem solving strategies should be tested and quantified. Concepts of the self and of the world should be elicited. Mood and affect must be observed.

TREATMENT

As befits an ill-defined group of disorders, the whole gamut of current psychological and chemical treatments have been recommended. Family counseling, family intervention, behavioral modification of child and family, individual psychotherapy with older children, child analysis, and family support systems all have their proponents.

As for psychopharmacology, our knowledge is as yet rudimentary. Rapoport sums up the present state of affairs. "The largest number of reports of antidepressant drug treatment deal with heterogeneous groups of patients described in for the most part uncontrolled trials and not employing objective criteria for improvement." Some enthusiasts for tricyclic and MAO antidepressants have demonstrated good results, better with dysphoric children than those with learning or speech underdevelopment.

It is common today to use drug response as a retrospective means of diagnosis. Such is not possible yet with depressed children.

SUMMARY

A concerted, government supported effort is now being made to better delineate and treat childhood depression (Schulterbrandt and Raskin 1977). We may soon have statistically valid diagnostic profiles to aid us. We will still be faced with the task of deciding when depressive affect is appropriate (to parental loss, death, illness), and we may have some guidelines to what sorts of depressive equivalents are appropriate to different ages. Current studies deal with depression in late latency and preadolescence, though we know that much younger children experience depression or its equivalents.

The concepts of Spitz, Mahler, Anna Freud and the English psychoanalysts (Winnicott 1958, Bowlby) can help us assess age adequate behavior.

We have at least progressed to the point where children have the right to be depressed and to deserve attention to their pain.

BIBLIOGRAPHY

Beck, A.(1972). Measuring depression: the depressive inventory. In *Recent Advances in the Psychobiology of the Depressive*

Illnesses, ed. T. Williams, M. Katz, and J. Shields. Washington: Government Printing Office.

Bibring, E. (1953). The mechanism of depression. In *Affective Disorders,* ed. P. Greenacre, New York: International Universities Press.

Bowlby, J. (1960). Grief and mourning in infancy and early childhood. *Psychoanalytic Study of the Child* 15:9–52. A controversial paper by an eminent British investigator of childhood depression.

Freud, A. (1965) Assessment of pathology. In *Normality and Pathology in Childhood.* New York: International Universities Press. The concept of developmental lines and their deviations.

Freud, S. (1917). Mourning and melancholia. *Standard Edition* 14.

Joffe, W., and Sandler, J. (1965). Notes on pain, depression and individuation. *Psychoanalytic Study of the Child* 20:-394–424.

Klein, M. (1948). *Contributions to Psychoanalysis.* London: Hogarth Press.

Mahler, M. (1961). On sadness and grief in infancy and childhood. *Psychoanalytic Study of the Child* 16:332–351.

Miller, J. (1971). Children's reactions to the death of a parent. *Journal of the American Psychoanalytic Association* 19:-697–719.

Rutter, M. Tizard, J., and Whitmore, K. (1970). *Education, Health and Behavior.* London: Longmans. The Isle of Wight Study.

Schulterbrandt, J., and Raskin, A. (1977). *Depression in Childhood.* New York: Raven Press. See especially articles by Kovacs and Beck.

Spitz, R. (1945). Hospitalism. *Psychoanalytic Study of the Child* 1:53–72.

Spitz, R., and Wolf, K. (1946). Anaclitic depression. *Psychoanalytic Study of the Child* 2:313–339.

Winnicott, D. (1958). The depressive position in normal emotional development. In *Collected Papers.* London: Tavistock.

Section B

Functional

and

Psychosomatic Disorders

Chapter 10

EATING DISTURBANCES

Ildiko Mohacsy, M. D

DEFINITION

Eating disturbances in childhood vary considerably both in focus and in degree. We shall describe five categories of disturbance: (1) failure to thrive in infancy; (2) anorexia nervosa; (3) obesity; (4) bulimia; and (5) intermediate feeding disturbances.

Failure to thrive is the name given to an infantile syndrome marked by refusal to eat and, consequently, retarded growth. This may be accompanied by vomiting or by rumination. (Rumination is the voluntary return of already swallowed food to the mouth. The food may then be spit out or reswallowed.) In the emotional sphere, the infant may seem depressed, apathetic, or whiny.

Beyond infancy (and into adulthood) the refusal of food, resulting in extreme emaciation, is termed *anorexia nervosa*. In girls past puberty, anorexia is frequently accompanied by amenorrhea. (The syndrome is very rare in males.) Sometimes the anorexic will have a spell of ravenous eating, followed by self-induced vomiting.

Obesity refers to the state of being overweight, most often as a result of excessive eating.

In *bulimia* the patient periodically experiences insatiable hunger and engages in ravenous overeating, often to the point of severe physical pain and/or vomiting. Bulimia can appear as part of the anorexic pattern.

Intermediate feeding disturbance is the term that we give to a wide spectrum of transient eating difficulties in childhood. These include food fads, finicky eating, refusal of specific foods, pica (the eating of nonedible substances such as dirt, plaster, and paint chips), or a refusal of food altogether. These intermediate disturbances are often connected with developmental stages. They almost invariably involve mother-child conflicts.

REVIEW OF LITERATURE

Since the 1930s, failure to thrive has been investigated, and successfully treated, as a problem in the mother-child relationship. Peto (1937) described the role of maternal depression in the baby's refusal to breastfeed. Provence and Lipton (1962) showed the effects of the caretaking environment on the biological rhythms of hunger and satiation. The successful treatment of the failure-to-thrive syndrome through treatment of the mother-child relationship has been described by Stein, Rausen, and Blau (1959), Ferholt and Provence (1976), and Shapiro, Fraiberg, and Adelson (1976).

Anorexia nervosa is generally viewed as a psychogenic disorder related to family conflicts (Kaufman and Heiman 1964). Branch and Bliss (1967) have delineated six different types of anorexia, each with its own particular style of malnourishment. The most widely recognized style is the female adolescent anorexic, whose refusal to eat is generally associated with a fear of aggression, oral impregnation, and cannibalistic impulses.

Obesity was first described as a symptom of psychopathology by Bruch (1940), who argued that the child might be trying, through his overeating, to convey a message of inner conflict. This line of argument has also been pursued by Anna Freud (1946), who proposed that the unhappy child may use food as a substitute for parental warmth and as a form of comfort in the face of fears of growing up.

Brody (1956) interpreted *intermediate feeding disorders* as a response to the mother's personality, as reflected in her feeding techniques. Anna Freud (1946) has divided intermediate feeding disturbances into three categories: (1) organic disturbances; (2) disturbances of the instinctive process; and (3) neurotic feeding disturbances. The last two categories are discussed below, under "Etiology."

INCIDENCE

A comprehensive study of normal children in a large California school showed a high frequency of parental complaints about poor eating. Moderately higher in girls, this peaked at age six when 37 percent of the girls were said to have insufficient appetites and 51 percent showed food finickiness. In a larger study of English schoolgirls, age eleven and older, done in 1972–1974 using rigorous criteria for anorexia nervosa, overall prevalence of this condition was 4.6 per thousand.

ETIOLOGY

It is generally agreed that a major cause of eating disturbances is conflict between parent and child. As Anna Freud points out, there are two types of psychological causation of *intermediate feeding disturbances.* First, the instinctively gratifying experience of feeding may be disturbed by struggles between mother and child. In this case, any number of behaviors associated with the child's developmental stage—food fads, eating with hands, smearing food, standing up in the highchair—may initiate the struggle, which ultimately leads to the child's loss of pleasure in, and refusal of, food. Second, in what Anna Freud calls the neurotic feeding disturbances, normal eating patterns are disrupted by libidinal or aggressive conflicts. Defending himself against oral-sadistic (cannibalistic) fantasies, anal tendencies, or phallic fantasies, the child may reject different kinds of food (e.g., meat or squishy foods), or he may reject food altogether. Whether these acute and transient disturbances turn into chronic disturbances depends, again, on the mother. If the child's pickiness is tolerated, it will generally pass. If it is not tolerated, then the child may develop serious and chronic eating problems.

The origin of overeating patterns again seems to lie in the parent-child relationship. In the typical pattern the child has overprotective parents who generally ignore his signals as to his own needs. The consequent feelings of ineptness, helplessness, and anxiety are then alleviated by eating, the child's one remaining area of control and comfort.

The development of *failure to thrive* and *obesity* as chronic patterns may be conceptualized as a circular process. They begin as transient feeding difficulties, which remain as the expression of severe, unresolved mother-child conflicts. *Anorexia nervosa,* on the other hand, generally appears as the symptom of a more pervasive psychopathology, such as obsessive-compulsive neurosis, schizophrenia, depression, hysteria, or phobia (Branch and Bliss 1967).

DIAGNOSTIC CONSIDERATIONS

Once organic causes are ruled out, psychological causation must be established by observing the mother-child interaction and by getting a thorough history of the child. The observation process is particularly essential, as it often reveals nuances of the mother-child relationship (e.g., hints of hostility and tension conveyed through tone of voice and "body language") that cannot be gleaned from seeing either mother or child separately. In the case of an adolescent anorexic, where the family dynamics may be particularly complicated, it is advisable to see the patient with the mother, then the patient with the father, then the parents alone, then the patient with both parents. This permits the psychiatrist to separate the different threads of the complex family interaction.

In the interview, the psychiatrist must determine whether the child has always been a difficult eater or whether the feeding problem constitutes a regression. In the former case, the problem might be attributed to personality or constitutional factors, or to chronic tension between mother and child. In the latter case, the traumatic cause of the regression must be sought in recent events affecting either the child (e.g., a change of residence or school) or the significant family members (e.g., the death of one of the mother's parents).

In the case of regression caused by trauma, the prognosis is generally good. In the case of fixation due to chronic mother-child struggles, the prognosis is generally poor.

TREATMENT

Whatever the etiology of the eating disturbance, it is the mother-child unit—and not the child alone—that the psychiatrist must treat. Even in the case of a strictly somatogenic disorder, the disorder itself may engender a mother-child conflict that must then be treated, along with the organic cause, if the child is to return to normal eating.

In the case of regressive intermediate feeding disorders and regressive obesity, the usual treatment would be short-term consultation with the mother and, if necessary, short-term psychotherapy with the child. The goal of these sessions would be, in Winnicott's words, to "unhitch the developmental catch," by working through the trauma with the child and by advising the mother on how to handle her feelings toward the child in general and his eating habits in particular.

In the case of the chronic and serious disorders, the treatment of mother and child is simply more intense. With failure to thrive, the child must of course be hospitalized if his life is endangered, if he needs close medical attention, or if the mother is unresponsive to home treatment. When the child is hospitalized, the mother, if possible, should stay in the hospital with him, so that the mother-child relationship can be treated simultaneously with the child's medical problem. A case of failure to thrive requires the attention of a multidisciplinary team consisting of pediatrician, nurse, social worker, and psychiatrist. However, the treatment of a hospitalized mother-child unit would be channelled largely through the nurse. By giving the child consistent tender care, a "mothering nurse" can elicit greater responsiveness from the child at the same time that she serves as a model and object of identification for the mother. Thus her attentions set up a feedback cycle of maternal attentiveness and infant responsiveness, which can eventually heal the relationship (Stein, Rausen, and Blau 1959).

If the child is in no vital danger and if the mother is able and willing to cooperate in the treatment, then hospitalization is not necessary. Rather, the mother-child unit would be treated at home. One member of a multidisciplinary team would visit them each day to dispense feeding instructions and informal therapy (Shapiro, Fraiberg, and Adelson 1976).

Anorexia nervosa also requires simultaneous medical and psychological treatment. In this case, the psychiatrist may elect family therapy. In any event, both parents must be dealt with in addition to the anorexic child or adolescent. At the same time the anorexic patient must be given individual psychotherapy for whatever psychopathology underlies the anorexia (e.g., depression or obsessive-compulsive neurosis). As with failure to thrive, the anorexic patient must be hospitalized if outpatient multidisciplinary treatment is unsuccessful or if there is a serious medical risk.

DISCUSSION

Eating, which serves the instinct of self-preservation, begins as a conflict-free sphere. Yet it can easily become conflict-ridden. Despite the child's absolute dependence on food for survival, he may reject it completely. In the case of the infant, eating is the nucleus of the mother-child interaction and is therefore extremely vulnerable to any conflict in this interaction. The somewhat older child soon discovers that eating patterns are extremely powerful means of communicating his emotional distress or of punishing his mother, for there is no other aspect of the child's functioning to which the mother responds as forcefully.

The best prevention of feeding disturbance is to avoid conflict over mealtime behavior and undue anxiety regarding transient feeding quirks. If feeding disturbance occurs, for whatever reason, then the mother-child conflict must be dealt with before the feeding problem can be resolved.

SUMMARY

Five forms of childhood eating disturbance were described: *failure to thrive, anorexia nervosa, obesity, bulimia,* and *intermediate feeding disturbance.* The literature on these disorders focuses on the causative role of psychosexual conflicts, personality factors, and, above all, tension between parent and child. It is generally assumed that parent-child conflict is a major cause. Even when the primary cause lies elsewhere, parent-child disagreement over the resulting eating abnormality generally aggravates the abnormality, and may convert a transient disorder into a chronic one. In diagnosis, it is important to observe the parent-child interaction and to determine whether the disturbance is a recent regression or a chronic fixation. Treatment of intermediate disorders and of regressive obesity may be limited to short-term consultation with the mother and, if necessary, short-term psychotherapy with the child. The more serious disorders of anorexia and failure to thrive can be treated either in the hospital or at home. In both cases, therapy is aimed at the parent-child unit rather than simply at the child.

BIBLIOGRAPHY

Branch, C., and Bliss, E. (1967). Anorexia nervosa. In *Comprehensive Textbook of Psychiatry,* ed. A. Freedman and H. Kaplan, pp. 1062–1063. Baltimore: Williams and Wilkins. A discussion of six "styles" of anorexic malnourishment, related to underlying psychopathologies.

Brody, S. (1956). *Patterns of Mothering.* New York: International Universities Press. A study of infant development, correlated with maternal behavior, especially feeding behavior.

Bruch, H. (1940). Obesity in childhood, V: the family frame of obese children. *Psychosomatic Medicine* 2:141–206. A report on research into the relationship between obesity in children and overanxious concern on the part of parents.

Ferholt, J., and Provence, S. (1976). Diagnosis and treatment of an infant with psychophysiological vomiting. *Psychoanalytic Study of the Child* 31:439–459. Discussion of psychotherapy of parents and child in the care of a profound disturbance in the mother-child relationship, manifested in the child's failure to thrive.

Freud, A. (1946). The psychoanalytic study of infantile feeding disturbances. *Psychoanalytic Study of the Child* 2:119–132. A description of feeding disturbance as the result either of instinctual conflicts or of mother-child conflicts leading to loss of pleasure in eating.

Kaufman, M., and Heiman, M., ed. (1964). *Evolution of Psychosomatic Concepts Anorexia Nervosa: A Paradigm.* New York: International Universities Press. A study of disturbed interactions in the families of anorexics.

Peto, E. (1937). Säugling und Mutter. *Zeitschrift für Psychoanalytische Pädagogic* 11:244–252. A study of several infants refusing to nurse as a result of maternal depression.

Provence, S., and Lipton, R. (1962). *Infants in Institutions.* New York: International Universities Press. A study of the depressed and retarded responses of institutionalized infants as a result of lack of mothering.

Shapiro, V., Fraiberg, S., and Adelson, E. (1976). Infant-parent psychotherapy on behalf of a child in a critical nutritional state. *Psychoanalytic Study of the Child* 31:461–491. Description of treatment of a severe feeding disturbance via therapy aimed at resolving the mother's childhood conflicts.

Stein, M., Rausen, A., and Blau, A. (1959). Psychotherapy of an infant with rumination. *Journal of the American Medical Association* 171:2309–2312. Description of successful psychotherapeutic management of both mother and infant in a case of infantile rumination.

Chapter 11

SPEECH DISORDERS: STUTTERING

AND ELECTIVE MUTISM

Leon Hoffman, M.D.,

Speech can be defined as the mechanism whereby sounds, when used together in certain accepted ways, produce verbal language. Verbal language refers to the symbolic meaning attached to these sound groupings. Children with speech disorders often manifest psychiatric disturbance and children with psychiatric disturbance often manifest some of their symptoms with a speech disturbance (Cantwell 1977). This chapter will discuss two syndromes of speech disturbance: stuttering and elective mutism.

STUTTERING: DEFINITION

Many authors make the comment that it is difficult to define stuttering. Often the "diagnosis" of stuttering is more apparent to the lay person than to the speech pathologist. Stuttering is a speech dysfluency manifested by repetition of words and syllables, hesitations, prolongations of sounds, interjections, and pauses. However, many of these characteristics are found in normal speech and with great frequency in children ages two to four. The definition of stuttering includes the speaker's reaction to his or her abnormality or anticipated abnormality as well as the formal abnormalities of his speech. It is crucial to remember that stuttering is unpleasant to both the speaker as well as to the listener. (Stammering is the term used in England.)

REVIEW OF LITERATURE

The literature on stuttering is vast (see particularly Bloodstein 1969, Fenichel 1945, Van Riper 1971, 1973, Freund 1966). The two major areas in the literature deal with the etiology of this disorder, i.e. psychosocial theories in contrast to organic theories, and the treatment of the disorder.

INCIDENCE

Four to five percent of the population in Western society will have stuttered at one time during a lifetime. Three percent will stutter for a period greater than six months. Most stutterers are children who undergo a spontaneous remission. Eight-five percent of stutterers begin their stuttering before the age of eight. There are two peaks: at two and a half to three and a half, when the child is starting to speak, and at six to eight when the child has just begun school, and is learning how to read. The early stutterers seem to be children whose spoken language is highly developed. During school age the prevalence is about one percent with a decrease beginning at about ten.

The male: female ratio is about 3:1 with some reports as high as 7:1. The sex ratio has been attributed to differences between boys and girls in constitution, physical maturation, speech and language development, and parental attitudes and expectations. None of these hypotheses has been conclusively proven.

Heredity may be a factor. Between 36 and 65 percent of relatives of stutterers also stutter. Twins are more likely to stutter (five times the expected frequency) and there seems to be a greater concordance among identical twins than among fraternal twins. If there is a genetic component, then it is most likely inheritance via polygenetic transmission.

Environment or culture seems to be an important factor. American Indians who had little contact with the general culture had a very low incidence of stuttering. Pressure for upward mobility leads to an increased incidence of stuttering. Greater permissiveness in child-rearing practices in the United States manifests itself in a lower incidence as compared to Europe. During the past few decades there has been a declining incidence of stuttering. This has been attributed to greater permissiveness as well as greater social acceptance of stuttering.

There is a high incidence of stuttering in mental retardation and a low incidence in deaf children. There are no systematic studies of stuttering among organic and psychotic children. At the Mount Sinai Medical Center In-Patient Child Psychiatry Unit, among severely disturbed children the prevalence of stuttering is about 1 percent or less.

The frequency of the stutter may vary from an occasional word to a stutter on the large majority of words. Most stutterers are "mild." The mean duration of a stuttering block is about one second with occasional severe stutterers blocking for more than a minute. Consonants are stuttered five times as often as vowels and 96 percent of stuttering incidents occur on the initial sound of words.

ETIOLOGY AND DYNAMICS

There have been many theories to account for the etiology of stuttering. Aristotle thought there was something wrong with the stutterer's tongue. In the 1840s a French surgeon, Dieffenbach, devised an operation to shorten the tongue. European authors have usually stressed organic factors whereas American authors have stressed environmental and psychological factors. Freud considered the etiology of Frau Emmy von R's stammer in the *Studies on Hysteria* (Breuer and Freud 1893–1895) to be related to a frightening event following a thunderstorm. Elsewhere he states that the origin of stammering may be related to a parapraxis (slip of the tongue) with a fear that the person may say a vulgar word. The stammer may thus be related to "upward displacement" of conflicts over excremental functions.

Fenichel (1945) elaborates this theory. He states that stuttering is mainly a result of anal-sadistic sexualization of the function of speech, even though other component instincts may be involved in the formation of the symptom. To the stutterer, the maxim "words can kill" is taken literally. The hesitations often express an aggressive act directed against the listener. Two situations in which the unconscious hostility is most intense exist when someone is particularly eager to prove a point and when he is in the presence of authority figures. In fact, stuttering increases in those situations in contrast to nonthreatening situations where there is no stuttering.

Analytic as well as nonanalytic authors stress the importance of the secondary gain involved in perpetuating the stuttering. Pity is aroused in the listener; special privileges may be had. The listener's attention is held and the stuttering may be used as an excuse for difficulties unrelated to it.

Bloodstein (1969) feels that psychoanalytic theories contribute to the understanding of the moment of stuttering but not to the understanding of its onset in childhood. He feels that the best conceptualization is to view stuttering as an anticipatory struggle. That is, the anticipation of failure in speech evokes a reaction of tension and fragmentation of speech. This struggle is a result of a communicative failure as perceived by the child. As a child, the eventual stutterer may have been chronically subjected to the threat of speech failure by a variety of obstacles. These threats may be a result of problems in the child such as cluttering,[1] retarded language development, perfectionism, low frustration tolerance, or overanxiousness for approval. Unrealistic parental expectations, anxieties, help, criticisms, and corrections unquestionably contribute significantly to the origin of the symptom. Thus the child, who may have been experiencing normal dysfluencies, becomes convinced that speech is difficult.

Learning theories are basically reformulations of the above constructions. Cybernetics models (servomechanism or feedback models) hypothesize that conflicts and parental reactions affect an already inbuilt delay in auditory feedback leading to stuttering.

DIAGNOSTIC CONSIDERATIONS.

The most critical issue in terms of diagnosis, especially in young children, involves the differentiation between stuttering and normal dysfluencies. Pauses, "ahs," interruptions, etc., occur in everyone's speech. Between the ages of two to

[1] See next Section

four, when the child is learning how to speak, one out of every four words of the child's speech consists of repetitions of words. One can easily imagine the effect of a parent who cajoles the child to "speak right."

Cluttering needs to be differentiated from stuttering. Cluttering is a developmental language disorder manifested by an exaggeration of the errors of speech made by a normal person as well as difficulties in writing and reading. The speech is characterized by rapid, confused, jumbled speech with repetitions and omissions of syllables and words. There may be associated maturational lags and traits similar to those of the child with minimal brain dysfunction. In contrast, the stutterer tends to be overcareful, anxious, rigid, and formal. Cluttering improves with effort and stress whereas stuttering worsens.

Many personality studies have been done on stutterers. The evidence is inconsistent (Bloodstein 1969, Cantwell 1977). There is no good evidence for a distinct neurosis, "severe maladjustment," or specific character trait. On the average stutterers are less well adjusted, have a lowered self-esteem, are less willing to risk failure and have a tendency to be somewhat hostile and anxious.

TREATMENT

A review of the literature of the treatment of stuttering leads one into a quagmire of confusing and contradictory proposals. Van Riper (1973) states the problem succinctly: "The trouble with treatments for stuttering is that almost all of them work for a while at least." Demosthenes used pebbles. This is an example of distraction. Suggestion, relaxation, and behavior therapies often fail when stresses recur.

Various kinds of psychotherapies, drug therapies, servotherapy (feedback) with auditory masking, rhythmic, timing, and rate control therapies have all been attempted.

The only "treatment" that is universally accepted by all speech pathologists, as well as by Gesell and by Spock, is the appropriate handling of stuttering in young children. In these cases the parent must refrain from criticizing the child. The parent-child relationship needs to be improved and environmental changes may need to be implemented. Stresses should be reduced, the parent needs to avoid being a nonresponsive listener and most importantly the child's conception of himself as a fluent speaker needs to be strengthened.

SUMMARY

Stuttering is predominantly a disorder of childhood more common in boys than in girls. The single outstanding factor to which a probable causal relationship has been established is competitive pressure for achievement. There is a high familial incidence but no constitutional or personality factor that can be clearly delineated as measured by standardized tests. There may be difficulties in speech and language delay and with articulation. A large percentage of the parents are demanding, overanxious, and perfectionistic in their child-rearing practices. There are a multitude of theories as to the etiology and treatment of stuttering.

ELECTIVE MUTISM: DEFINITION

Elective mutism is defined as partial speech avoidance whereby the child speaks to a few select intimates (parents and siblings) but not to others. The problem commonly begins when the child starts school. He is seen by the teachers to be timid and stiff, often to the surprise of the parents since he acts differently at home.

REVIEW OF THE LITERATURE

The earliest reference to this entity was by Kussmaul in 1877 who used the term "aphasia voluntaria"—voluntary mutism in association with insanity. Since that time many terms have been used. The most commonly accepted term is elective mutism coined in 1934 by Tramer in the German literature. Tramer differentiated elective mutism from language retardation, schizophrenic or hysterical mutism.

INCIDENCE

Elective mutism is quite rare with a prevalence in a general population of school age children of less than .05 percent. In immigrant children the prevalence is much higher. This is not accounted for by a language difficulty. At the Mount Sinai ward various degrees of elective mutism are seen with a fair frequency (1–2 percent).

ETIOLOGY AND DYNAMICS

Factors that have been implicated in the genesis of this disorder can be placed within the context of psychodynamic and learning theories. There is fairly universal agreement that there is significant intrafamilial pathology.

Marital dissatisfaction leads to a pathological mother-child dependency; the parents have conflicts over talking and its consequences and thus "secrets" are common. When the child's dependent relationship to the mother is threatened, he becomes aware of his own hostility. This leads to anxiety and fear of total abandonment. He chooses not to speak selectively; this is a compromise of his fear that he will reveal his mother's secret.

Other factors have been implicated: (1) a traumatic event at the time of speech formation which may lead to fixations and regressions; (2) predisposing constitutional hypersensitivity to instinctual drives; (3) fear of the child's own voice; and (4) hostile retentive aspects (Elson 1965).

The silence is used as a weapon by the child in an attempt to control oral aggressive and anal destructive fantasies. The silence can be conceptualized as a protective reaction to an environment perceived as hostile and rejecting.

DIAGNOSTIC CONSIDERATIONS

Some authors exclude schizophrenic children from the diagnostic category of elective mutism whereas others do not. All of the children are characteristically immature and can be described as Chess's tempermental type "slow to warm up." They are concerned over their feelings of inferiority. Halpern (1971) conceptualizes the mutism as a speech phobia arising out of an overvaluation by the child of the power of his speech (i.e. magical speech).

TREATMENT

Milieu therapy is an important treatment modality for elective mutism (Elson 1965). This has been corroborated by our impression at Mount Sinai with severely disturbed children. Family therapy or some kind of family involvement in addition to individual therapy is crucial because of the familial factors involved in the etiology of this disorder (Browne 1963).

An example of a behavior therapy technique is gradually accustoming the child to the feared situation (classroom talking) via graduated cue requirements (requiring more and more talking) before the child can leave the classroom plus specific advice to the parents as to how to improve the individuation of the child.

In the psychological treatment of these children one must stress the importance of being aware of potential counter-transference reactions. The patient's silence may be difficult for the therapist to tolerate because he senses the child's underlying aggression. The therapist should particularly avoid retaliatory silence.

SUMMARY

Elective mutism is a condition whose dynamics are related to intrafamilial conflicts. The treatment of choice requires active involvement of the family in addition to treating the child.

CONCLUSION

This chapter discussed two disturbances in speech functioning: stuttering and elective mutism. Both can be viewed from the psychoanalytic point of view as manifestations of anal erotic and sadistic conflicts; from the learning point of view as maladaptive responses; and from the interactional point of view as reactions to intrafamilial conflicts and pressures. The first is relatively common and the second rare. Both require multimodality forms of treatment.

BIBLIOGRAPHY

Bloodstein, O. (1969). *A Handbook of Stuttering.* Chicago: National Easter Seal Society. A comprehensive survey of the field.

Breuer, J., and Freud, S. (1893–1895). Studies on hysteria. *Standard Edition 2.* The classic studies in the infancy of psychoanalysis.

Browne, E. (1963). Diagnosis and treatment of elective mutism in children. *Journal of the American Academy of Child Psychiatry* 2:605–610.

Cantwell, D. (1977). Psychiatric disorder in children with speech and language retardation. *Archives of General Psychiatry* 34:583–591. An excellent overview of the subject.

Elson, A. (1965). Follow-up study of childhood elective mutism. *Archives of General Psychiatry* 13:182–187. Best review on the subject.

Fenichel, O. (1945). *The Psychoanalytic Theory of Neurosis.* New York: Norton. The classic psychoanalytic model of the disorder.

Freund, H. (1966). *Psychopathology and the Problems of Stuttering.*

New York: Charles C. Thomas. Freund, himself a stutterer, describes an overview: historical as well as current.

Halpern, W., Hammond, J., and Cohen, R. (1971). A therapeutic approach to speech phobia: Elective Mutism reex-
amined. *Journal of the American Academy of Child Psychiatry*
10:94–107.

Van Riper, C. (1971). *The Nature of Stuttering.* Engelwood
Cliffs, N.J.: Prentice-Hall.

———C. (1973). *The Treatment of Stuttering.* Englewood Cliffs,
N.J.: Prentice-Hall. Two standards in the field.

Chapter 12

SLEEPING DISTURBANCES

Ildiko Mohacsy, M. D.

DEFINITION

Childhood sleeping disturbances, particularly common in the second year of life, include any disruption of the normal patterns of sleep. The child may wake repeatedly during the night, have upsetting dreams, wet his bed, walk in his sleep, or—often in consequence of one of the above—refuse to go to sleep at all.

In children, as in adults, *insomnia* is the inability to fall asleep or to remain asleep for a normal period. The child may take hours to fall asleep, or he may awaken repeatedly during the night. (The latter is also called *nightwaking.*)

In addition, there are a number of disturbances that occur during sleep. The most familiar is the *anxiety dream,* which occurs during REM[1] sleep. The anxiety dream usually involves a rather complicated and elaborate series of imagined

---

[1]Rapid-eye-movement (REM) sleep, which occurs cyclically throughout a night's sleep, is the closest stage to waking. In this stage, the eyes dart back and forth under the closed eyelids. The muscles are relaxed, but the brain waves are similar to those of the waking state.

events, with well-disguised imagery. (In a typical case, for example, a child whose grandfather had recently died and who was just beginning nursery school dreamed that he lost his lunchbox.) The anxiety dream arouses mild to serious anxiety but not panic. It may be accompanied by some verbalization and a gradual increase of pulse. When the dreamer awakens, he quickly reestablishes contact with reality, calms down, and can often remember the dream in considerable detail.

Less common and much more intense is *pavor nocturnus,* or *night terrors.* This type of dream occurs during stage IV[2] sleep and usually involves a single image in which the dreamer is threatened with or subjected to violent destruction. The resulting terror far surpasses that of the anxiety dream. The dreamer undergoes pronounced physiological changes (increased pulse and respiration rates, extreme activation of the autonomic nervous system), shows intense motor activity (thrashing, sitting up, somnambulism), and often utters piercing screams. When awakened, he is disoriented, difficult to subdue, and usually amnesic for the dream. While anxiety dreams are common in both children and adults, night terrors are far more common in children than in adults. The latter observation is almost certainly related to the fact that stage 4 sleep decreases with age. Young adults spend only half the time that children spend in this stage, and the elderly have no stage IV sleep at all.

Another form of disturbance that occurs in stage IV sleep is simple *somnambulism,* or sleepwalking, without night terrors. Typically, the child gets out of bed and walks through the house, sometimes with a very clear purpose. (For exam-

[2]Stage IV sleep, the deepest stage of sleep, is characterized by high-amplitude, low-frequency brain waves. The amount of time spent in stage IV sleep decreases with age.

ple, the oedipal child may try to invade the parents' bed.) A serious problem with somnambulistic children is that they are prone to hurt themselves (e.g., fall downstairs) in the course of their wanderings.

A final form of childhood sleep disturbance is *secondary nocturnal enuresis,* in which the child, after having mastered nighttime bladder control, loses this control and begins wetting the bed regularly. It is also frequent in somnambulistic episodes. *Secondary nocturnal encopresis,* in which the regression takes the form of soiling, is extremely rare. (Both enuresis and encopresis are more fully covered in separate chapters.)

REVIEW OF LITERATURE

The developmental aspect of sleep disorders is stressed by Gesell and Ilg (1943), who treat sleep disturbance as a normal developmental problem between the ages of fifteen and twenty months—and one that in most cases remits spontaneously. Nagera (1966) explores in detail the relationship between sleep disturbance and the vicissitudes of normal development. The connection between anxiety dreams and traumatic events is treated by Fraiberg (1950) and Solnit (1972). According to Fraiberg, the anxiety dream, by reenacting the traumatic event, is an example of the typical childhood effort to gain mastery through repetition. She stresses the role of ego functions in disturbed sleep and suggests that the insomnia so common in the second year is caused by the fear of losing newly gained ego controls, especially bowel control.

Keith (1975) provides a comprehensive discussion of pavor nocturnus, and a thorough review of the literature on this syndrome. Freud (1900) considered pavor nocturnus a variant of the anxiety attack and was the first to attribute this problem to repressed sexual impulses. The relationship between pavor nocturnus and psychosexual conflicts, particularly those rooted in the oedipus complex, has since been discussed by Klein (1932).

In the 1960s a new era in the study of sleep disturbance was inaugurated by the establishment of sleep laboratories. In such laboratories sleeping subjects are given continuous EEG's and are monitored for physiological change. In the event of a night terror or anxiety dream, they are awakened and asked to relate the content of the dream. Such laboratory research led Gestaut and Broughton (1965) to two significant discoveries: (1) that pavor nocturnus occurs in stage 4 sleep; and (2) that most children who suffered from night terrors were otherwise psychologically normal, whereas the opposite was true of adults. Fisher and his colleagues (1974) have done considerable laboratory research on pavor nocturnus. They argue that lowered psychological defenses, with consequent ego regression, precipitate the dream. They have also been able to elucidate somewhat the content of the dream: it "revolves around pregenital and oedipal content relating to primal scene experiences or fantasies, with the projection of intense, murderous oral-sadistic impulses."

INCIDENCE

Authoritative figures on the incidence of sleep disorders are not yet available, but current research suggests that in children from five to twelve years old, 1 to 3 percent have experienced at least one episode of night terrors and 15% have experienced at least one episode of somnambulism (Kales, Jacobson, and Kales 1968).

ETIOLOGY

Like eating disturbance, sleeping disturbance, whatever form it takes, is usually a symptom of underlying psychological conflict. As with eating disturbance, the psychological problem may be of a purely transient developmental nature. In the second year of life, the most fertile period for sleeping problems, the child is subject to a number of developmental challenges. In the first place, the separation-individuation process is still going on. To be sent off to bed means losing mother, a deprivation that can arouse intense anxiety, particularly in view of the fact that the child regresses as he becomes tired. Furthermore, a child in the throes of separation-individuation has not yet integrated the good and bad images of his mother. When separated from her, the bad image, split off from the good, may come to the forefront, while the good image becomes impossible to conjure up. This is a fearful experience that the child would sooner avoid by avoiding sleep altogether.

Secondly, the child in the second year is required, rather abruptly, to develop impulse-control—in particular, to regulate his bladder and bowel functions and to restrain aggression. To avoid losing his parents' love, the normal child will comply with these demands. But in sleep, when the distractions of the day are removed and the unconscious comes to the forefront, the primitive impulses threaten to reassert their dominance. The child may wet his bed, or he may dream of enacting his forbidden aggression against siblings or parents. Thus, once again, sleep becomes a dangerous state—something to be avoided.

In addition to developmental stressors, trauma of course can also cause sleep disturbance, especially anxiety dreams and consequent insomnia.

Finally, it should be noted that the very young child has an

extremely limited repertoire of coping devices—a fact that
may cause or exacerbate sleeping problems. To facilitate the
transition between daytime activation and the relaxation of
sleep, the older child can read a book, listen to the radio,
even count sheep or baseball players. The younger child has
no comparable relaxers. And what tension-reducing devices
he does have—thumbsucking, masturbation, a transitional
object, a bedtime bottle—may at this time become forbidden,
as part of the "time-to-grow-up" regime.

For the only child, the resulting anxiety and helplessness
may be all the more intense. He alone is exiled from his
parents' company; he alone is imprisoned in a dark room
with his tabooed thoughts.

DIAGNOSTIC CONSIDERATIONS

Once a medical examination has ruled out organic causation (any chronic health problem, such as headache, indiges-
tion, or inner ear infection, can cause persistent sleep disturbance), the psychiatrist should see the parent and child
together, as such a joint interview may reveal parent-child
conflicts implicated in the sleeping disturbance. From a separate interview with the parent, the psychiatrist must determine the frequency, intensity, and duration of the disturbance. The greater these three indicators, the more likely it
is that the sleeping problem is the result of a serious psychological conflict rather than a transient developmental difficulty. Another important factor is whether the sleeping disturbance was precipitated by a traumatic event. If so, and if
the trauma is fresh and on the surface, without a shell of
defenses, then the problem can probably be solved more
swiftly and directly. Finally, the age of the child is an important diagnostic consideration. As a general rule, sleeping

disturbance in the older child is more serious. Beyond the age of approximately thirty-six months, the child presumably has greater ego strength, more coping devices, a more accurate picture of reality, and a better-defined image of himself and his parents. Thus, a chronic sleeping problem beyond this age can no longer be viewed as a developmental hitch. On the contrary, it suggests more serious pathology.

TREATMENT

When the diagnostic indicators listed above indicate a developmental problem, giving the parents therapeutic advice may be sufficient treatment. Parents of a child undergoing separation-individuation should be told to increase peek-a-boo and hide-and-go-seek games. Any bedtime tension-reducers that have been withdrawn should be restored, and new ones (bedtime stories, a flashlight, a permanent night light, a small radio, a picture book) should be offered. Furthermore, it is helpful if child-training regimens (especially toilet-training) are discontinued or at least modified until the sleeping problem subsides. In cases where the sleeping problem has been caused by a traumatic event, the parent should encourage the child to talk about the event freely, giving vent to his fear, anger, or sorrow. If the parent is unable to draw the child out, the therapist may take one or two sessions to talk with the child about the trauma.

When these remedies fail, or when the diagnosis suggests that the sleeping problem is due to more serious underlying pathology, the appropriate treatment is child psychotherapy, directed to uncovering the unconscious conflict and helping the child cope with it.

Whatever the treatment, the therapist should offer the parents support and suggestions for coping devices that *they* might use, such as taking turns handling the bedtime scene. A child who refuses to sleep can arouse intense hostility in the most loving parents. The therapist should try to mitigate this hostility, as it can only exacerbate the child's problem.

Somnambulism and night terrors can often be relieved with imipramine (10–50 mg), though the mechanism of the drug's action is unknown. Diazepam (2–5 mg), which reduces stage IV sleep, has also proved successful in eliminating night terrors.

DISCUSSION

The transition from the constant twilight state of the newborn to a bi-cyclic pattern of deep sleep at nighttime and sustained wakefulness during the day is a matter not only of neurophysiological maturation but also of psychological development. As the child's capacity for attention increases, the mother helps him develop and refine his cognitive faculties. But the transition is a gradual one, and any psychic threats —whether conflicts in the mother-child relationship, traumatic events, or simply developmental hurdles—can upset the nascent sleeping pattern or, if it is already established, overturn it altogether.

Furthermore, it must always be taken into account that nighttime is the hour of the id. Whatever unconscious struggles the child is waging in the effort to establish ego control over his impulses, these struggles will surface in his sleep. If they are sufficiently intense, the pattern of normal sleep may be disrupted for weeks, months, or even years. Thus sleep is probably the most fragile of the child's vegetative functions. It is no surprise that one of the most common reasons for bringing a child to a psychiatrist is sleep disturbance.

SUMMARY

Five childhood sleeping disorders—insomnia, anxiety dreams, pavor nocturnus, somnambulism, and secondary nocturnal enuresis—were described. In the second year of life disturbed sleep is so common as to merit classification as a normal developmental occurrence. The literature on sleep disturbance stresses its developmental nature, particularly its connection with the child's fear that he will lose the ego controls he has been forced rather hastily to develop in the second year. In the young child, most sleep disturbances remit spontaneously, as the developmental difficulty is finally mastered. The usual treatment is to advise the parents as to how they can increase the child's coping devices and ease the transition from waking to sleep. In addition, if trauma is involved, the child must be encouraged to discuss the trauma with parent or therapist. In the older child sleeping disturbance is likely to indicate a more deep-seated psychological conflict. Such a conflict must be addressed through psychotherapy.

BIBLIOGRAPHY

Fisher, C., Kahn, E., Edwards, A., Davis, D., and Fine, J. (1974). A psychophysiological study of nightmares and night terrors: III. Mental content of stage 4 night terrors. *Journal of Nervous and Mental Diseases* 158:174–188. A discussion of the content of night terrors, based on verbalizations of sleep-laboratory subjects.
Fraiberg, S. (1950). On the sleep disturbances of early childhood. *Psychoanalytic Study of the Child* 5:285–309. An interpretation of childhood sleep disturbance as the con-

sequence of anxiety in the face of demands on the immature ego, especially in the anal period.

Freud, S. (1900). The interpretation of dreams. *Standard Edition* 4/5.

Gesell, A., and Ilg, F. (1943). *Infant and Child in the Culture of Today.* New York: Harper and Row. A guide to normal child development and normal developmental problems within the context of modern culture.

Gestaut, H., and Broughton, R. (1965). A clinical and polygraphic study of episodic phenomena during sleep. In *Recent Advances in Biological Psychiatry,* vol. 7, ed. J. Wortis, pp. 197–221. New York: Plenum Press. The first sleep-laboratory study of the physiological and psychological aspects of night terrors.

Kales, J., Jacobson, A., and Kales, A. (1968). Sleep disorders in children. In *Progress in Clinical Psychology,* vol. 8, ed. L. E. Abt and B.F. Riess, pp. 63–73. New York: Grune and Stratton. A discussion of somnambulism, enuresis, and night terrors as disorders of stage IV sleep.

Keith, P. (1975). Night terrors: a review of the psychology, neurophysiology, and therapy. *Journal of the American Academy of Child Psychiatry* 14:477–489. A thorough review of the literature on night terrors and especially of the recent sleep-laboratory research. Included is an excellent table outlining the differences between night terrors and anxiety dreams.

Klein, M. (1932). *The Psycho-Analysis of Children.* London: Hogarth Press, 1963. A discussion of the interpretation of dreams and play in child analysis.

Nagera, H. (1966). Sleep and its disturbances approached developmentally. *Psychoanalytic Study of the Child* 21:393–447. An examination of sleep disturbances characteristic of different developmental stages, with emphasis on the universality and normalcy of sleeping problems, particularly in the preschool child.

Solnit, A. (1972). Aggression: a view of theory building in psychoanalysis. *Journal of the American Psychoanalytic Association* 20:435–450. A study of aggression in a child with sleeping problems, to demonstrate the relationship between psychoanalytic theory-building and the interpretation of an individual case.

Chapter 13

ENURESIS

Arnold R. Cohen, M.D.

DEFINITION

Enuresis may be defined as urinary incontinence occurring in children who are of an age when bladder control should be expected. Most children are dry at night and during the day by three years of age. Most authors would agree, though, that an incontinent child should not be termed enuretic until age six and unless they wet more than monthly. Enuresis may be diurnal, occurring while the child is awake, or nocturnal with the enuretic event occurring during sleep. Enuresis can be primary (continuous) or secondary (acquired). Primary enuretic children continue to be incontinent from infancy onward without a significant period of dryness. Secondary enuresis refers to incontinence beginning after a sustained period of bladder control (about six months). Finally, enuresis may be functional, that is without demonstrable urinary tract pathology, or organic, that is, incontinence found in association with demonstrable urinary tract pathology. In common usage, if organic pathology is felt to be the cause of the enuresis, the problem is referred to simply as urinary incontinence. This chapter deals primarily with functional enuresis and more specifically with nocturnal enuresis. Nocturnal enuresis is the most common and well-studied form of enuresis.

INCIDENCE

Essen and Peckham (1976) studied the prevalence of nocturnal enuresis in a large sample of English children. These authors found that 10.7 percent of the children were enuretic at age seven. One third of this number were still wetting at age eleven. There was no sex difference among enuretic children at age seven, but by age eleven the boy:girl ratio was 2:1. These authors found enuresis to be most common among lower socioeconomic class children. These figures are similar to those in other epidemiological studies. In the United States, the figures differ between socioeconomic and geographically different groups.

In general, there is a spontaneous cure rate of about 15 percent a year. As the numbers of primary enuretics decrease yearly, the total number of age adjusted enuretic children does not fall as rapidly because of the addition of secondary enuretic children.

ETIOLOGY AND REVIEW OF LITERATURE

Most nocturnal enuresis is thought to be functional. Hallgren (1957) found organic genitourinary pathology in 1–3 percent of a large series of children. Although this is the commonly held urological view, there are a few urologists who are proponents of the theory that most enuresis is due to minor, usually overlooked urinary tract pathology. They claim that the organic pathology creates an irritable bladder which in turn causes incontinence.

Enuresis (and encopresis) are not common in lower animals. Many animals are capable of retaining their bodily waste for varying periods of time. The animal then releases the waste at specific places or times. This in turn allows the wastes to be used for marking territorial boundaries or to entice the members of the opposite sex (scent marking). Eliminating away from the nest prevents predators from raiding the nest and killing the young. Thus, in animals and probably in man, the ability to control the bladder and rectal sphincter is a normal maturational accomplishment. The ability of people to delay their response to the micturition reflex while awake probably gave rise to the long held idea that enuresis was usually the result of willful or unconsciously motivated behavior.

Freud stated that enuresis, unless related to epilepsy, corresponded to a nocturnal emission. Abraham in 1917 associated enuresis and the passive flow of semen in ejaculatio praecox. Freud, in the Dora case, suggested that enuresis represented the male and female elements of intercourse, equating the micturition with ejaculation and the resulting wetness with the vaginal lubrication.

Gerard (1938) wrote a classic paper in which she espoused analytically-oriented psychotherapy for enuresis. She found enuretic boys to be passive and fearful of assertive activity, while enuretic girls were seen as boylike and assertive. Gerard's boy patients exhibited evidence of masturbation guilt and castration anxiety, with the passive release of urine viewed as a compromise solution to neurotic conflict and representing a feminine identification. Enuretic girls, wrote Gerard, identified with their fathers and wet the bed as an expression of the wish/fear of incestuous longing.

A. Katan (1946) wrote of her experiences with enuretic children. Katan felt that some children wet as an expression of regression following temporary loss of a love object or subsequent to the birth of a new sibling. Other children were thought to wet as a result of neurosis induced by sexually traumatic occurrences such as molestation or medical operations. Katan made the important observation that all enuretic children view their genitals as damaged.

M. Sperling (1965) felt that enuresis was related to sexual precocity and that it represented a substitute for masturbation in sexually overstimulated children. She felt that the observed disappearance of enuresis in adolescents was due to a shift to genital sexuality and was replaced by nocturnal emission and masturbation. Silberstein and Blackman in 1965 suggested that most enuresis was due to a lack of motivation or faulty training while the rest could be explained psychodynamically.

Faulty learning was also the explanation advanced by behavior therapists. This view was reinforced by the fact that so many enuretic children have responded to the "bell and pad" deconditioning devices (to be discussed later). Other data led to the observation that enuresis tends to run in families and in twin studies as well as family studies, genetic predisposition can be shown. Genetic predisposition, deep sleep, bladder irritability, small functional bladder capacity have all been advanced as nonpsychiatric etiologies for enuresis. Dreaming was also considered etiological by some. This view was strengthened by the observation that enuretics often dream of wetting or being wet.

It remained for Broughton (1968) to describe the pathophysiology and to identify enuresis as a disorder of arousal and sleep metabolism. Broughton showed that enuresis is a function of slow wave sleep (stage IV, III) and that the enuretic event occurs along a continuum of increasing arousal. The enuretic event is signaled first by increased muscle tone followed by tachycardia, tachypnea, or apnea and decreased skin resistance as well as other signs of emerging arousal. The micturition occurs in stage IV sleep or, more commonly, as the subject goes into stage III or II. Broughton also found that the older a patient was, the longer the interval between beginning arousal and micturition. Some psychological factors may have intervened because the subjects suffered fewer enuretic events in the lab than at home.* The awakening enuretic appears to be in a confusional state, is nonreactive to normal stimuli and exhibits automatic behavior. These pathophysiologic phenomena are shared with two other disorders of slow wave sleep and arousal, namely somnambulism and night terrors. Broughton suggests that the abrupt arousal from deep sleep causes a confusional state not inducible in normals.

In addition to these abnormalities of sleep, enuretics demonstrate other relevant symptoms. Enuretic children have more frequent and more intense spontaneous contractions of the primary detrusor muscle in non-REM sleep than do normal children. These bladder contractions can be evoked by noise. In addition, enuretic children have higher bladder pressure regardless of whether an enuretic event occurred during the experimental period. Other observations made were that enuretic children have higher heart rates and blood pressures than do normal children prior to sleep, in stage IV sleep, and upon awakening. It appears that there are various

---

*The same observation is often made about children who wet less frequently when they are guests, are away at camp or are in institutions. One explanation may be that the slow wave sleep is not as intense and therefore arousal does not proceed in the same way.

autonomic occurrences, which in conjunction with possible psychological factors, lead to pathological arousal and micturition. The autonomic abnormalities suggest neurophysiological immaturity, possibly subcortical in origin, which then may be altered by cerebral input.

Most recent reports place emotional factors on the sideline when discussing the etiology of enuresis and suggest that the psychological effects of enuresis are secondary, not primary. Many authors feel that enuretic children are as emotionally healthy as other children. Enuresis is not associated with any particular childhood psychiatric syndrome with the exception of hyperkinetic syndrome and its impulse disorder sequelae in adolescence (Mendelson, Johnson and Stewart 1971).

The lack of association between enuresis and other psychopathology is especially true of primary enuretics. Secondary enuretics, particularly if diurnal enuresis (without organic pathology) is present, are more likely to have signs of emotional disturbance. Rutter examined enuresis and deviant behavior and found enuretic boys only slightly more disturbed than nonenuretic boys, but enuretic girls significantly more deviant than nonenuretic girls. Rutter also found that signs of emotional disturbance often preceded the onset of secondary enuresis. E. Ritvo (1969) demonstrated two types of enuretic events in a small sample of boys. One kind of enuretic episode occurred early in sleep and during Stage IV; the other, a late night episode, occurred during periods of arousal. The later phenomena seemed more common in the more neurotic subsample. This suggests that neurotic input may trigger the later kind of enuretic event.

Douglas (1973) followed up a large sample of English children born in 1946. Douglas was able to demonstrate that traumatic events in early childhood predisposed children to subsequent enuresis. For example, in the population studied, 50 percent of children who had been separated from their parents and who were placed in unfamiliar surroundings were still enuretic at age six. This study suggests that the acquisition of bladder control may be affected by emotional stress. It may be that there is a "sensitive period" in which normal neurophysiological maturation allows for bladder control, but the balance during this "sensitive period" may be upset so that normal development is delayed for long periods of time.

Kolvin and Taunch (1973) elaborate a dual theory of enuresis. According to these authors, primary enuresis is a biological disorder caused by faulty maturation because of genetic or pathophysiological factors. Kolvin and Taunch feel that secondary enuresis on the other hand may have important emotional determinants. We would suggest that enuresis is a disorder of sleep metabolism and the arousal mechanism. The confluence of stimuli from within (pathophysiological factors) and emotional stress may produce the particular enuretic event. The speed with which a child acquires dryness will depend upon his hereditary maturational rate, neurophysiological immaturity, the presence of stress during the "sensitive period" and later anxiety which may cause regression back to an enuretic state. Brazelton (1962) demonstrated that enuresis almost never occurs in the children of parents who are counseled and trained to refrain from placing pressure on the child to be dry at night and who toilet train permissively.

Neurophysiologically immature children may be more sensitive to the presence of emotional stress. The frequent association of minimal brain dysfunction syndrome and enuresis suggests this possibility. Central neurophysiological controls may be lost under the pressure of anxiety and a regression to enuresis may occur in a vulnerable child.

Beyond the analytic literature, there is little evidence of specific behavior patterns or emotional illness associated with enuresis other than the above mentioned hyperkinetic, minimal brain dysfunction and antisocial behavior disorders. It does seem likely that Katan's observation that enuretic children experience themselves as damaged may explain the anxiety that occurs in some enuretic children and their families. For this reason diagnosis and treatment are important.

DIAGNOSTIC CONSIDERATIONS

The diagnosis of enuresis depends upon the reporting of the symptom. Physical examination and urinalysis can screen out the presence of genitourinary disease. The presence of diurnal enuresis as well as nocturnal should alert the examiner to the possibility of urologic or psychiatric etiology. Family history, frequency of the enuresis and whether it is primary or secondary help determine whether further urological investigation should be pursued. Urologists differ upon what constitutes a sufficient urological workup to exclude organic causes. Some feel that a urinalysis and IVP are sufficient. Others feel that retrograde cystoscopy is necessary to rule out the abnormalities that can cause incontinence.

TREATMENT

In general, especially in a younger child, reassurance and education may be sufficient treatment. Restricting fluid intake at night and waking the child a few hours after the onset of sleep are usually tried before the child is brought to a

physician. Because of the child's and parents' anxiety, further treatment in an older child is often indicated.

Pfaunder, in 1904, devised an apparatus to be used on a pediatric ward with enuretic children. The device caused an electrical circuit to be closed when a child was enuretic. When the circuit was closed, an alarm rang to alert the nurse who could then go and change the child. It was soon discovered that the children often stopped being enuretic. This approach did not become popular until many years later when Mourer reported good success in the arrest of enuresis using a similar device. The basic design of this device consists of a power source connected to an electrical grid which is placed between sheets on the child's bed. This is connected in turn to an alarm. The circuit is open until urine provides an electrical conductor to close the circuit which then causes the alarm to sound. The child is instructed to sleep on the grid without pajama bottoms. For the first few days the apparatus is not connected to the power source. Then the child is told that if he wets, the alarm will ring. The child is to get up, dry himself and reset the device.

The results of this behavioral treatment are somewhat difficult to evaluate. Most reports do not differentiate primary and secondary enuretics or the frequency with which they wet prior to treatment. Doleys (1977) in a review of the literature reports an average arrest rate of 75 percent with a 41 percent relapse rate. With retreatment another 68 percent are successfully treated. Treatment usually continues until there are twenty-one consecutive dry nights. The average length of treatment is two and one-half months. Doleys reports that an intermittent schedule of alarm presentation increases the arrest rate.

Other behavioral treatments have been advanced. One such method is retention control, in which children are given large quantities of fluid to drink. The children are then encouraged to delay micturition for as long as possible. This supposedly increases the functional bladder capacity. No statistics for this method are available yet.

The psychoanalytic influence in the treatment of enuresis has been strong. Gerard (1938) reported excellent results for treating enuresis with psychoanalytically oriented psychotherapy. Nonanalytic authors state that psychotherapy is of no value, especially in primary enuresis. There are suggestions that psychotherapy is of greater value for secondary enuretics, but only if other psychiatric symptoms are present.

Bindglass (1968) published his finding that imipramine caused an arrest of enuresis. Since that time there have been numerous papers attesting to the efficacy of imipramine (or other tricyclic antidepressants) in enuresis. The value of imipramine has been variously ascribed to its antidepressant effect, or its anticholinergic effect on the urinary bladder sphincter. The main effect of imipramine may be upon the depth of stage IV sleep. Imipramine may act centrally to alter the quality of that sleep or it may act upon immature neurophysiological systems. Whatever the mechanism, imipramine often stops enuresis—but unless the child is one who would have become spontaneously dry in the interim, the wetting recurs when the drug is stopped. Imipramine is useful for the short-term control of enuresis, to demonstrate to the child that he can become dry, or to prevent further dysfunction in a pathological home environment where the parents are destructive to the child because he wets his bed. Imipramine may have occasional adverse effects and, at doses over 4 mg/kg of body weight per day, cardiac arrhythmia and lowered seizure threshold can occur. Its use is not recommended in children under six years of age. It is usually given in doses of 25 mg to 75 mg before bedtime. Imipramine is a common cause of self-induced poisoning in children and it should be prescribed with caution. In hyperkinetic enuretic children requiring medication for the hyperkinesis, imipramine can be employed to treat both problems. Some children who do not improve with behavior modification or with imipramine alone, do improve when both are used together.

Esman (1977) recommends that treatment should focus on parental guidance and reassurance of the child. In children over seven years of age, Esman recommends psychotherapy to undo the psychological consequences of enuresis. Esman also suggests either medication or the bell-pad to promote quick removal of the symptom and thereby enhance self-esteem. Others recommend behavioral treatment in preference to imipramine because it can quicken true arrest of enuresis and imipramine cannot.

DISCUSSION

Enuresis is a common condition of childhood in which urinary incontinence occurs either diurnally or nocturnally. Most nocturnal enuresis seems to be a manifestation of disturbed slow wave sleep and arousal from it. Enuresis tends to run in families. Emotional stress during the "sensitive period" when dryness is usually established, may interfere with this maturational step and delay full bladder control. Secondary enuretics are more likely to manifest emotional problems but, other than MBD, there is no specific psychiatric syndrome associated with enuresis. In susceptible children the presence of anxiety and a neurophysiological predisposition may create a "confluence of events" that then leads to the specific enuretic episode. In other children, the neurophysiological substrate may be sufficient cause for bedwetting.

Enuresis leads to impairment of self-esteem and possibly feelings of genital incompleteness. Treatment of the symptoms is warranted for this reason. Support, education and guidance are the initial treatments. The bell-pad device is useful in receptive families. Imipramine can bring about dramatic short-term improvement if necessary. Psychotherapy should be reserved for enuretic children with other evidences of emotional disturbance.

Nocturnal enuresis is a common childhood problem. Current thinking places development and neurophysiological problems ahead of psychogenic issues as causative in enuresis. With the exception of the hyperkinetic disorder of childhood and impulse disorders of adolescence, there is no correlation between enuresis and specific psychopathology in childhood. Abraham's observation about enuresis and ejaculatory dysfunction in adulthood has not been challenged. One may assume that even if the enuresis is not primarily psychogenic in origin, it may contribute to a sense of genital inadequacy and heighten sexual anxiety and conflict in some children.

The relationship between hyperkinesis and enuresis probably speaks to a common underlying minimal brain dysfunction problem. The fact that imipramine controls both problems may be related to a common central nervous system action.

In general, reassurance and family counseling are sufficient treatment, especially for primary enuretics. Psychotherapy is warranted when secondary enuresis is accompanied by other psychiatric problems. Because the enuresis may compound other anxieties, the clinician must decide whether the use of a bell and pad device or imipramine should be used to control the symptom rapidly. Reports suggest that the bell and pad are well accepted by most users and that adverse effects are rare; thus it should be considered in uncomplicated enuresis in highly motivated families.

SUMMARY

Nocturnal enuresis is a condition that affects one of every ten seven-year-old children. There is a spontaneous cure rate of about 15 percent of enuretic children with each passing year of age. Primary enuresis is thought to be a developmental problem and specifically a disorder of sleep metabolism, often familial in origin. Psychological stress may increase the likelihood of an enuretic event in a vulnerable child. Psychological factors may be more important in secondary enuresis. Persistent enuresis may compound the sense of genital damage or inadequacy and conflict in some children.

Before treatment is instituted, organic disease must be ruled out. After family counseling and simple measures such as fluid deprivation, there are several specific treatments that can be offered. They include behavior modification, medication and psychotherapy.

BIBLIOGRAPHY

Bindglass, R., Dec, G., and Enos, F. (1968). Medical and psychosocial factors in enuretic children treated with imipramine hydrochloride. *American Journal of Psychiatry* 124:1107–1112.

Brazelton, T. (1962). A child oriented approach to toilet training. *Pediatrics* 29:121.

Broughton, R. (1968). Sleep disorders: disorders of arousal?

Science 159:1070–1078. A comprehensive review of sleep disorders.

Doleys, D. (1977). Behavior treatment for nocturnal enuresis in children: a review of the recent literature. *Psychological Bulletin* 84:30–54.

Douglas, J. (1973). Early disturbing events and later enuresis. In *Bladder Control and Enuresis,* ed. I. Kolvin, R. MacKeith, and S. Meadow, pp. 109–117. Philadelphia: Lippincott.

Esman, A. (1977). Nocturnal enuresis: some current concepts. *Journal of the American Academy of Child Psychiatry* 16:150–158.

Essen, J., and Peckham, C. (1976). Nocturnal enuresis in childhood. *Developmental Medicine and Child Neurology* 18:577–589.

Gerard, M. (1938). Enuresis. *American Journal of Orthopsychiatry* 9:48–58. A classic paper on the psychotherapeutic intervention in enuresis.

Hallgren, B. (1957). Enuresis. *Acta Psychiatrica Supplement* 114:1–139.

Katan, A. (1946). Experiences with enuretics. *Psychoanalytic Study of the Child* 2:241–255.

Kolvin, I., MacKeith, R., and Meadow, S. (1973). *Bladder Control and Enuresis.* Philadelphia: Lippincott. A complete and comprehensive review of the problem of enuresis.

Kolvin, I., and Taunch, J. (1973). A dual theory of nocturnal enuresis. In *Bladder Control and Enuresis,* ed. I. Kolvin, R. MacKeith, and S. Meadow, pp. 156–172. Philadelphia: Lippincott.

Mendelson, W., Johnson, J., and Stewart, M. (1971). Hyperactive children as teen-agers: a follow-up study. *Journal of Nervous and Mental Diseases* 153:273–279.

Ritvo, E., Ornitz, E., Gottlieb, F., Poussaint, A., et al. (1969).

Arousal and non-arousal enuretic events. *American Journal of Psychiatry* 125:77–84.

Sperling, M. (1965). Dynamic considerations and treatment of enuresis. *Journal of the American Academy of Child Psychiatry* 4:19–31.

Chapter 14

ENCOPRESIS

Robert T. Porter, M.D.

DEFINITION

The term *enkopresis* appeared in the German literature in 1925 and 1926 to describe cases of fecal soiling in children over two years old who manifest no organic illness. Bellman (1966) defined encopresis as passing a lump of feces into the clothing at least once a month for at least three months, but concluded it is inadvisable to set a very precise age limit even though the child's fourth year is the period during which bowel control is normally established. Several kinds of encopresis have also been described, including primary or continuous (where bowel control has never been achieved), secondary or discontinuous (where control had been achieved but then broke down with a resumption of soiling), and retentive (where there is fecal retention either as a persistent or intermittent phenomenon).

REVIEW OF LITERATURE

While references to the problem of soiling go back to the 1880s, with the suggestion of many different treatments, most of the serious studies date from the 1950s. For a quite comprehensive bibliography (eighty references) and review of the literature up through the early 1970s, see Halpern (1977). Many of the interesting attempts to develop concepts of etiology, treatment, and prevention stemmed from careful studies of one or a few clinical cases. Huschka (1942) was able to work analytically with a three and a half year old boy with psychogenic megacolon who was having no bowel movements except when one was effected by enemas given every four days. He had been quickly trained by his nurse from the age of three or four months. Huschka became interested in the effects of what she defined as coercive bowel training (i.e., started before the age of eight months). She was able to obtain definite data on when bowel training had been started for 169 children seen in a pediatric out-patient clinic, and for 91 it had been before the age of eight months. She was also able to ascertain what the reactions of 163 children had been during bowel training, and concluded "nearly a half reacted in what might be called a self-damaging manner. There is no basis in the findings of the study for saying that these children, like the boy analyzed, have developed neurosis, but it is significant that their immediate response to exacting bowel training was in terms of the stuff by which neurosis often manifests itself: constipation, loose stools, anxiety, rage, negativism, excessive cleanliness, guilt."

Garrard and Richmond (1952) carefully studied six children with megacolon and were able to establish that it was psychogenic and quite distinctively different from Hirschsprung's disease (congenital aganglionic megacolon). Fecal soiling was the admitting complaint in five of the six, and in the sixth it developed later. Bowel training was coercive. In five of the six patients the first three months of life were characterized by painful gastrointestinal experiences (enemas, anal fissures, colic).

Anthony (1957) conducted one of the few extensive research projects on this subject. One hundred children passed through the research clinic, of whom seventy-six were set aside for full investigation. Ages ranged from four to fifteen. Boys outnumbered girls about 6:1. He calls attention to the important differences between the children who are in effect never trained and those who have been trained but whose training then breaks down. His composite picture of the "continuous" child is "a dirty child from a dirty family, burdened with every conceivable sort of social problem." Enuresis is commonly associated. Toilet training can be characterized as neglectful. His composite of the "discontinuous" child is "the compulsive child of a compulsive family. He is overcontrolled and inhibited in his emotional life and scrupulous with regard to his habits. The toilet "leakage" is his dark secret and toward it he manifests a mixture of shame and anxiety." The "retentive" child undergoes a severe toilet training, and responds to it not with soiling or a precarious continence, but with stubborn constipation out of which encopresis later develops.

Bemporad and his co-workers (1971), at a child psychiatry clinic serving dependents of Air Force personnel, gathered a total of seventeen cases of encopresis, of whom only one was a girl. Fourteen of the seventeen displayed an unexpected similarity in terms of additional symptoms, character structure, and family dynamics. The parents of eight had been divorced; of the remaining six, the fathers were either completely absent from the home (as on overseas military assignment) or away from home a great deal (holding two jobs) and had essentially no involvement in the family interactions. The mothers of the fourteen were domineering, overly involved in their children's everyday life but inclined to complain about the encopretic son, and seven of the mothers were clinically depressed. The fourteen boys presented a remarkably similar physical appearance: all were small, pale children with a distinctly sickly look. They had histories of poor coordination, and none enjoyed sports. They were described as obstinate and withdrawn, and none had good peer contacts. The majority spent most of their time after school watching television or in other solitary pursuits. There was a sad lack of spontaneity or curiosity in most of them. All fourteen had lower Verbal than Performance subscale scores on the WISC, though all had at least normal intelligence. This corresponded to a clinical finding of a severe language disorder in six, and historical information on an additional three who were noted to be developmentally slow talkers, which was consistent with an overall clinical picture of what is often called the "maturational lag syndrome." Other associated symptoms were enuresis (8), headache (2), asthma (1), and nocturnal tooth-grinding (2). Four occasionally soiled in school, but the remaining ten soiled only at home and usually in the proximity of their mothers. Eleven of the fourteen had been toilet trained prior to eighteen months of age, and the training had been reported as difficult, coercive, or prolonged. Eight had actually achieved continence, whereas six had achieved a modified form of continence with occasional accidents. In twelve, it was possible to trace the onset of encopresis, or the time when soiling became clinically significant. In two, it began at age two, after a period of continence of at least five to six months, coincident with the birth of a sibling. In three, it began between three and four years of age and was related to separation from the mother, or to parental separation or divorce. In five, it began at age six, shortly after starting school. One developed it at age seven when his mother had to be hospitalized for surgery, and another at age nine when he was switched to a new school. An unexpected finding was that in six of these boys the fecal soiling rapidly abated or completely stopped when the fathers returned home from military tours or when the fathers were induced to spend more time with their sons.

Baird (1974), reporting on her experience with approximately forty encopretic children, found it difficult to accept the toilet training experience as being of prime etiological importance. She believes the key is a family interactional problem with the encopretic child as symptom bearer for the family. She found in each case of encopresis there were four characteristic and coexisting interaction patterns: (1) withholding; (2) infantilization; (3) mishandled anger; and (4) miscommunication.

INCIDENCE

There have been very few careful studies of large, unselected populations. Some of the older figures cited were for children referred to child guidance clinics. Others were of populations too small to give valid figures, or lumped together children of widely different ages. Bellman (1966) found 132 Stockholm first graders out of 8683 were still encopretic at an average age of seven and three-quarters years, an incidence of 1.5 percent. For boys it was 2.3 percent and for girls, 0.7 percent. In this same large sample, the incidence of enuresis at the same age was 5.8 percent (7.2 percent for boys, and 4.4 percent for girls). From a questionnaire filled out by parents of the entire study population (8683), it was possible to ascertain the ages at which the children had acquired control of urination and defecation. By their third birthday, 8.1 percent still did not control defecation (11 percent of the boys, 5.2 percent of the girls) while 18.4 percent were still enuretic (22.2 percent of boys, 14.6 percent of girls). By their fourth birthday, soiling was reduced by more than half (to 4.3 percent of boys and 1.4 percent of girls) while enuresis was halved (to 11.7 percent of boys and 7.6 percent of girls). It is much higher in such populations as the severely mentally retarded.

ETIOLOGY

Theories of why some children do not become continent of feces and why others, having established apparently reliable bowel control, later have extensive breakdown of this control, center principally upon the timing and manner of toilet training and the complex interpersonal factors between child and mother predating, accompanying, and following the actual period of training. Other factors considered important by nearly all investigators are such things as the constitutional endowment of the child, including possible maturational lags, but these are difficult to measure precisely. The importance of the entire family and social matrix are also increasingly recognized, especially as these support and enhance the caretaking functions of the mother or interfere with her ability to carry these out well. In this regard, the impact of absence or noninvolvement of the father seems to be very significant from some of the clinical studies. Other factors which emerge from clinical observation are the variety of traumatic experiences which may lead to breakdown of bowel control in vulnerable children. These include such events as illness, hospitalization, birth of a sibling or other situations which seem to represent separation or threatened loss of the mother, such as maternal depression, entering school, and divorce or separation of the parents.

Since the vast majority of children do become trained, even under very adverse circumstances, it seems important to see the issue in terms of normal development, and for this purpose the work of A. Freud (1963) remains very helpful. She delineated the development "from wetting and soiling to bladder and bowel control" and noted four stages: (1) complete freedom to wet and soil; (2) a cathectic shift from the oral to the anal zone so that anal products become highly cathected with unfused libido and aggression; (3) bowel and bladder control accomplished through identification with mother, though dependent on positive relations to her; and (4) autonomous control disconnected from object ties. She emphasizes that as long as the oedipal and preoedipal conflicts are not resolved, the intense disappointments with mother may lead to loss of bowel and bladder control and interfere with development to stage four. She stated: "A child who is severely disappointed in his mother . . . may not only lose the internalized urge to be clean but also reactivate the aggressive use of elimination."

Anthony (1957) concluded from his research that "toilet training is the most important and most influential of the variables involved", but he cautions against thinking of Huschka's "coercive" training solely in terms of how early it may be. It must be seen within the context of the total mother-child situation.

DIAGNOSTIC CONSIDERATIONS

Soiling has significant adverse consequences, including rejection by family and schoolmates and damage to the child's self-esteem, as well as the impact of the often noted denial on the child's reality testing. Accordingly, a careful assessment is indicated whenever this problem is encountered. A thorough history should cover any painful bowel experiences of early life, including colic, constipation, diarrhea, anal fissures, or enemas, as well as the nature of toilet training. The latter should tactfully elicit not only when training was initiated and completed, but what methods were employed, what difficulties may have been encountered, as well as whether continence of bladder and bowels was ever really established or whether a pattern of retention developed. It is worth asking how this process went with any siblings, too. In discontinuous encopresis, careful inquiry should focus on events and circumstances just prior to its onset. Although it is more difficult to learn retrospectively, maternal depression or emotional stresses operating at the time of training of the child should be looked for, as well as the conscious reactions of the mother and other family members if there was never any period of bowel continence, or after there was any prolonged breakdown in this. A full psychiatric evaluation will consider the entire family and its overall emotional health and mode of dealing with problems, though seeing the family together in a family interview may not be indicated, especially if the investigator is not trained in family therapy. Interviews with the encopretic child may employ tactful questioning, play techniques, and such readily available projective tests as figure drawings or a drawing of the family. Referral for full psychological testing may be indicated if clinical appraisal remains difficult.

Usually before psychiatric evaluation is sought, there will have been an ample medical investigation by the pediatrician of possible physical factors. Differentiation of psychogenic megacolon from aganglionic megacolon will usually be in the province of the pediatrician and radiologist, but from history it is noted that encopresis is uncommon in the latter.

TREATMENT

Anthony suggested that prolonged psychotherapy is indicated for discontinuous encopresis, where he found the child was often deeply disturbed. For the child who never had become trained, he felt a program of habit training under happier circumstances (i.e., with a warm, interested but relaxed person operating under a more consistent regime than was ever available at home) should be the main focus. He cautioned about the need for expert handling of the mother of the child needing extended therapy, lest she withdraw the child from treatment.

An interesting note on quick, effective therapy of a four-year-old boy who refused to be toilet trained was reported by Rosen and Landsberg (1952). It consisted entirely of brief counseling of the child's parents. The authors conclude that such good outcome in so short a time was possible because of a fortunate combination of circumstances: receptivity of the parents to outside help, a sympathetic and noncritical relationship between the mother and the pediatrician, and ready availability to the pediatrician of psychiatric counseling and ongoing exchange of ideas and data.

Although many authors have suggested complex family problems, there are few reports of a true family therapy approach having been effective, and it has been speculated that unless prompt remission of the presenting symptom is attained, therapy may not be sustained.

On the other hand, the symptom of soiling is such a clear and definite one, and failure to learn or mislearning seem such a basic part of the problem that it is not surprising that it has attracted much interest and effort in the area of behavior modification. There are numerous reports of successful use of this approach. Careful instructions are given to parents on how to refrain from punitive approaches to soiling and how to plan a new positive schedule for utilizing the toilet, with positive reinforcement for successes by praise, rewards suggested by the child, and more rewarding time spent with the child by the parents. However, as with all approaches, there have been disappointments with behavior modification too, including relapses after apparent improvement.

Sullivan, Dickinson, and Wilson (1963) reported on an essentially medical and pharmacologic management of fecal incontinence, initially for a group of children with definite anatomic causes (spinal cord damage, or lacking anal sphincters). They employed dioctyl sodium sulfosuccinate (Colace, Coxinate) to keep the fecal mass soft, and bisacodyl (Dulcolax) in suppository form to effect a timed, complete evacuation once or twice a day, but only after first clearing any fecal impaction. In approximately one hundred children, 80% of those who conscientiously followed the program were able to avoid both constipation and soiling. They felt the same program was helpful for many children with functional encopresis, since in so many cases it followed constipation, frequently with impaction dilating the rectum allowing soft fecal material to escape with flatus and continual soiling.

Halpern (1977) has advocated an eclectic approach, based on the belief that one technique will not suffice in the therapy of encopresis. A careful assessment involves medical clearance and history gathering from parents and child, during which family interaction and motivation are evaluated. Usually parents and child strongly wish to overcome the problem, and the child is asked for suggestions of items he values which can be used in a reinforcement schedule. The physiology of retention and soiling is explained and a rationale given for the establishment of the control over defecation which the child desires. Dulcolax (bisacodyl) suppository is used for its quick action on the large bowel, so that conveniently timed evacuation will give the child an immediate success experience for which he can be promptly rewarded. With this combination of organic therapy and behavior modification, most children quickly regain both cleanliness and regular movements. For those few who do not respond to this method, usually when phobic concerns are also present, the child and his parents are offered collateral or family therapy, which may include systematic desensitization of the child to the feared situation. In those cases where the child quickly forms hard stools which are pushed out with discomfort or fear of possible pain, a stool softener such as dioctyl sodium sulfosuccinate is added to the regimen.

In any of these approaches where symptom relief is attained, it would appear desirable to maintain some contact not only for follow-up, but to offer any other therapeutic help which may be needed, either for problems which may have precipitated the soiling or for the conflicts and damaged self-esteem which may follow upon family and peer reactions to the problem.

DISCUSSION

The possibility that the children with this problem may be predisposed by constitutional type or maturational lags does not lessen the destructive impact on their social development if they encounter rage or rejection from their parents. Some of the traits described in the children (withdrawn, obstinate, poor peer contacts, lacking in spontaneity, etc.) might well be consequences of the rejection and shaming they encounter. At the same time, some authors reflect strong disapproval of attitudes of the mothers toward their children even though they noted these mothers to have compulsive personality features and frequently depression of a clinical level.

While Huschka (1942) noted too-early toilet training and regarded this as "coercive" (in the sense it was being imposed before the child was sufficiently mature to be able to reliably comply), it is easy to forget the cultural factors which contributed to such too-early training. Huschka pointed out that the United States Children's Bureau publication on Infant Care, in as recent an edition as 1935, stated: "Training of the bowels may be begun as early as the end of the first month. It should always be begun by the third month and may be completed during the eighth month." It also urged "absolute regularity," emphasizing the importance of this by a picture of a mother and a baby with a clock nearby and advised "not varying the time by five minutes," and followed this with detailed instructions for using the soap stick as an aid in conditioning the rectum.

The most enlightened instructions on toilet training may be those of Winnicott (1957), addressed to the "ordinary, devoted mother." In six brief pages he gives the mother some of the physiological explanations which are rarely understood, and in a very acceptable manner conveys something of the intensity of gratification which not only can but should accompany this phase of development. Throughout he emphasizes the understanding on the part of the mother which will enable her to facilitate the normative development of the child. For example, he says: "If the movement is held by the baby at the last stage in the rectum, it gets dried; water is absorbed from it as it waits there. The movement is then passed on as a solid thing which the baby can enjoy passing; in fact, at the moment of passing it, there can be such a localized excitement that the baby cries from excess of feeling. You see what you are doing by leaving the matter to your baby (although helping insofar as the baby cannot manage alone)? You are giving every possible chance for him to find from experience that it feels good to hold a bowel movement for a while before passing it on, and to discover that the result is interesting; in fact to discover that if all goes well defecation can be an extremely satisfactory experience." He goes on to explain how, even before the baby can talk, there are ways in which he may communicate to the mother that a movement has been passed, and later even when there is going to be one, and the mother may indicate her interest not because she is afraid he will make a mess or because she feels she ought to be teaching him how to be clean, but because she loves him and whatever is important to him is also important to her. "So you will not mind if you got there late, because the important thing was not keeping the baby clean, but answering the call of a fellow human being. Later on your relationship to the infant in these terms will become richer. Sometimes a baby will feel frightened of the movement that is coming, and sometimes he will feel that it is something valuable. Because what you do is based on the simple fact of your love, you soon become able to distinguish between the times when you are helping your baby to be rid of bad things, and when you are receiving gifts. . . . When this is what happens, and when it is kept up over a period of time, what is called training can follow without much difficulty, because the mother has earned the right to make such demands as are not beyond the infant's capacity."

Fraiberg (1959), too, gives very perceptive explanations of what the child is going through so that the mother can adapt appropriately. She also gives examples of some of the kinds of difficulties which may occur even when parents are in tune and not impatient, and how they may be dealt with.

With the availability now of excellent guidelines for more patient and understanding training, and the convenience of automatic washing machines and disposable diapers, it could be hoped that through well-baby clinics and pediatricians, more mothers and child caretakers could be helped with this potentially troublesome phase of the infant's development, and that not only encopresis but the many other problems associated with difficult toilet training might be reduced or prevented. If problems do arise, early intervention by pediatricians probably can correct many of them before they become firmly established or mar the mother-child relationship. For those not responsive to pediatric counseling, early psychiatric consultation might lessen the risk of serious sequelae and would almost certainly require less effort and time than intervention at a later age.

BIBLIOGRAPHY

Anthony, E.J. (1957). An experimental approach to the psychopathology of childhood: encopresis. British Journal of Medical Psychology 30:156–162, 172–174. Reprinted in *Childhood Psychopathology: An Anthology of Basic Readings,* ed. S. Harrison and J. McDermott, pp. 611–625. New York: International Universities Press.

Baird, M. (1974). Characteristic interaction patterns in families of encopretic children. *Bulletin of the Menninger Clinic* 38:144–153.

Bellman, M. (1966). Studies in encopresis. *Acta Paediatrica Scandinavika, Supplement 170.* An excellent research study, in English.

Bemporad, J., Pfeifer, C., Gibbs, L., Cortner, R. and Bloom, W. (1971). Characteristics of encopretic patients and their families. *Journal of the American Academy of Child Psychiatry* 10:272–292.

Fraiberg, S. (1959). *The Magic Years.* New York: Scribner. An excellent, integrated approach to childhood development. For bowel training, see pp. 91–103; for the related topic of discipline, see pp. 244–250.

Freud, A. (1963). The concept of developmental lines. *Psychoanalytic Study of the Child* 18:245–265.

Garrard, S., and Richmond, J. (1952). Psychogenic megacolon manifested by fecal soiling. *Pediatrics* 10:474–483.

Halpern, W. (1977). The treatment of encopretic children. *Journal of the American Academy of Child Psychiatry* 16:478–499. An excellent review article of the literature, with a very complete bibliography.

Huschka, M. (1942). The child's response to coercive bowel training. *Psychosomatic Medicine* 4:301–308.

Rosen, V., and Landsberg, E. (1952). Short term management of a child behavior disorder. *Pediatrics* 10:484–487.

Sullivan, D., Dickinson, D. and Wilson, J. (1963). The conservative management of fecal incontinence in children. *Journal of the American Medical Association* 185:664–666.

Winnicott, D. (1957). *Mother and Child.* New York: Basic Books.

Chapter 15

BRONCHIAL ASTHMA: AN EXAMPLE OF

PSYCHOSOMATIC DISORDER

Norman Straker, M.D.

DEFINITIONS

Psychosomatic disorders are a group of somatic disorders in which psychosocial processes are believed to play an important role in the etiology and course of the disease. The area of psychosomatic medicine includes the study of the relationships between the emotional, biochemical, and physiological responses of the organism (Stein 1972).

Historically, the modern study of the psychosomatic diseases began in the late 1930s and early 1940s and was primarily psychoanalytic. Since that time the study has widened to include behavioral, physiological, and biochemical measures. Controlled clinical studies have augmented the earlier clinical case reports.

Among the psychosomatic disorders of childhood, *bronchial asthma* is probably still the most prevalent. The interrelationships between multiple concomitant factors has led to the elaboration of a great number of theories of the etiology and pathogenesis of asthma. However, rather than continue the dichotomy of psyche and soma, the principle of a summation of various factors underlying the etiology of childhood asthma is beginning to be accepted by the various disciplines that are involved in the treatment of these children. Bronchial asthma is presented as an example of a psychosomatic disorder.

Bronchial asthma is a symptom complex characterized by an increased responsiveness of the trachea, major bronchi and peripheral bronchioles to various stimuli. It is manifested by extensive narrowing of these airways. This results in a prolonged expiratory phase of respiration and is noted clinically by wheezing and difficulty in breathing. The bronchial obstruction and resulting impairment of air exchange is the result of a combination of bronchospasms, edema, and mucous plugs. The various stimuli which trigger the symptom complex include allergens, infection, and psychological stresses.

REVIEW OF LITERATURE

It has become increasingly evident from clinical and animal research studies that the emotions can effect bronchial function via the autonomic nervous system, and by modifying the immunological and allergic processes. In addition, the individual's coping style influences the subjective distress of the patient and may affect the type of medical decisions made regarding the use of corticosteroids. (Kinsman 1977)

French and Alexander (1941) were the first psychoanalysts to report their clinical observations. Since then, psychoanalytic studies have consistently reported that the main conflicts in these patients are related to repressed aggression and separation anxiety.

M. Sperling (1968) described what she termed "a psychosomatic mother-child relationship." This she defined as a relationship in which the child is rejected when he is healthy and strives towards independence, while he is rewarded by close attention and caring when ill and helpless. She reported that the child's aggression was discharged through the asthmatic symptomatology. She noted that overt aggressive behavior often followed psychotherapy of asthmatic children, as the asthmatic symptomatology decreased. She suggested that the basic developmental phase during which asthma emerges is the anal phase, ages one to three years.

Sandler (1964, 1965) and Wenar, Handlar, and Garner (1962) have carried out two independent studies of asthmatic children (four to seven years; six to eleven years) and their mothers in order to test the hypothesis of a particular mother-child relationship. Sandler's group of mothers characteristically used the threat of removal of love as an instrument of discipline. Wenar found the mothers he studied to be lacking in motherliness and tending to engage in a close but frustrating relationship with their own mothers.

A frequently reported observation is the improvement of an asthmatic child's symptomatology upon removal from his home environment ("parentectomy," a term coined by Peshkin). Jessner, et al. (1955) suggested that the freedom from symptoms while a child is hospitalized for a short time may be due to the anaclitic relationship that the child establishes with hospital staff. Attempts to systematically study this phenomenon were carried out at the Children's Asthma Research Institute and Hospital in Denver. Children were divided into subgroups after being in hospital residence for six months, based on whether they could be removed from steroids or remained dependent upon them. (Purcell, Turnbull, and Bernstein 1962).

Recent clinical and experimental observations have started

to focus on the role of aggression in the development and precipitation of asthma. In a clinical study (Straker 1971) of intractable asthmatic children on a child psychiatric inpatient unit, a clinical improvement in asthmatic symptomatology correlated highly with a concurrent increase in aggressive behavior. These patients were not unlike those described by Sperling (1968). They repressed aggression as a means of defending against fears of separation. Initially, they all improved after admission to the ward, without changes in medication, presumably because of the temporary "parentectomy" and the development of dependent relationships with nurses, physicians, and therapists. While undergoing intensive psychotherapy most of these children exhibited a change in overt behavior on the ward. They were initially quite guarded and inhibited in their expression of angry feelings or aggressive behavior and tended to respond to frustration with wheezing or withdrawal. Later, however, most of these children responded to frustrating experiences on the ward with more aggression. Temper outbursts, screaming, and fighting emerged. This shift in behavior occurred in most of the children and was accompanied by a lessening of asthmatic symptomatology. The one child whose asthmatic symptomatology remained relatively unchanged was the most ill psychologically, and the least able to be in contact with her angry feelings. Two other children in this study manifested transient but completely reversible psychotic episodes in the course of their psychotherapy while hospitalized (Straker 1977). These transient psychotic episodes were defenses against conflicts and their emergence in the transference. Since the asthmatic symptoms remained quiescent, this illustrates that the old controversy of whether asthma and psychosis may alternate (alternation hypothesis) could better be understood in a context of choice of defense.

A study designed to look at the relationship between asthmatic symptomatology and aggressive expression was carried out as a follow-up, in the natural setting of a summer camp exclusively for asthmatic children. It was found that the "treated group" (defined on the basis of requiring medical treatment which could include steroids, hospitalization, or epinephrine injections during a defined period of time) and whose bronchial function was significantly more impaired than the untreated, were shown to be significantly less expressive of aggression as measured by a modification of the Conner's Scale (Straker 1974).

The above findings are in agreement with recent experimental studies which suggest that the inhibition of aggressive impulses plays a role in the etiology of bronchial asthma. Mathé and Knapp (1971) compared six male college students with perennial asthma with six matched controls prior to and during two experimental stressors. The authors reported that asthmatics as compared to controls had significantly less manifest hostile emotions prior to and during stress. Extensive interviews revealed that "asthmatics showed a trend toward more anxiety, depression, guilt, disgust-shame; hostility ratings were much higher in healthy controls." In addition, they reported that asthmatics had lower urinary epinephrine values during both stress and control periods. Their measurement of respiratory indices showed that asthmatics had lower airway conductance and respiratory rate and an opposite direction of change in these indices under stress as compared to control subjects.

Similarly, Hahn (1966) reported that eighteen asthmatic children's response to criticism was more timid, self-reproachful, and less manifestly angry as compared to controls. The asthmatic subjects' concurrent physiological response to criticism resembled the initial stages of an asthmatic attack.

The above studies illustrate how the psychosocial experiences of hospitalization, parentectomy, and changes in the ability to experience and express aggression are reflected in changes in bronchial function. The actual mechanism whereby changes in bronchial function occur is unclear, but it is thought to be the result of changes in amount of autonomic nervous system activity and the hypothesized beta adrenergic deficit which will be elaborated shortly (see Etiology and Dynamics). Also, the finding of lower urinary epinephrine in asthmatics vs. controls, both during control and stress periods, is of interest and requires further study.

Another avenue of research has been to study the effect of suggestion. The original study was the presentation of an artificial rose to a patient with a "rose allergy." Bronchospasm resulted. Luparello (1968) in a more elaborate study of this phenomenon induced bronchospasm in subjects by telling them they were inhaling allergens when they were actually inhaling nebulized physiological saline. Nineteen of forty subjects responded with a significant increase in airway resistance. Full-blown asthmatic attacks occurred in twelve subjects and were reversed with an injection of saline. The use of atropine which blocks the vagus nerve, blocked the experimental effect. The induction of stress through hypnosis or movies, or the lessening of stress through hypnosis or biofeedback techniques have also been reported by Vachon (1976) and Weiss (1976).

Stress also has effects on the immunological system. These have been reported rather extensively by Stein (1976). Lesions in the anterior hypothalamus in guinea pigs affect the levels of circulating antibodies as well as the animals' response to histamine.

Kinsman (1977) reports that one of the important determinants of chronicity or intractability in asthma is the coping style of the child. Using a symptom checklist, those children scoring highest on the panic-fear and irritability items were perceived by physicians to be more ill, whether or not they had poorer bronchial function than others. These perceptions by their doctors affected the decision as to whether they were treated with corticosteroids.

INCIDENCE

Bronchial asthma is thought to affect approximately 4.5 million people in the United States. Three million of these are estimated to be children. The number with chronic asthma is 300,000. The number of deaths per year attributed to bronchial asthma has been estimated at 9,000. Boys are more frequently affected than girls. It is also reported that up to 45 percent of children lose their symptoms by puberty.

ETIOLOGY AND DYNAMICS

The etiology of bronchial asthma is unclear, as noted earlier, but it is thought to be multifactorial. There is increasing consensus that one factor is an instability of the bronchial system which overreacts to allergic, infectious, and psychosocial stimuli. In order to more clearly understand this "beta adrenergic theory" as originally espoused by Szentivanyi (1968), a short review of the autonomic and neurotransmitter control of the bronchomotor tree would be helpful.

Bronchomotor tone is the result of a balance between parasympathetic and sympathetic influences. The parasympathetic influence is via the vagus nerve and constricts the bronchioles. The sympathetic nervous system's influence on bronchiole size is via two neurotransmitters, epinephrine (E) and norepinephrine (NE) which affect the alpha and beta receptors of the bronchial tree. NE and E affect alpha receptors which result in bronchoconstriction. E alone affects beta receptors and allows for bronchodilation. The sympathetic nervous system is activated by stress, infection, the products of the antigen-antibody reaction and noxious fumes. These influences are usually· adjusted by the homeostatic mechanisms of the autonomic nervous system.

The bronchial hyperactivity of the asthmatic is postulated to be due to a reduced functioning of the beta adrenergic receptor system. This leads to an alpha dominance and a consequent increase in bronchoconstriction in response to those stimuli that activate the sympathetic nervous system. The deficit is postulated to be an inherited or acquired enzyme deficiency of the beta receptor, adrenyl cyclase.

The immunological abnormality in some of those affected with bronchial asthma is the production of reagin antibody as a result of a constitutional hypersensitivity to allergens. The problem with infection is that in addition to the inflammation, and the resulting mucus and edema, bronchospasm may result from an allergy to the infecting agents.

The psychodynamics involved in bronchial asthma were reported earlier in the Review of Literature. As was noted, the emphasis on aggressive conflicts that threaten separation from a maternal figure have an importance both in precipitating and maintaining asthmatic symptomatology. The need to repress and/or suppress aggressive impulses derives from either the family constellation or the level of ego development of the individual. In some children the direct discharge of aggressive impulses is not tolerable because of the threat of retaliation, or direct threats of abandonment. For others, threats of loss of maternal support are intrapsychic and based on the fear that death wishes might be fulfilled, or fears of projected aggressive impulses. Asthmatic wheezing can serve to discharge both aggressive feelings and longings for continued object contact while direct aggressive expression is inhibited. As noted earlier, Mathé and Knapp suggested that the asthmatics' inability to express aggression is of etiological significance. Their finding of decreased blood levels of epinephrine both under control and particularly under experimental conditions when aggression is stimulated, as compared to nonasthmatics, may have some important bearing on the reduced functioning of the beta receptors and consequent bronchoconstriction.

DIAGNOSTIC CONSIDERATIONS

Bronchial asthma must be distinguished from physiological concomitants of anxiety that are manifested in the respiratory system. These include deep sighing, hyperventilation, breath-holding, a sense that one can not get enough air, and coughing. The main differential feature here is that only bronchial asthma involves increased bronchial resistance. Thus, pulmonary function tests and x-rays of the chest are important in the diagnostic assessment.

Once a diagnosis of bronchial asthma has become clear, it becomes important to tease out precipitating and/or maintaining factors. A thorough history of allergies and infections should be taken and emotional triggers should be searched out. Note should be taken of hereditary factors.

A careful allergic history and skin testing may serve to allow for the elimination of allergens that might be of crucial importance. Similarly, a psychiatric and psychological evaluation of the child's development, conflicts and family relationships might point to emotional triggers and causes of chronicity. The diagnostic workup all too commonly leaves out a careful elucidation of the emotional factors involved. Too often emotional factors are noted but dropped from further consideration for therapeutic intervention.

TREATMENT

A detailed discussion of the treatment of bronchial asthma is beyond the scope of this presentation. Symptomatic treatment is often accomplished by the use of bronchodilators of various types, given orally, or by aerosol. At times when bronchospasm fails to respond to these measures, epinephrine is required subcutaneously. Cromolyn sodium might be indicated on a continuing basis for chronic asthma. Some children may only respond to corticosteroids in acute attacks. Others might require them on a continuing basis and are destined to have numerous side effects of these drugs. Recently, steroid aerosols have been introduced and seem to result in symptomatic improvement for some patients without the systemic side effects.

In addition to the symptomatic measures noted above, attempts should be made to search out and lessen allergic and emotional triggers. Allergic desensitization might be indicated, as might some form of psychiatric intervention. A careful evaluation of the child's psychological development and family relationships would indicate which of the possible interventions would be most suitable: individual psychotherapy, family therapy, treatment of the child and parents separately, or residential treatment. A careful liaison with the pediatrician or pediatric allergist is essential during all phases of the treatment. Actual separations from the therapist, as well as aggressive conflicts that the child fears could lead to such separation, often lead to asthmatic wheezing until the patient becomes less anxious with the expression of aggressive feelings. The working through of such conflicts is essential to the success of the treatment. In addition, parents should be helped to accept and cope with an increase in their child's assertive and aggressive behavior as the psychotherapy unfolds. It is important to recognize that many of these youngsters need to be helped to acquire the verbal skills to handle aggressive conflicts rather than wheeze or act them out behaviorally.

DISCUSSION

Childhood asthma is an illness that is rather extensive in terms of the numbers of children affected, and is usually not treated by the child psychiatrist until it has become intractable or institutional treatment is being contemplated. It is at that time that the dynamics that have been described are apparent: namely, extensive conflicts over aggression and fears of abandonment and separation. While it is true that working through these conflicts in psychotherapy does lead to less repression of aggression and less anxiety over separation and a concomitant decrease in asthmatic symptomatology, there seems to be an unanswered question: is the dynamic constellation in part the result of having been chronically sick, or is it due to a life-threatening illness which in itself induces regression by intensifying dependency and earlier conflicts over issues of separation? A collaborative study of allergic children by allergists and child psychiatrists prior to the development of asthma would allow this problem to be sorted out. However, from a clinical point of view, child psychiatric evaluation, intervention, and psychotherapy can offer important therapeutic benefit.

SUMMARY

A rather extensive review of the psychological literature basically elaborates upon the earliest observations of French and Alexander who first reported the asthmatic patient's conflicts with separation. More recent studies have focused on various aspects of the family dynamics, the effects of separation from parents when children are hospitalized, institutionalized, or at camp, and the effects of psychotherapy. The latest studies have included documenting clinical findings and psychological measures with measures of pulmonary function and biochemical laboratory tests. It is this kind of collaboration that holds the most promise for understanding the pathogenesis of this syndrome.

BIBLIOGRAPHY

French, T., and Alexander, F. (1941). Psychogenic factors in bronchial asthma. *Psychosomatic Medicine Monograph 4.* Washington: National Research Council.

Hahn, W. (1966). Autonomic responses of asthmatic children. *Psychosomatic Medicine* 28:323–332.

Jessner, L., Lamont, J., Long, R., et al. (1955). Emotional impact of nearness and separation for the asthmatic child and his mother. *Psychoanalytic Study of the Child* 10:-353–375.

Kinsman, R., Dahlmen, N., Spector, S., et al. (1977). Observations on subjects symptomatology, coping behavior and medical decisions in asthma. *Psychosomatic Medicine* 39:102–119.

Luparello, T., Lyons, H., Bleeker, E., et al. (1968). Influences of suggestion on airway reactivity in asthmatic subjects. *Psychosomatic Medicine* 30:819–825.

Mathé, A., and Knapp, P. (1971). Emotional and adrenal reactions to stress in bronchial asthma. *Psychosomatic Medicine* 32:323–340.

Purcell, K., Turnbull, J., and Bernstein, L. (1962). Distinctions between subgroups of asthmatic children. *Journal of Psychosomatic Research* 6:283–291.

Sandler, L. (1964). Child rearing practices of mothers of asthmatic children, I. *Journal of Asthma Research* 2:109–116.

———(1965). Child rearing practices of mothers of asthmatic children, II. *Journal of Asthma Research* 2:215–256.

Sperling, M. (1968). Asthma in children. *Journal of American Academy of Child Psychiatry* 7:44–58.

Stein, M. (1972). The what, how and why of psychosomatic medicine. In *Modern Psychiatry and Clinical Research,* ed. D. Offer and D. Freedman, pp. 44–58. New York: Basic Books.

———, and Schiavi, R. (1976). Influences of brain and behavior on the immune system. *Science* 191:434–440.

Straker, N. (1971). Unpublished study.

———, and Bieber, J. (1977). Asthma and the vicissitudes of aggression. *Journal of American Academy of Child Psychiatry* 16:132–139.

Straker, N., and Tamerin, J. (1974). Aggression and childhood asthma: a study in a natural setting. *Journal of Psychosomatic Research* 18:131–135.

Szentivanyi, A. (1968). The beta adrenergic theory of atopic abnormality in bronchial asthma. *Journal of Allergy* 42: 203–232.

Vachon, L., and Rich, E. (1976). Visceral learning in asthma. *Psychosomatic Medicine* 38:122–130.

Wenar, C., Handlar, M., and Garner, A. (1962). *Origins of Psychosomatic Disturbances.* New York: Hoeber.

Weiss, J., Lyness, J., Molk, L., et al. (1976). Induced respiratory change in asthmatic children. *Journal of Psychosomatic Research* 20:115–123.

C. Other Disorders

Chapter 16

GENDER DISTURBANCES

Robert T. Porter, M.D.

DEFINITIONS

Transvestism is, literally, cross-dressing, or putting on the garments of the opposite sex, but most commonly the term has been used to describe what would be more precisely called "fetishistic cross-dressing," where putting on the clothes of the opposite sex "produces clear-cut, unquestioned genital excitement, generally leading to masturbation and orgasm. . . . Fetishistic cross-dressing is unreported in women; while women cross-dress, they do not become sexually excited by the garments they put on. . . . Fetishistic cross-dressing is an activity indulged in primarily by heterosexual men, and it is rare for men who are homosexual in preference to be sexually excited by women's clothes. . . ." according to Stoller (1971).

Homosexuality has been variously defined, from simply quantitative or manifest behavioral sexual activity with the same sex to qualitative aspects recognizing the emotional intensity of attraction and arousal. Marmor (1965) prefers to define "the clinical homosexual as one who is motivated in adult life by a definite preferential erotic attraction to members of the same sex and who usually (but not necessarily) engages in overt sexual relations with them. . . . Homosexuality, as a psychosexual phenomenon, ought to imply the same kind of strong and spontaneous capacity to be aroused by a member of one's own sex as heterosexuality implies in regard to members of the opposite sex." Money and Ehrhardt (1972) distinguish *facultative homosexuality* (optional homosexuality, which does not exclude heterosexuality, so that the person is, in effect bisexual) from *obligative homosexuality* (compelling or exclusive, leaving no bisexual or heterosexual option).

Transsexualism is, in essence, where an individual of one sex has such a deep identification with the opposite sex that he or she chooses to live as a member of that sex. Money and Ehrhardt (1972) define it as "behaviorally, the act of living and passing in the role of the opposite sex, before or after having attained hormonal, surgical and legal sex reassignment; psychically, the condition of people who have the conviction that they belong to the opposite sex and are driven by a compulsion to have the body, appearance and social status of the opposite sex." A research program at Stanford University employs the term *gender dysphoria syndrome* to include "classic" transsexuals, some effeminate homosexuals, and some transvestites all of whom claim great dissatisfaction with the gender role of their anatomical sex.

REVIEW OF LITERATURE AND ETIOLOGY

Green (1974), in an excellent historical and cross-cultural survey, summarizes that "males and females discontented with the sex roles expected of them because of their anatomy are unique neither to our culture nor our time. . . . Evidence from classical mythology, ancient, Renaissance, and more recent history, as well as cultural anthropology points to its long-standing and widespread occurrence. . . . Thus, many people have lived out their lives in an opposite-sexed role in many places and in many times. . . . Regrettably missing from these historical and cross-cultural accounts are data on the origins of such behavior. How did it come about? What early experiences were associated with the desire to adopt the opposite sex role? This process is not clear."

Homosexuality and transsexualism both clearly fail to fit the innate biological norm of adult preferential heterosexuality, and transvestism seems to represent some difficulty in the area of gender role (cross-dressing) even when it serves heterosexual goals. Among some homosexuals there is at least one other deviation from the usual gender role: an adopt on of some of the mannerisms and dress of the opposite sex.

The three main levels at which such deviations or reversals are noted are: (1) core gender identity or the inner conviction of being male or female; (2) gender role, which has to do with the manifest behavior as it is thought to comply with the social norms for one sex or the other. (3) sexual object choice, usually combining not only the sexual arousal felt toward the object but yearnings for an emotional attachment of the kind labeled love.

Some confusion arises because not all three levels need be disturbed in a given individual. It is possible (and usual) in transvestism for the gender identity to be male, sexual object choice heterosexual (female object), and gender role confused (i.e., in many if not most situations, gender role is masculine, but for sexual arousal and release cross-dressing is necessary). In homosexuality in both sexes, gender identity may be compatible with the biological sex, but sexual object choice is the reverse of the norm, and gender role may be that compatible with biological sex and gender identity, or it may be more compatible with the opposite sex. It is probably not common, however, for an effeminate male homosexual or a very masculine female homosexual to have a completely unambiguous gender identity. In transsexualism of the "classic" kind, it has been customary to think of the core gender identity as being strongly that of the opposite sex; then if gender role and sexual object choice are also those which would be expected in someone of the opposite sex, they would seem compatible with gender identity but not with the physical (biological) sex—and it can be understood how such individuals might feel everything would be harmonious if they could simply have their bodies changed.

Stoller (1971) has offered a composite or typical history, derived from the early childhood of a number of transvestites who were carefully studied. Allowed to develop in a clearly masculine direction for the first two or three years and thus develop a masculine core gender identity, the little boy then encounters a female who is irritated by precisely this masculinity and attacks it in the child by putting female clothes on him. This creates a fear in the boy that his sense of belonging to the male sex may be destroyed. This initial experience seems not to have been sexually exciting, but in time the original traumatic experience seems to be converted into a triumph, so that what was originally humiliating becomes sexually exciting. Later, his highly valued penis is impotent and nonejaculatory without the fetishistic stimulus of female attire.

Socarides (1968) does an excellent and thorough job of summarizing the literature on the etiology of homosexuality; it is too lengthy and complex to digest here. Marmor (1965) also reviews some of the most interesting hypotheses, but comments that most modern psychoanalysts do not agree with Freud's theory that homosexuality is a normal phase of libidinal development. Rather, they view it as an ego adaptation to certain environmental vicissitudes, which result in "hidden but incapacitating fears of the opposite sex." Marmor concludes "for our time and culture, the psychoanalytic assumption that preferential homosexual behavior is always associated with unconscious fears of heterosexual relationships appears valid." Money and Ehrhardt (1972) believe that certain sexually dimorphic traits or dispositions are laid down in the brain before birth, but are too strongly bivalent to be exclusive and invariant determinants of either homosexuality or heterosexuality. The primary origins of these conditions lie in the developmental period of a child's life after birth, particularly during the years of late infancy and early childhood, when gender identity differentiation is being established. They conclude that "the present state of knowledge does not permit any hypotheses that will predict with certainty which biographical conditions will ensure that an anatomically normal boy or girl will become erotically homosexual, bisexual, or heterosexual."

The term transsexual is a recent one, coined after the wide publicity of a sex-change operation in 1952 encouraged many individuals to seek such surgery themselves. The need to define a group for which such a drastic procedure might be indicated led to intensive study of relatively small groups of individuals at several leading medical centers. Gradually some tentative hypotheses began to be offered about the origins and etiology of this condition, although it was recognized early that applicants for such surgical procedures seemed to be well acquainted with all the literature on the subject and tended to present histories in conformity with those in the medical literature whether by conscious intent or not. Nonetheless, an early history of crossed gender role behavior has been given by most transsexuals, and in many cases this has been confirmed by the reports of other family members and by pictures in family albums. More important, it is postulated that their gender identity has also been crossed from very early, and this is usually described as being so complete that their gender role behavior is convincingly correct for the opposite sex, not a caricature of it. Stoller in 1968 described a typical background from which a male transsexual might emerge. A woman whose own mother did not recognize or encourage her daughter's femaleness grows up to marry a passive man for a relationship which is unsatisfactory for both but often enduring. When this depressed woman bears a beautiful son, she is thrilled, and an intense, blissful symbiosis is established between mother and infant which nothing can unlock as the years pass, and certainly the father does nothing to break it, tending to stay away from the home. Excessive physical and emotional closeness to the mother for too long creates feminine identifications and behavior which secretly please the mother who thus positively reinforces them. Stoller believes this is a nonconflictual learning process, akin in some ways to imprinting; in contrast he regards the homosexualities and transvestism as end products of defense against the trauma of dangerous, painful interpersonal relationships.

More recently, Stoller (1972) has offered a tentative formulation for the conditions for development of female transsexuals, which may be not quite comparable to those for male transsexuals. In his series of ten female transsexuals, he found the mother had been psychologically removed from the family, usually by depression, early in the girl's development, and the father instead of supporting his wife in her suffering offered the transsexual-to-be daughter in his place. In his series, each remembered always feeling very protective toward her mother, with conscious thoughts of taking care of her as a husband would (but not with conscious sexual fantasies), and that her mother reciprocated, openly encouraging her to serve in this protective way. Since to be a proper protector she will have to take on masculine attributes, as the months pass these will begin accumulating. The daughter's own depression, the result of having a mother who cannot mother, is then "cured" only when she does something to which her mother will respond warmly, as when the girl acts like a protecting husband. This mechanism Stoller finds more akin to homosexuality in that the aberration begins as a defense against trauma. Only later does the nonconflictual part of the process emerge, as encouragement augments the masculinity; the child is really loved and admired as she develops boyish traits.

Person and Ovesey (1974) postulated a different etiology based on their study of twenty male transsexuals. They considered five of the twenty to be effeminate homosexuals, another five to be transvestites. The remaining ten they termed primary transsexuals (i.e., they had progressed toward a "transsexual resolution of their gender and sexual problems without a significant history of either heterosexuality or homosexuality"). Although the ten primary transsexuals had envied girls and all had cross-dressed surreptitiously beginning sometime between the ages of three and ten, none actually believed he was a girl, and nine of them gave no history of feminine behavior in childhood and were not referred to as "sissies." What seemed more important was that they were childhood loners with few age-mate companions of either sex, and had feelings of anxiety, depression, and loneliness. Also they remained relatively asexual, and a major component of this asexuality was a specific self-loathing of male physical characteristics. Person and Ovesey did not find the core gender identity of the primary transsexuals to be female, but flawed or ambiguous, and they see their wish to be female as based on a fantasy of symbiotic fusion with the mother as a way to deal with extreme separation anxiety. They feel these patients fall in the range of the borderline syndrome diagnostically, characterized by separation anxiety, empty depression, sense of void, oral dependency, defective self-identity, and impaired object relations. They suggest that transsexualism, transvestism, and effeminate homosexuality reflect different ways of handling unresolved separation anxiety occurring during progressive steps of the separation-individuation phase of development: transsexualism first, transvestism and effeminate homosexuality later. In contrast to transsexualism, separation anxiety in transvestism and homosexuality is allayed not by the fantasy of symbiotic fusion with the mother, but by resort to transitional and part-objects—less primitive mechanisms than symbiosis.

INCIDENCE

No reliable figures on the incidence of transvestism were found, perhaps because only those who present themselves for therapy or who have been arrested under statutes against cross-dressing could be identified.

Widely quoted figures on the incidence of homosexuality are still those published by Kinsey in 1948 and 1953. While questions remain over their reliability based on speculation over what kind of self-selection operated among those who volunteered for this pioneer inquiry into human sexual behavior, they do support the concept that there is a wide range of human sexual behavior, with a considerable number of individuals, especially men, functioning in what might be termed a bisexual manner. For males, he found 50 percent were exclusively heterosexual throughout life and had never become aware of any tendency to respond to homosexual stimuli. Four percent of males were exclusively homosexual throughout their lives, after the onset of adolescence. Eight percent of males had been exclusively homosexual for a period of at least three years, and 13 percent of all adult males have more of the homosexual than the heterosexual in their histories over a period of at least three years. Of the 50 percent who were not exclusively heterosexual, 37 percent had had at least some overt homosexual experience to the point of orgasm between adolescence and old age, while another 13 percent have experienced manifest homosexual urges without ever having had overt homosexual contact to the point of orgasm. For females, the cumulative incidence reached 28 percent who had had either overt sexual experience or psychic responses to other women; 13 percent had had overt contacts to the point of orgasm. Only about half to one third as many females as males in any age period were primarily or exclusively homosexual.

In a much more recent study by Sorenson (1973) of adolescent sexuality, boys again reported more homosexual experiences than did girls. Among those from sixteen to nineteen years of age, 17 percent of boys and 6 percent of girls reported one or more homosexual experiences at some time in their lives, but only 2 percent of boys and virtually no girls indicated ongoing or current homosexual behavior. Sorenson's study was very carefully designed, both in choosing a representative sample and in the questions asked. Younger adolescents may have been somewhat reluctant to report such experiences. It is quite unlikely that there was any over-reporting.

In Sweden, Walinder reported prevalence of transsexualism to be 1:37,000 for males and 1:100,000 for females over the age of fifteen, but from his experience he estimates the actual frequency to be at least twice that high.

DIAGNOSTIC CONSIDERATIONS

In older adolescents and adults who present themselves for sex-change surgery, it is important to be certain that their gender dysphoria is long-standing and of a serious nature, and to screen out those who may simply be trying to find a way out of a situational crisis or who are psychotic. It is generally agreed that before an irreversible and expensive procedure is undertaken, the individual should have demonstrated his or her ability to live and work in the role of the sex to which they wish to change. Accordingly, if they have not already done so, they usually are counseled to live in that role for an extended time, with whatever help they may find in reversible or less serious measures such as hormone therapy, depilation, or plastic surgery on the Adam's apple. Often quoted criteria for recognizing "classic" transsexuals include: history of a lifelong wish to be the opposite sex, including a growing conviction that they are "trapped in the wrong kind of body"; gender role behavior so coherent and convincing that interviewers describe feeling as if they are speaking with someone of the sex to which the transsexual wants to be reassigned; loathing for their breasts (in women) or their penises (in men); and usually a preference for "straight" individuals of their own biological sex.

In children and even younger adolescents, an appraisal of the final personality picture and gender role, as well as the direction of the sexual drive, may not be reliable until mid to late adolescence. On the other hand, at least some of the children at risk may be recognized fairly early in childhood. On the basis of the frequency with which feminine behavior in childhood was reported in several studies of male transsexuals and male homosexuals, Green (1974) elected to study feminine boys to understand the origins of gender identity and gender role. He noted that masculinity or tomboyishness is much more common in girls than is femininity or sissiness in boys, although in adulthood far more males appear to experience sexual identity conflict. Moreover, tomboyishness is much more socially accepted than is sissiness (probably with good reason, since the latter is not the opposite of the former, but a cluster of avoidances and fears which tend to isolate the feminine boy). In any event, feminine boys and their families will be more likely to experience growing social distress, and might be more motivated to seek help and to participate in such a study. Green noted the typically feminine boy, from the early years of life, cross-dresses, prefers girls as playmates, is rejected by boys, prefers girls' toys, avoids the rough-and-tumble games of boyhood, and takes a female role in fantasy games. They have also been noted to show an unusually strong interest in play-acting and also to be unusually adept at acting. Adolescent and adult follow-up studies on several groups of feminine boys who had been evaluated in childhood showed that out of twenty-seven, nine had a homosexual orientation, three or four were transsexual, and one was a transvestite. Green has used interviews with feminine boys as young as five in which some of the children unequivocally express the wish to be girls. He has also used a variety of psychological tests which seem to separate out many of the play choices and attitudes of boys from those of girls, and on these tests the feminine boys showed a striking similarity to the performances of the girls and distinctly different from the average boys of the same age.

Green believes another study which needs to be done is one which will identify those tomboys for whom this behavior may not be just a passing phase, which will probably mean finding a way to discern which tomboys show not only a masculine gender-role preference but also a basic male sexual identity. Ehrhardt has recently noted that inability to accept breast development and menses may distinguish those girls whose tomboyishness is not just a passing phase. Green also recognizes that there are numerous individuals who are homosexual at maturity where there is no history of obvious cross-gender behavior in childhood.

TREATMENT

For adults who are deeply conflicted about problems of gender identity and homosexuality, various forms of psychotherapy are available, and a number of authors emphasize that a good outcome is possible for at least a significant portion of those seeking help. Bieber's group reported in 1962 that of seventy-two patients who began treatment as exclusively homosexual, 19% became heterosexual. This offers hope to some adolescents and young adults who are strongly motivated and who probably have at least some heterosexual orientation.

For children with ambiguities in their gender role, such as the feminine boys described by Green, there is not only social hardship even in childhood, but they appear to be at fairly high risk for one of the serious disturbances of gender role in adolescence and adult life, so that difficulties of societal censure and personal disappointment will probably continue to cause suffering despite growing social tolerance. Green emphasizes that therapy for such boys does not aim "to suppress sensitivity and compassion, nor to promote a thirst for aggression and violence, but rather to impart greater balance where a radically skewed development has precluded a comfortable range of social integration." Green offers these tenets upon which his treatment approaches are based: (1) developing a relationship of trust and affection between a male therapist and the feminine boy; (2) educating the child as to the impossibility of his changing sex; (3) stressing to the child the advantages of participating in some of the activities enjoyed by other boys, and promoting greater comfort in such activity; (4) educating the parents as to how they may be fostering sexual identity conflict in their child; (5) advising the parents of the need for them to consistently disapprove of very feminine behavior and to consistently encourage masculine behavior, if they desire change in their sons; and (6) enhancing the father's or father-substitute's involvement in the feminine boy's life. Green has used three specific strategies of intervention: (1) individual sessions with the boy and separate sessions with his parents; (2) group sessions with several boys plus group sessions with their mothers and group sessions with their fathers; and (3) teaching parents to act as therapists by instructing them on specific aspects of behavior which should be systematically encouraged or discouraged at home. He points out that as yet there are no long-term follow-up studies of such boys who received treatment in childhood.

DISCUSSION AND SUMMARY

The evidence from studies of animals and humans whose hormonal exposure prenatally has been disturbed experimentally or by various accidents or natural causes indicates that some of the behavioral traits usually labeled masculine or feminine may be influenced by such prenatal impact on the central nervous system. Two excellent books bringing together most of the current research data in these areas are by Money and Ehrhardt (1972) and Friedman, Richart, and Vande Wiele (see bibliography, Person and Ovesey 1974).

There is also overwhelming evidence that the developing personality of the infant needs social experience with feedback, and that differentiation of gender identity and gender role not only requires but normally receives it by way of parental responses to the perceived sex of the infant and whatever innate behavioral differences the infant shows from birth on. Essentially, clear and unambiguous gender identity with congruous gender role and sexual object choice (emerging clearly in adolescence) develop through learning complementation to members of the opposite sex and identification with members of the same sex. This is made possible by the reciprocal consistency with which both complementation and identification are responded to by parents in particular but to some extent by all significant people in the environment. If people in the environment are inconsistent in their own representation of gender roles, or if they respond inconsistently to the child's sorting out of complementation and identification, or if they selectively reinforce inappropriate gender role, then confusion or incongruity in gender identification and role may develop and this may be reflected in adolescence by the emergence of erotic preference of a homosexual or other paraphiliac kind. Complexities of the childhood interactions with environmental influences are so great that at present predictions of outcomes of various kinds of childhood histories are not reliable, but profoundly skewed parental influences are felt to be necessary for the most extreme incongruity, transsexualism.

Those concerned with the healthy development of children will wish to be familiar with patterns of family life or early childhood behavior which appear to correlate with later disturbances of gender identity and sexual object choice. There is a great deal of evidence that gender identity is becoming consolidated by age two and is probably quite strongly established by age six. Money and Ehrhardt, whose book is most strongly recommended for richness of material and imaginativeness of description as to how the infant and child develop their gender identities and learn their gender roles, state that the majority of humans have a gender identity, plus or minus paraphiliac complications, that is so firmly set by the time of puberty that it cannot be changed. Accordingly, optimal times for intervention will be in early childhood and certainly before puberty, if there are indications of any disturbances in gender identity and gender role.

There remains a clear need for further study of how gender identity develops and consolidates, and of how children reveal serious difficulties in this area. There is also need for dissemination and discussion of what is now known and what is being learned from research relating to this complex, fascinating, and important aspect of child development.

BIBLIOGRAPHY

Friedman, R., Richart, R., and Vande Wiele, R., eds. (1974). *Sex Differences in Behavior.* New York: Wiley.

Green, R. (1974). *Sexual Identity Conflict in Children and Adults.* New York: Basic Books.

Marmor, J. (1965). Introduction. In *Sexual Inversion,* ed. J. Marmor. New York: Basic Books.

Money, J., and Ehrhardt, A. (1972). *Man and Woman, Boy and Girl.* Baltimore: Johns Hopkins Press. A superb, thoroughgoing exploration of differentiation and dimorphism of gender identity from conception to maturity, utilizing research findings from all the relevant disciplines and intelligently focusing on the interaction between genetic and endocrine factors and environmental influence.

Person, E., and Ovesey, L. (1974). The psychodynamics of male transsexualism. In *Sex Differences in Behavior,* ed. R. Friedman, R. Richart, and R. Vande Wiele. New York: Wiley. A valuable volume, containing papers by most of the leading students and research workers in this field from all disciplines presented at a conference. The quality of the papers is high, the research is up-to-date, and there are excellent discussions by the participants of the papers in each section.

Socarides, C. (1968). *The Overt Homosexual.* New York: Grune and Stratton.

Sorenson, R. (1973). *Adolescent Sexuality in Contemporary America.* New York: World.

Stoller, R. (1971). The term "transvestism." *Archives of General Psychiatry* 24:230–237.

——— (1972). Etiological factors in female transsexualism: a first approximation. *Archives of Sexual Behavior* 2:47–64.

Chapter 17

SUICIDE

Murray I. Kofkin, M.D.

DEFINITION

Suicide may be simply defined as knowingly taking one's
own life. The study of suicide, and particularly of suicide in
children, however, is complicated by several factors, revolv-
ing primarily around the "knowingly" aspect. Can very
young children knowingly commit suicide when their appreciation of death is so limited? Do older children (also adolescents and adults) despite their rational appreciation of the
finality of death actually on a deeper level "knowingly" seek
extinction? Similarly, when considering suicide attempts, a
good deal of intuition goes into deciding what actually constitutes a "knowing" but "unsuccessful" attempt at self-
destruction.

There are relatively few studies and reports of suicides in
children as distinct from adolescents. They are often considered together, but the following discussion, with some indicated exceptions, refers to children only.

REVIEW OF LITERATURE

Lukianowicz (1968) reviewed the world literature and noted that articles describing suicide in children have been occasionally appearing for over one hundred years, first in the French and German literature. One of the earliest investigators he quoted was Durand-Fardel, who reviewed twenty-one cases of suicide in France between 1835 and 1844 by children below the age of fourteen. He noted then that the tendency to suicide in children increases with age. Morselli in 1881 surveyed several European countries (Australia, Belgium, Denmark, England, France, Germany, Italy, and Sweden) and came to the conclusion that the tendency to commit suicide was more frequent in children living in towns than in the country. Emminghaus made a similar observation in 1887 and concluded that "with the progress of culture (industrialization) the tendency to suicide seems to be increasing."

Bakwin (1957) in his review of the world literature notes that there was ample reason for interest in the suicides of children and adolescents during the latter part of the nineteenth century and the early part of the present century because the rates were not only exceedingly high, especially in Prussia, France, and Russia, but were also rising. He mentions, for example, that the rate in Saxony in the ten to fourteen year age group during the period 1903–1907 was almost ten times as high as comparable U.S. figures for the year 1954. He noted seasonal fluctuations. The incidence is highest in May, decreasing in summer and autumn, is lowest in December, and then rises till the peak in May.

In reviewing ideas about causality, it has been noted that writers in the period 1880–1900 blamed the romanticized treatment of suicide in the novels of the time. From 1915 to 1935 an emphasis was placed on constitutional factors, stressing the psychotic and hereditary aspects. Freud stressed the psychological and motivational aspects. Television themes may be added to the list of current cultural influences.

INCIDENCE

When considering the reported incidence of suicide and suicide attempts in children, several factors must be kept in mind. In many cases of threatened or attempted suicide in children, parents may not take the gesture seriously enough to seek medical advice. On the other hand, many parents, however strongly they may have been disturbed and upset, do not report the event, being afraid of publicity, social embarrassment or disgrace. Parents may also hush up the incident for fear of an investigation and possible prosecution for neglect or cruelty. In one study of adolescents quoted by Lukianowicz (1968) only 3 percent of families sought medical advice after a suicide attempt despite routine encouragement to do so by the police. It is felt by many investigators that what are reported as accidents are actually suicides or suicide attempts. Accidents in childhood may correspond in this respect to automobile and firearm accidents of adolescents and adults. As other causes of death in children decrease (e.g. infection) the importance of accidents and suicide increase, with suicide listed fifth, and accidents first, as causes of death in children (Schuyler 1975).

With respect to the incidence of attempted suicide Shaffer (1974) reports there are many more threats and attempts compared to the relatively few actual suicides. The number of serious threats or attempts for each completed suicide is estimated by various authors from 15:1 (Morrison 1969) to

100:1 (Jacobziner 1960). It is to be noted, however, that actual suicides have often been preceded by suicidal gestures.

The sexual differences in suicide and suicide attempts is a striking feature. As a general rule females make more attempts than males, but males outnumber females in actual deaths by suicide for all ages, with a few exceptions for adolescents in Japan, Ireland, and Italy.

According to Bakwin (1957), not only is suicide more common in males than in females, but it is more common in whites than in nonwhites, in urban than in rural areas, and in the professional than in the nonprofessional groups (parents).

ETIOLOGY AND DYNAMICS

Any assessment of suicidal motivation in children must take into account the developing nature of the child's concepts of death. Various writers (Ackerly 1967, McIntire, Angle, and Struempler 1972, Nagy 1959) describe different ages and stages in the developing appreciation of the meaning of death. They generally agree, however, that up to ages four to six death is equated with reversible separation, departure, and sleep; from five to nine it is conceived of more in terms of murder, violence, retribution, and retaliation; and only from nine to ten does the child acquire a causal, logical explanation of death as a result of biological, irreversible processes. Some writers (Rochlin 1965) attributes this knowledge of irreversibility to children as young as three to four, although the persistence into adulthood of the concept that death is not final is the more frequent finding. McIntire, Angle, and Struemplor (1972) found (through questions about pets) that in about 20 percent of their thirteen to sixteen-year-old group there was a persistence of the belief of continued cognition after death. They found also in a study of 1000 subjects ages six to eighteen that self-destructive behavior is more likely if the individual does not consider death to be a total cessation of life. Very young children will make suicide attempts, in accordance with their ideas of lethality, by swallowing paste, ink, sea water, alcohol, dirty handkerchiefs, flowers, smoking cigars, or putting on lots of lipstick. As the concepts of death become more refined so do the motivations for suicide seem to develop from the impulsive unpremeditated act of the younger child to the more internalized, conflict-resolving attempt of the older child.

The impulsive attempts of younger children often follow some slight or rejection that may seem minor and unimportant to adults. They do not seem preoccupied with death but seem to respond to their feelings of the moment. There are young children however who make repeated, impulsive, serious suicidal attempts and do indeed seem bent on self-destruction. The young child's suicide attempt is seen as an effort to escape from an intolerable situation, an expression of aggression, or an attempt to manipulate or to gain love or sympathy from others. Ackerly (1967) described the precipitating events as varying from the seemingly minor rebuffs to severe circumstances such as separation, loss, or death of a parent. He found separations by divorce or death in one-third of all cases of suicide attempts. Morrison (1969) found that 76 percent of his suicide group had experienced a significant loss, separation, or the anniversary of such a loss within days or weeks of their suicide attempts. The losses and separations included death, illness, and hospitalization. Sobel (1970) feels similarly that self-poisoning in children (ages two to five) can be seen as acts of defiance, a bid for attention, a coercive attempt to achieve dependency, or an expression of anger deflected from a parent (usually mother) to the self. Accidental poisoning was related to the emotional disorders of childhood, but the more significant association was between accidental self-poisoning of the child and family psychopathology including marital and sexual dissatisfaction, mental illness, and poor ego strength. Other significant correlates were with family stress and strain, and a disturbed parent-child relationship.

When we consider the older children, the motivation for suicide begins to resemble more the adolescent and adult. The older child's attempts are in part responses to the stress of events and circumstances that exist for younger children but derive also from the accumulated interplay of internal forces producing conflict, depression, regression, etc.

Ackerly (1967) describes the older child's motivations as follows:

> When a latency-age child threatens to kill himself or wishes to die, he is expressing a complex of multiple psychic forces. These forces arise from: (1) his aggressive drives (primary oral sadism); (2) his narcissistic expectations; (3) his archaic superego; (4) his withdrawal of libido from objects (transient or prolonged); (5) the alteration of his ego by identification (usually with a suicidal mother); (6) his disappointment at not being able to achieve the aspirations of his ego ideal; (7) his loss of a sense of well-being or ideal self; (8) his struggle with his early emerging conceptions of death; (9) his attempt to overcome his state of helplessness; and (10) his wish for rebirth or reunion with the all-giving mother (state of primary narcissism) or the phoenix motif. In those children who attempt to kill themselves, we see further a major break with reality, intensified despair, hopelessness, and overwhelming aggressive response to frustration and disappointment.

Morrison (1969) stresses the role of the family in a child's suicide attempt, and sees suicide (as well as many other childhood conditions) as frequently symptoms not only of individual upheaval but of underlying family disruption. He stresses the function of suicide as a communication within the family. As an indication of the importance of the suicide attempt in the family economy, he describes an adolescent girl treated successfully for a severe attempt, only later to have her mother commit suicide.

The events preceding and precipitating suicide attempts (separations, deaths, divorces) are similar to those described as preceding acute psychotic episodes, the various psycho-physiologic crises, and the onset of serious physical illness. What then makes the suicidal child different from other disturbed children? Kreitman (1970) suggests that the difference lies in the suicidal child's familiarity with the phenomenon of suicide itself. This familiarity derives from living in a subculture (the family) where suicidal behavior is a recognized form of communication between people, and where he hears much talk about suicide and death and may have seen untreated suicidal attempts. He postulates a kind of suicidal modeling.

DIAGNOSTIC CONSIDERATIONS

Since the expression of the wish to die is not unusual for children, the assessment of underlying motivation may be difficult. Every attempt, however, is a serious attempt since it may result in inadvertent death because of insufficient recognition of the risks. The children who actively attempt suicide have experienced a major break with reality, or at the least, a massive disruption of adaptive mechanisms. Ackerly

(1967) felt that his group of four boys (ages six to eleven) were seriously disturbed, and seemed to be expressing a deep and profound wish to die, and he considered them to be psychotic or borderline. The three girls were preadolescent and their attempts were reminiscent of hysterical adolescent girls. Some of the symptoms found in association with suicide attempts in children include: school refusal and truancy, sexual confusion and/or promiscuity, boredom and withdrawal, a variety of physical symptoms, compulsive hyperactivity, threats of physical assault, running away, and the use of drugs and alcohol.

It is probably more practical and useful to consider a suicide attempt or threat as a significant event in itself, requiring psychiatric exploration of the child and the family, and to defer to a later date the establishment of a definitive diagnostic classification. Besides the conventional psychological and psychiatric investigation of the child and the family, critical information can often be obtained from those in contact with the child at the time of the event (teachers, friends, the maid, janitor, etc.).

TREATMENT

Diagnosis and treatment in actual practice often are not sharply demarcated, so that an initial family diagnostic interview where the family sits together dealing with a significant family crisis may be an auspicious beginning of treatment. This initial interview is best done as soon after the incident as possible, and following whatever life saving procedures are necessary. Ample time should be provided for this initial interview which may on occasion go for several hours. The two main foci of treatment are the family relationships, and the child himself. Family interviews serve to focus attention on the suicide attempt or gesture as an indication of a disturbance of the family and not only as a symptom of some mental disease process entirely within the child. These family disturbances may surface readily during the first interview or may require several meetings. The initial family interviews may reveal similar symptomatology in other siblings or parents. Some families can move readily from centering on the child's symptoms to considering the complex family dynamics. For other families considerable tact and timing may be needed to shift attention from the suicide attempt itself. The initial family interviews may continue to serve as the main treatment modality or may lead to various modifications. Individual treatment may be indicated for the child, and/or sibling, and/or parents, with or without concurrent family treatment. Some families cannot sustain the intense relatedness needed for family work, and may leave treatment soon after the crisis has subsided. A later crisis in the same child or a sibling may again lead the family to another fleeting therapeutic contact.

Emphasis is being placed here on the family interview for diagnostic and therapeutic purposes, but in some circumstances the child or parent is seen first individually, with the family dynamics being elucidated only later. A child's suicide attempt may serve to unite his separated or divorced parents in their concern. Individual treatment, that is, psychotherapy, with or without the use of psychopharmacologic agents, may then become not only the treatment of choice but the only one possible.

Family treatment, when feasible, is directed toward clarifying first the external situation that provoked the crisis, and then the family's internal susceptibilities, defects of communication, and deficiencies of mutual support. Concrete suggestions to the parents about how to protect the child in a responsible and realistic fashion should be given as soon as they can be elucidated.

The goals of individual treatment of the child will reflect the dynamic understanding of the child, and include such objectives as altering the archaic superego so that he doesn't always expect retribution for his anger, helping him to see the world as not exclusively destructive and withholding, modifying the demands of the idealized image toward more realistic expectations, softening the intensity of previous hurts, fostering identification with more benign figures, etc. Treatment often centers around his relationship to someone important to him who has died, perhaps by suicide.

Along with attentiveness to the family, and work with the child's internal difficulties, a third critical factor is the continued availability of the therapist which must be made known to the child. The testing of digits forward can easily lead to memorizing the therapist's telephone number during the very first interview.

Case Illustration. Sean, age nine, who had no previous psychiatric contact, swallowed his mother's barbiturates, was hospitalized, and when first seen after gastric lavage, was still reacting to the drugs. His parents were both at the hospital. They were separated, but each parent maintained a separate household with a paramour, and was unable to divorce the other. David described his feeling of being two people since age four (the time of the separation). His suicide attempt reflected many of the motivations described above, including an attempt to unify his environment and himself. Conjoint therapy of both parents was unsuccessful. David and his parents each continued in individual therapy with only moderate success. David and his mother subsequently moved to another city. This case illustrates the dynamics of desperation inherent in a child's suicide attempt, the inner and outer fragmentation and some of the problems of treatment.

DISCUSSION

Suicide attempts by children are increasing. Many contributing factors have been identified, but involvement of the family in diagnostic and therapeutic procedures is critical, and universally accepted. In addition to the flexibility and ingenuity required in dealing directly with children, quick action may also be necessary, particularly for those children who seem bent on self-destruction and make frequent serious attempts. Children's suicide, like child abuse, is profoundly stirring to whoever comes in contact with it; and like abuse, its seriousness and import is often denied. Just as the index of suspicion about abuse is rising, so also must all "gestures" be taken seriously until clearly shown to be otherwise.

SUMMARY

The rising incidence of suicide in children, as distinct from adolescents, was described with reference to the world literature. The dynamics within the child and the family were outlined, with emphasis placed on considering the attempt as a symptom of family disorganization and not only childhood psychopathology. Treatment procedures were reviewed. Similarities to child abuse were drawn with respect to increasing incidence, emotional impact, and the need for alertness to its existence.

BIBLIOGRAPHY

Ackerly, W. (1967). Latency age children who threaten or attempt to kill themselves. *Journal of the American Academy of Child Psychiatry* 6:242–261. A good discussion of the psychodynamics of the latency aged child.

Bakwin, H. (1957). Suicide in children and adolescents. *Journal of Pediatrics* 50:749–769. An international, statistical, sociological review with many references to early writings.

Jacobziner, H. (1960). Attempted suicides in children. *Journal of Pediatrics* 56:519–525. A study of children and adolescents in New York City.

Kreitman, N. (1970). Attempted suicide as language: an empirical study. *British Journal of Psychiatry* 116:465–473.

Lukianowicz, N. (1968). Attempted suicide in children. *Acta Psychiatrica Scandinavika* 44:415–435. A relatively recent international review.

McIntire, M., Angle, C., and Struempler, L. (1972). The concept of death in midwestern children and youth. *American Journal of Diseases of Children* 123:527–532. An extensive questionnaire survey of a large clinic and nonclinic population.

Morrison, G., and Collier, J. (1969). Family treatment approaches to suicidal children and adolescents. *Journal of the American Academy of Child Psychiatry* 8:140–153. A clear exposition of the family approach.

Nagy, M. (1959). The child's view of death. In *The Meaning of Death,* ed. H. Feifel, pp. 79–98. New York: McGraw-Hill. A classic study in a classic book.

Rochlin, G. (1965). *Griefs and Discontents: The Forces of Change.* Boston. Little, Brown. A psychoanalytic study of life's disappointments.

Schuyler, D. (1975). When a child dies, accident or suicide? *RN* 38:21–23. A short editorial.

Shaffer, D. (1974). Suicide in childhood and early adolescence. *Journal of Child Psychology and Psychiatry* 15:275–291. A study of coroners, schools, hospitals, and social service records.

Sobel, R. (1970). The psychiatric implications of accidental poisoning in childhood. *Pediatric Clinics of North America* 17:653–685. An excellent study of poisonings in younger children, and their families.

Chapter 18

ALTERED AND DISSOCIATIVE STATES OF CONSCIOUSNESS

Anna J. Munster, M.D.

DEFINITION

Altered states of consciousness or awareness (these terms will be used interchangeably) are best defined as *states of mind in which clear consciousness, i.e., total alert wakefulness or vigilance has undergone modifications, due to diverse and numerous factors.*

From the normal or conscious state to unconsciousness, there is a continuum of phenomena, and we all recognize that our awareness of the world around us fluctuates constantly. *Awareness is an active process of maintaining a readiness to respond.* Anything that infringes upon the organism will change awareness, if only temporarily, the more so if the event is meaningful for the individual. Both external and internal influences act as powerful modifiers upon the brain, e.g., drugs, infections, metabolic conditions, toxic substances, as well as strong emotions and/or unconscious processes.

Conditions producing altered states of awareness include physiologic conditions, e.g., sleep, dreams; externally induced conditions, e.g., biofeedback and hypnosis; personally induced conditions, e.g., meditative states and trances; and pathologic conditions, e.g., dissociative states.

An alphabetical listing of altered states of awareness would include: amnesia, biofeedback, catatonia, coma, deliria, delusional states, dissociative states, ecstatic states, fugue states, hallucinosis, head trauma, hunger, hypnagogic experiences, hypnotic states, metabolic conditions, multiple personalities, seizure disorders (pre-ictal, ictal, post-ictal states), sensory deprivation, sleep, sleep deprivation, stupor, trances, transcendental meditation.

Certain altered states of consciousness occur in childhood. We will define them below beginning with:

Dissociative states frequently manifest in hysterical neurosis. Defined in general terms, these are *conditions in which a group of psychological activities, possessing a certain unity among themselves, lose contact with the rest of the personality and function independently.* In the psychoanalytic literature, dissociative states are treated as a defense mechanism representing a splitting of the ego which, operating unconsciously, protects the person, through detachment, from an emotion, idea or subject, and keeps feelings out of awareness. This process produces varying degrees of alienation from the self or environment, creates feelings of depersonalization, strangeness or unreality, and can give rise to selective amnesia, fugues, multiple personalities or somnambulism.

Coma wherein the subject is totally unresponsive; *stupor* wherein the individual can, at times, be aroused, though responsiveness is seriously disturbed; and *delirium,* wherein orientation is totally lacking and delusional thinking prominent, are all observed in children, as is *hallucinosis,* wherein orientation is preserved and the sensorium is quite clear but the subject is bothered by auditory hallucinations and paranoid delusions.

Hypnagogic experiences, frequently reported by children,

occur in the semiconscious state before falling asleep, and are characterized by auditory hallucinations or more commonly by visual imagery.

Sleep deprivation which alters external as well as internal perceptions ought to be considered with overtired, undernourished, poorly functioning children.

Numerous manifestations of altered states of awareness are observed in the seizure disorders. The *absence* is a blotting out of awareness lasting only for a few seconds with total unawareness of the event. The *aura* or warning preceding certain focal or grand mal seizures is a *pre-ictal* phenomenon consisting of strange feelings, smells, or other hallucinatory experiences. It often reveals the focus of the damaged neurons producing the "fit" (ictus). During the ictus itself, there is total unconsciousness. In the *post-ictal state,* consciousness remains cloudy or is overcome by deep sleep, followed by total amnesia. The myriad automatisms, at times preceding seizures, at other times substituting for the seizure itself, manifest themselves in forms from simple lip-smacking, to more complicated motoric functions, infrequently reaching the complexity of the *epileptic fugue* wherein, as in the *hysterical fugue,* the individual may engage in complex, organized activities, sometimes over a span of time, before regaining consciousness, without subsequent memory of the events occurring during the fugue state.

REVIEW OF LITERATURE

Kanner (1972) in his classical *Textbook of Child Psychiatry* describes, enumerates and cites incidences of altered states of consciousness in reference to diagnosis, etiology, prognosis, and treatment. Gastaut and Broughton (1972) treat the subject extensively in their book on seizure disorders. *Stedman's Medical Dictionary* (1976) gives succinct definitions while Rycroft (1968) and Moore and Fine (1968) concern themselves entirely with elaborate definitions and comments on dissociative states from the psychoanalytic point of view. *Altered States of Awareness* (1972) reports and reviews experiments and observations of researchers using different approaches (encephalography, sleep, dream research, sleep deprivation, split-brain and localizing studies) with the ultimate aim of a comprehensive view of the brain's organization and functioning. The studies reported are tentative and as yet inconclusive. Lassek (1970) reviews and revives Hughling Jackson's classical studies on the subject, presenting a comprehensive view of the brain's organization, which permits us to understand altered states of awareness. This view will be presented below. Angel (1961) and Ey (1962) concern themselves with Jackson's work. The former incorporates psychoanalytic views, the latter puts forward a new "organo-dynamic" view of psychopathology including altered states of consciousness. Gottschalk (1973) stresses the importance of psychotherapy with children suffering organic conditions producing altered states of consciousness, such as the seizure disorders. Monroe (1973) approaches the subject from an organic and psychodynamic point of view based on his own and others' reviewed case studies (800 in number). He concludes that many subjects bearing a variety of psychopathological diagnoses also suffer from altered states of awareness, frequently fleeting, during which they execute diverse actions, which afterwards are alien to them. *Psychiatric News* (1975) reminds its readers about the danger of drugs and medication as well as the vulnerability of children (and older people) to various agents, and draws attention to the altered states of awareness they can induce.

INCIDENCE

Exact figures as to conditions producing altered states of awareness have not been established.

The infectious diseases affect children more readily than they do adults. The ensuing high fever commonly produces delirium as well as convulsions, which are especially prevalent during the first two years of life. Hallucinosis is rare but dissociative states, sometimes responsible for fugues, are seen in children, and more easily diagnosed and treated above the age of eight or nine years.

Of the seizure disorders, the petit mal absence is observed mainly in school children, while the grand mal type of convulsion is rare above the age of two but becomes more prominent again during preadolescence and adolescence, though it still remains a condition of low incidence (estimated epileptics for the population, 4–6 percent).

ETIOLOGY, DIAGNOSIS, AND TREATMENT

Etiology, diagnosis, and treatment are intimately tied to each other. Diagnosis is often derived from etiological factors, and treatment follows etiology, wherever the latter is clear-cut. Etiology, even where known, is rarely simple, as most of the time many factors, such as pre-, peri-, and postnatal influences, might contribute to the manifestations of illnesses producing altered states of awareness.

Antibiotics, fever depressants, drug withdrawal where indicated, as well as anticonvulsive medications, are used according to the case. In young children as in some adults, the deliria are due to: (a) illness such as microbial or viral diseases; (b) traumata such as head injuries; (c) slow emergence from coma of any cause, be it traumatic or postoperative (mainly after heart, kidney, or transplant surgery); (d) metabolic conditions due to liver and pancreas deficiencies; (e) nutritional conditions such as severe avitaminosis or hunger; (f) sensory and sleep deprivation; (g) toxic conditions due to legitimate or illegal drugs because of overdoses, wrong combinations, and/or high susceptibility to drugs. The drugs most commonly responsible for deliria in children are atropine, belladona, the barbiturates, and, more recently, the psychotropic medications sometimes used in children.

Hallucinosis was observed, according to Kanner, as an aftermath of acute rheumatic fever, when it could last up to five weeks. In adults, hallucinosis is common after alcohol withdrawal, and is beginning to be seen in juvenile alcoholics from age eight on, as well.

Because of the greater permeability of the blood-brain barrier in children (and older people) many conditions affect the brain more readily, and may cause deliria and sometimes complications such as encephalitis or meningitis, leaving, at times, permanent sequelae expressed in neurological or psychological deficits including the seizure disorders. Often these sequelae manifest themselves much later in life.

In the dissociative states, an entirely psychological etiology is generally assumed and therefore the treatment of choice will be psychotherapy, preferably long-term. The seizure disorders are assumed to be of organic origin and are treated with anticonvulsants. These certainly diminish the seriousness and frequency of seizures, but often give erratic results, which can be improved with the addition of psychotherapy. Differential diagnosis between hysterical and true fits, and between the dissociative and epileptic fugues is often delicate. Hysterical children (starting at age three) can imitate true convulsions perfectly. Here, however, medication rather than containing the seizures, usually makes them worse. In the epileptic fugue, the subsequent amnesia is impenetrable whereas in dissociative states, it can, at times, be reversed with treatment. A positive electroencephalogram leads to a sure diagnosis, but its absence does not eliminate a seizure disorder, which can coexist with a hysterical neurosis.

The etiology for some of the altered states of consciousness seems clear, but the mechanisms which produce them are not. Specific treatment as well as symptom-relieving medication are always in order, and may render some patients symptom-free; but underlying factors, if not resolved, may result in relapses or permanent disability as in certain seizure disorders or dissociative states in which frequent altered states of awareness overwhelm the subject.

DISCUSSION

The complexity of etiological factors and ensuing treatment are attributable to man's biological nature as a living organism, whose personality is formed by a constant interplay of inherited genes and environmental influences. This interplay, which precedes birth in terms of the quality of food, rest, or emotional stability of the mother as that bears on the intrauterine milieu, continues after birth with the care given, affective bonds established, illnesses contracted, and over- or understimulation received, and influences all physiologic and psychologic responses throughout life. These influences, as well as the sum total of life experiences, will determine and mark, to a great extent, later personality.

Thus external as well as internal influences merge to produce the total picture in any illness. The latter often lays bare formerly well-inhibited or repressed feelings and will point to physical vulnerabilities as well. Thus, in treatment and prevention, all aspects of a patient's life history have to be taken into consideration.

Psychophysiologically, altered states of consciousness can be understood by adopting Hughling Jackson's view of the brain's organization. A pioneering British neurologist, Jackson drew his inferences about the brain's function from astutely and thoroughly observed neurological cases (with later autopsy) which he called "experiment in disease." In brief, Jackson saw the central nervous system as a series of levels, wherein every part of the body was represented in every part of the brain (the split-brain experiments seem to attest to this). Any permanent or temporary alteration to the cortex of the brain will not only affect this functional part but will disinhibit areas usually under higher control, e.g., Jackson showed that postparalytic rigidity caused by head injury or strokes was due to damage of the voluntary cortical motor function, which released the involuntary tonic cerebellar function as expressed in the rigidity.

The following two case histories concerning patients with seizure disorders demonstrate the interplay between organic and psychological factors which become understandable in the light of Jackson's views.

The first case was seen privately at age sixteen because he had been involved in delinquent activities detected by the local police. The second offspring of two professionals who were practicing Catholics, he had attended parochial schools until the high school level and had originally intended to become a priest but later hoped to be a biologist.

An older sister born with a congenital heart defect had undergone closed and open heart surgery and had required much care most of her life, until she stabilized and went away to college. A younger brother presented no problems. The parents were at a loss to understand their son, and the mother wondered if he suffered from a "split personality."

The patient himself was more concerned with "dazes," lapses in attention which came on without warning and left no memory. He was accused of inattentiveness by teachers as well as by friends and smashed the family car in their driveway during one such instance. Beer, which he indulged in secretly and with friends, increased the occurrence of "dazes." One such lapse was observed during mental status examination, and subsequent electroencephalogram revealed a spike and wave pattern over the left temporal lobe. Medication controlled the "dazes" and the patient got well. Psychotherapy uncovered and clarified the content of his behavior in these episodes and showed why in his disinhibited state, delinquent behavior came to the fore.

The second case was an emergency consultation in a pediatric acute care clinic. This eleven-year-old bilingual girl and known epileptic, treated with anticonvulsant medication, had presented increased seizure activity, which did not yield to higher doses of medication. On the contrary, she had become violent, careless of danger, running over highways, in front of cars, and was unable to be contained or restrained. When seen, she was ataxic, staggering, unsteady, woozy, as well as explosive (cursing, destructive, pounding on her mother and any object around her). The interaction with the mother revealed a severe mother-child conflict, understandable in the light of the child's history.

The mother was an x-ray technician working towards a master's degree. The father had left the family when the daughter was three years old, did not give child support, and visited rarely. The mother went back to work when the child was one year old, and a series of caretakers looked after her until age six when she went to boarding school. At age seven, while in boarding school, she had fallen from a monkey bar and was knocked unconscious. Details were unknown to the mother. At age ten, she was sent to Puerto Rico to live with a friend of her mother. During a visit, the mother observed a seizure and brought the child back to New York for investigation and treatment. A diagnosis of seizure disorder was made, and anticonvulsant medication was prescribed.

The mother described the child as dutiful and obedient prior to her illness. In fact, she had always seen her as accomplishing great things and becoming famous.

The drug toxicity and side effects were not only expressed in the patient's neurological symptoms, but also in her feelings, previously well repressed, towards a mother whom she saw as inflicting suffering upon her. The feelings were conveyed through wishes to "never go back to Puerto Rico or to a hospital" (she had been hospitalized three times for seizure control) and "to be left alone."

Withdrawal of medication resulted in a return to premorbid behavior, but also in a recurrence of seizures, which had to be controlled again with medication. In addition, psychotherapy with child and mother was recommended.

In both these cases, the altered state of consciousness revealed an underlying problem which needed treatment in itself, specifically psychotherapy, apart from the treatment needed for the condition which had produced the altered state of awareness.

SUMMARY

A continuum of altered states of consciousness was reported, presenting normal as well as pathologic manifestations. The behavior and content revealed in these altered states reflect individual life experiences. By reaching layers of consciousness not accessible during vigilant states, the emergence of significant events and their clarification can facilitate the understanding and treatment of underlying factors.

BIBLIOGRAPHY

Angel, R. (1961). Jackson, Freud and Sherrington on the relation of brain and mind. *American Journal of Psychiatry* 18:193–197.

Ey, H. (1962). Hughling Jackson's principles and the organic dynamic concept of psychiatry. *American Journal of Psychiatry* 18:673–680.

Gastaut, H. (1972). *Epileptic Seizures.* Springfield, Ill.: Charles C. Thomas.

Geriatric Drug Abuse, a virtually ignored problem (Abstract). *American Psychiatric Association Psychiatric News,* p. 24. September 17, 1975.

Gottschalk, L. (1973). Effects of intensive psychotherapy in epileptic children. In *Childhood Psychopathology,* ed. S. I. Harrison and J. F. McDermott. New York: International Universities Press.

Kanner, L. (1972). *Child Psychiatry,* 4th edition. Springfield, Ill.: Charles C Thomas.

Lassek, M. (1970). *The Unique Legacy of Doctor Hughling Jackson.* Springfield, Ill.: Charles C Thomas.

Monroe, R. (1973). *Episodic Behavioral Disorders.* Cambridge, Mass.: Harvard University Press.

Moore, B., and Fine, B. (1968). *A Glossary of Psychoanalytic Terms and Concepts.* New York: American Psychoanalytic Association.

Readings from the *Scientific American* (1972). *Altered States of Awareness.* San Francisco: W. H. Freeman.

Rycroft, C. (1968). *A Critical Dictionary of Psycho-Analysis.* New York: Basic Books.

[Stedman] (1976). *Stedman's Medical Dictionary,* 23rd ed. Baltimore: Williams and Wilkins.

Chapter 19

HALLUCINATIONS IN CHILDHOOD

Roberto M. DePaula, M.D.

DEFINITION

When listening to an adult patient reporting experiences of "hearing voices," one will have no difficulty establishing the fact that this person might be experiencing a perceptual disorder. It is generally agreed that *hallucinations are false sensory perceptions in the absence of external stimulation.* Even though they can interfere with any of the senses—hearing, vision, smell, taste, and touch—the first two seem to be the ones most affected.

The interest in hallucinatory experiences dates back to ancient times. Anthropological studies show some cultures considered them as sacred or divine, granting an affected person some extraordinary powers and virtues.

The term *hallucination* was first used by Esquirol in 1817 when he suggested it be applied to false sensory impressions in the absence of any disease of the sensory organ. The absence of external stimulation helped the differential diagnosis from illusions, which are misinterpretations of evident and detectable stimuli. While hallucinations are experiences

usually occurring combined with other psychological disturbance, the term hallucinosis is usually used when some evident perceptual alterations occur isolated from any other
sign of mental illness.

REVIEW OF LITERATURE

Although widely studied in adults, very few authors have
looked into the phenomenon of hallucinations as they occur
in childhood. Moureau and Bouchut in France seem to be the
first to have written about hallucinatory experiences in children toward the end of the last century. Others such as Levin
(1932), Bender and Lipkowitz (1940), Despert (1948), and
Brenner (1951) turned their attention to the problem of hallucinations in children in the absence of detectable psychosis
or organic illness. Weiner (1961) attempted to classify the
common points in the etiological factors in hallucinations.
Wilking and Paoli (1966) classified hallucinatory experiences
according to the sources of stress which could be interfering
with the developmental process. Based on such an approach,
five different types of hallucinations in children were presented: (1) hallucinations in a "normal" child; (2) hallucinations in a "deprived" child; (3) hallucinations in a child with
organic defect or dysfunction; (4) hallucinations in a neurotic
child; (5) hallucinations in a schizophrenic child. Despert and
Bender discussed the differences in experience and content
of hallucinations in schizophrenic and nonschizophrenic children, those of the former being more bizarre, incoherent,
and delusional. Bender (1970) described the maturational
pattern of these experiences in children.

INCIDENCE

Hallucinations seem to be a fairly common experience in children, sometimes combined with an evident illness. Egdell and Kolvin (1972) in a review of literature on hallucinations in children cite various authors who, between 1948 and 1972 described these experiences in different groups of children (psychotic, epileptic, schizoid, neurotic, and children with behavior disorder). The incidence of hallucinations ranged from 59–100 percent in the psychotic group and 0–45 percent in the nonpsychotic one. Not all ten authors had the same percentage findings and the different criteria for the diagnosis of hallucinations seemed to play a part in the discrepancy among these findings.

ETIOLOGY

While most studies have attempted to explain and classify perceptual disorders, no isolated cause has been found. Because these states occur in a variety of conditions, it seems that immaturity of the nervous system and of the ego structure make children very susceptible to hallucinatory experiences. Organic, emotional, and social factors often play important roles triggering these phenomena. When hallucinations occur, these factors interrelate, though any one may predominate at different times.

These experiences are often ego-alien and cause great anxiety in a youngster, especially in the nonschizophrenic. The majority of cases of hallucinations in children who are nonpsychotic and without any evident organic problem will show youngsters overwhelmed with emotional stress and often terribly depressed. The affective component of these patients ought to be explored further, as a possible cause for these perceptual problems.

Some of the dynamic aspects involve the use of a combination of projective and introjective mechanisms in an attempt to resolve a particular conflict.

Hartman (1975), while describing hallucinations and their origins, mentions studies with epinephrine and norepinephrine acting as mediators in the maintenance of attention and in the patterning of functions. While not denying the importance of the psychodynamic component of these children, the organic theory mentioned by Hartman would help to explain the impaired perception.

There have also been other organic theories relating the depressive spectrum to perceptual disorders. A fruitful field for research in the future might be the exploration of such possible hereditary predispositions.

DIAGNOSTIC CONSIDERATIONS

The younger the child, the more difficult it is to elicit an accurate account of any hallucinatory experiences, both because of the immature state of their language development and insufficiently developed ability to differentiate inner from outer stimuli.

For didactic purposes, different authors have tried to classify these states according to several arbitrary factors. The presence or absence of an evident illness led Weiner (1961) to a classification of primary and secondary hallucinations. The primary group included those appearing in the absence of clear diagnosable disease. Among these dreams, hypnagogic states, eidetic imagery, imaginary companions, and hallucinosis are mentioned. The phenomenon of pavor nocturnus could also be added to this list.

Clinical observations of children have shown that hallucinations occur not only in the dreaming state but also may be present while awake, as when wishing for a gratifying object.

Because of its immaturity, the mental apparatus of children seems to be more susceptible to changes in the perceptual area. Children between the ages of three and five will often vividly describe play objects or an imaginary companion as if they were real. These states, normal for the age, are incorporated in the fantasy and imagery of a child. In situations where there is a delay or arrest of the emotional growth, these events seem to occur beyond the chronological age of three to five to compensate for some unmet needs. Some young individuals are also able to intentionally produce vivid images which can usually be separated from reality. These are called *eidetic imagery* and progressively disappear as the child grows older.

In the process of falling asleep or awakening one will often experience hypnagogic hallucinations. It seems that in getting to and from the unconscious state, the perception of reality blurs, causing the healthy individual to hallucinate. The phenomenon of hallucinosis among children is today, more than ever, a point of great interest. It seems that these experiences are more frequent in children than previously thought. Frequently children with a history of deprivation and neglect, and presenting a behavior disorder, will report hallucinations. These will be mostly auditory in nature. Voices may give commands to "act bad" or superego-like comments commending or criticizing the child's behavior. The absence of thought disorder or other signs of psychosis characterizes this syndrome as hallucinosis.

The phenomenon of pavor nocturnus is also considered by some authors as a form of hallucination, because despite the fact that the child is awake, he is unable to recognize the surroundings or reestablish contact with reality as he emerges from stage IV of sleep.

The secondary types of hallucinations in Weiner's classification are the ones related to an evident diagnosable illness. Delirium, sensory deprivation, migraine, epilepsy, organic brain syndrome, and schizophenia are some of the diseases mentioned in which hallucinations can occur.

TREATMENT

When hallucinations occur as part of a clinical picture in a particular illness, the therapy is usually directed towards the presumptive causes of such illness. On the other hand, the appearance of perceptual disorders unrelated to an evident psychosis or organic problem usually requires more attention on the part of the therapist. Due to cultural and-/or transference factors children will often deny or not acknowledge till later in therapy the presence of perceptual problems. The anxiety caused and the fear of being considered "crazy" will frequently lead to withholding this information from the therapist. Not infrequently hallucinosis will disappear after psychotherapy and/or chemotherapy (tranquilizers, antidepressants) are instituted. It seems that a combination of both provides the most effective treatment method.

DISCUSSION AND SUMMARY

Further studies and understanding of hallucinatory experiences in children are needed. The origins of hallucinations and their relationship to the different situations of occurrence still provide areas for fruitful research.

The presence of hallucinatory experiences in children occur in a variety of situations. An attempt is made to understand these phenomena and the different situations in which they may occur. The possible cause and treatment of perceptual disorders are described.

BIBLIOGRAPHY

Bender, L. (1954). Imaginary companions: hallucinations in children. In *Dynamic Psychopathology of Childhood.* Springfield, Ill.: Charles C Thomas.

———— (1970). The maturation process of hallucinations in children. In *Origin and Mechanisms of Hallucinations,* ed. Keup, pp. 95–101. New York: Plenum Press.

Bender, L., and Lipkowitz, H. (1940). Hallucinations in children. *American Journal of Orthopsychiatry* 10:471–490.

Brenner, C. (1951). A Case of childhood hallucinosis. *Psychoanalytic Study of the Child* 6:235–243.

Cohen, D., and Young, G. (1977). Neurochemistry and child psychiatry. *Journal of the American Academy of Child Psychiatry* 16:353–411.

Despert, J. (1948). Delusional and hallucinatory experiences in children. *American Journal of Psychiatry* 104:528–537.

Egdell, H., and Kolvin, I. (1972). Childhood hallucinations. *Journal of Child Psychology and Psychiatry* 13:279–287.

Eisenberg, L. (1962). Hallucinations in children. In *Hallucinations,* ed. L.J. West, pp. 198–207. New York: Grune and Stratton.

Esman, A. (1962). Visual hallucinosis in young children. *Psychoanalytic Study of the Child* 17:334–343.

Hartman, E. (1975). Dreams and other hallucinations: an approach to the underlying mechanisms. In *Hallucinations,* ed. R. K. Siegel and L. J. West, pp. 71–79. New York: John Wiley.

Levin, M. (1932). Auditory hallucinations in non-psychotic children. *American Journal of Psychiatry* 88:1119–1152.

Lukianowicz, N. (1969). Hallucinations in non-psychotic children. *Psychiatria Clinica* 2:331–337.

Weiner, M. (1961). Hallucinations in children. *Archives of General Psychiatry* 5:544–553.

Wilking, V., and Paoli, C. (1966). The hallucinatory experience: an attempt at a psychodynamic classification and diagnostic significance. *Journal of the American Academy of Child Psychiatry* 5:431–440.

Part III

Neurologically Based and Allied Conditions

Chapter 20

NEUROLOGIC CONDITIONS

Alan M. Aron, M.D.

ACUTE TOXIC REACTIONS

In the course of certain bacterial infections, particularly pneumococci, children may experience frightening visual hallucinations. With temperature elevation in the 103°–105° range and concomitant symptomatology of toxicity, children are especially vulnerable between the ages of five and twelve years. The hallucinations are usually frightening. They may take the form of seeing monsters or rodents coming through cracks in the wall. The patient appears agitated and frequently screams to be comforted. The child is usually able to communicate what he is seeing. The hallucinatory activity can last for several hours. It tends to be self-limited as soon as temperature control is achieved and the infection is treated with appropriate antibiotics. The hallucinations may be experienced in association with pneumococcal pneumonia and from other sources of infection outside the nervous system. The treatment of the acute toxic delirium is the treatment of the underlying bacterial infection and of the temperature elevation. It is usually best to refrain from employing any specific sedating or tranquilizing agents.

HYSTERIA—CONVERSION REACTIONS

Among the commonest manifestations of hysterical symptomatology in childhood are sudden blindness and sudden ataxia of gait. This usually occurs in a child where there is a history of somatic preoccupation. An associated headache or abdominal pain of a recurrent nature is common. When a child complains of blindness, a brief testing should be performed. Do the eyes react to light? Is there a response to threatening gesture? Can optokinetic nystagmus be induced with a moving tape or drum? In order to induce optokinetic nystagmus, one must be able to fixate and to see a target. The patient will not be able to interfere with the normal horizontal nystagmus which is induced with a moving tape. Hysterical blindness, therefore, can be rapidly diagnosed.

The individual who is uncoordinated immediately seeks to widen his base. The patient with functional ataxia has a narrow base and displays a bilateral circumduction with scissoring. There are usually increased adventitious hand movements employed frequently in a wild fashion as a balancing maneuver. There is an attempt to hold on to objects in the environment for support. When these supports are removed, however, the patient carefully guards against any actual falling.

Other syndromes, such as hemianesthesia, tend to be less frequently encountered in younger children, but can be seen in the adolescent. They are delineated by failure to conform to appropriate anatomic dermatomes. There is frequently splitting of the sternum with a tuning fork or with a pin in reporting sharp sensation. Frequently, the patient will report the hypesthesia or anesthesia stops at the midline in the frontal region. It is important also to examine each of these complaints in context. Are they occurring in isolation or are they manifestations of other complaints affecting the nervous system? Hysterical symptomatology frequently can be delineated by its lack of other suggestions of organic involvement of the nervous system. It is also important to emphasize that functional symptomatology does not preclude the concurrent presence of an underlying organic disease of the nervous system. There are patients, for example, who have both bona fide seizures and hysterical seizures. There are patients with tumors of the nervous system whose initial presentations involved only functional complaints. Functional symptomatology, therefore, can pose one of the most difficult problems for the clinician. The physician must guard against overlooking an organic involvement which can coexist with the functional presentation.

ORGANICALLY DRIVEN HYPERACTIVITY

The well-described syndrome of hyperactivity has been associated with the child with minimal cerebral dysfunction. Such behavior can also be found in association with a variety of affections of the nervous system. This includes chronic convulsive disorders, mental subnormality, and diffuse brain damage. The behavior is characterized by an inability to attend. There is generalized restlessness, fidgetiness, and frequently a desire to touch and handle all objects in the environment. The behavior is readily apparent when such a child enters the office. Objects on the desk suddenly land on the floor. Desk drawers are opened. The telephone receiver is removed. In short, mayhem rapidly develops. Such children have a low frustration tolerance and balk at controls. They are easily distractible and react without an ability to delete extraneous environmental influences. Such behavior makes control in a classroom difficult. Management at home becomes a thoroughly frustrating parental experience. Hyperactive children have a particularly high incidence of exhibiting paradoxical responses to barbiturates. Instead of being quieted, they are further excited. It is for this reason that barbiturates as a class of drugs should be avoided. If anticonvulsants are required, a choice of a hydantoin, a diazepam analog, or carbamazepine would be preferable.

There is nothing specific or diagnostic about hyperactivity per se. It can be associated with many different disease states. Its importance cannot be underestimated because it interferes with teaching efforts in the classroom and makes home and environmental management a problem. The first approach to handling the behavior is to establish its genesis. A thorough history, detailed physical and neurologic examination, and psychiatric evaluation represent an initial starting point. When it is determined that the behavior is organically determined, first efforts should center on simple environmental manipulation. An attempt should be made to screen out extraneous influences, and to create a calm environment with clearly defined limits. Techniques of positive reward and operant conditioning may be of value. For the child who has not benefited from these efforts, a trial of chemoprophylaxis should be considered. This would involve utilizing agents such as amphetamines, pemoline, or Ritalin. These drugs can be particularly useful for the child with minimal cerebral dysfunction manifesting learning disability. For the more uncontrollable patient, use of phenothiazines such as Thorazine or Mellaril can be considered.

IMPAIRMENT OF MEMORY

Transient amnesic episodes in childhood are most frequently associated with head trauma or with seizure states. With head trauma, producing concussion or contusion, it is common to have amnesia from the time of trauma until some period after the resumption of consciousness. This has been referred to as anterograde amnesia. Loss of memory for the events prior to the episode of head trauma (retrograde amnesia) is more rarely seen. Depending upon the neurological status, full recovery of memory capacity would be anticipated with simple head trauma. The details of the specific memory loss, however, may never be fully recovered.

Patients with seizure disorders may experience a variety of transient impairments of memory. The patient with a major motor seizure undergoes a total loss of consciousness, and is invariably amnesic for the entire episode. On regaining consciousness, there may be recognizable clues from which the patient infers he had a seizure. This may include tongue soreness, bruising of the body during a fall, or similar signs. For the child with a petit mal seizure disorder, the lapses of contact are usually sufficiently brief so that they may not be fully appreciated. They may be perceived only as momentary confusion. The patient with a psychomotor seizure may experience a variety of sensations which may produce illusionary phenomena, which will be described subsequently. The duration of a psychomotor attack may last from thirty seconds to several minutes. The interruption of sensorium may be only partial. The child may show a disorientation and a confusion which lasts for seconds to minutes at the conclusion of the episode. He may be totally amnesic for the episode, or have a partial awareness that he "had one."

ALTERED STATES OF CONSCIOUSNESS PECULIAR TO SEIZURE DISORDERS

The auras of psychomotor seizures can produce a variety of sensations which initially may sound bizarre. In childhood, visual sensory distortions producing micropsia or macropsia are not uncommon. The child describes objects in the environment altering in size. This may generate great terror. One child expressed extreme panic when he saw his mother reduced to midget proportions. He feared she would go down the drain with the water receding from the bathtub in a vortex. Another child expressed terror at seeing his teacher become gigantic. He screamed, "Watch out. You're going through the roof!" For the complete psychomotor seizure to be realized, these auras must then be followed by a sensorial interruption in which lip-smacking movements are frequent, and automatic behavior may be seen. Other characteristic auras of psychomotor seizures involve a sudden feeling of familiarity when none really exists, the so-called *déjà vu* phenomenon. Contrastingly, a feeling of sudden unfamiliarity can arise—the *jamais vu* phenomenon. Patients may experience unpleasant tastes or smells. These sensations are uncinatory phenomena, from their origin in the uncus-hippocampal region of the brain. The sensations frequently are difficult to qualify, and are described in vague terms as a generally unpleasant or disagreeable sensation.

It is possible to have the status state of petit mal or psychomotor seizures. Status epilepticus is defined as one seizure merging into the next without a resumption of consciousness. A child with petit mal status may present with behavioral disturbances. This can take the form of negativism and aggressivity. When the patient is carefully examined, it becomes clear that the child is having recurrent episodes of fading in and out, which may be accompanied by eye-blinking. The diagnosis is confirmed by electroencephalography which shows continuous bisynchronous three per second spike and dome wave abnormalities.

The status state of psychomotor seizures may produce behavioral changes which can vary from a fuguelike state to a sociopathic pattern. It is on this basis that a legal defense can be fashioned in a trial. It is argued that the accused acted during a prolonged seizure state, and was, therefore, unaccountable for the act because it occurred during a psychomotor seizure. During the actual status state of psychomotor seizures, it is possible to have sufficiently minimal blunting of sensorium to allow the patient to perform certain activities. One such patient, a university undergraduate, got to the local airport, charged an airfare on a credit card, and flew one thousand miles away. She was picked up because of wandering on a subway and bumping into people. Initially suspected of taking drugs, she was delivered to an emergency room where it was recognized that she was in the status state of psychomotor seizures. When the status state was terminated by appropriate intravenous medication, the patient had no memory for the event, and was shocked to find herself in another city.

During the status condition of psychomotor seizures, the patient may appear intermittently obtunded. He may stare off into space, and then have intermittent returns of consciousness which allow a partial contact. The patient may exhibit bizarre behavior, or may appear frankly demented. For example, a patient reached for a box of Kleenex and began eating it. There is frequently a motor restlessness in which picking of the clothes may be seen. More strikingly, a generalized tremorous activity can involve all four extremities. When the diagnosis is confirmed with EEG, a dramatic resolution can be evidenced when intravenous Valium or phenobarbital is administered, with the prompt restoration of appropriate behavior.

The status state of minor seizure disorders may produce a behavioral syndrome of irritability, contrariness, and even demoniacal activity. This more often affects the child from two to five years of age. The child cannot be comforted. There is a motor restlessness which resists usual efforts to cajole and can interfere with sleeping and ability to relax. The intensity of this behavioral state can rise to such heights that the parents are unable to handle it, and seek medical help to ameliorate the child's "horrible behavior." Most often, the parents are unaware of an underlying seizure state. The physician can suspect minor motor seizures by noting intermittent eye rollings, or subtle body jerkings. The impression must be confirmed by electroencephalography. As soon as the seizure state can be controlled, the return to a previous baseline of normal behavior can be startling. It is frequently difficult to control minor motor seizures on a long term basis with standard anticonvulsants. Utilization of the ketogenic diet may be required and is an excellent method for the preschool youngster.

ORGANIC MENTAL SYNDROME

The evolution of an organic mental syndrome is relatively uncommon in the childhood and adolescent population, except for the transient state induced by drugs or alcohol. More permanent impairment may be seen in certain degenerative diseases. In Schilder's disease, and subacute sclerosing panencephalitis, the mental changes may be particularly prominent. This can vary from acute confusional states to inability to recall previously learned facts. The patient may lose direction and may be unable to find his way home. Short-term memory is particularly impaired. The examiner, on being called to the telephone, can return to the patient and not be recognized. The patient may show difficulty in dressing. This may involve putting clothes on backwards or in a total helter-skelter fashion. Certain patients lose their ability to recognize letters and numbers, and undergo sufficient mental deterioration to become illiterate and unable to calculate.

The patient may perform acts which appear to be of psychotic nature. One adolescent would rise after midnight to go into the garden to communicate with the stars. He heard special voices summoning him, and was observed to have conversations directed to celestial bodies. This was the first manifestation of what was to become a rapidly progressive deteriorating neurological state which went on ultimately to include myoclonic seizure phenomena, and ultimately to a severely impaired decorticate state. The central feature in such conditions is the setting in which the behavioral abnormalities occur. An organic basis becomes established by discerning concomitant neurologic dysfunction.

With certain supratentorial brain tumors, particularly those involving the temporal lobes, bizarre behavioral states may be encountered. Not only may one encounter transient episodic phenomena secondary to seizures as described above, but more persistent depressive states, or even maniacal states may result.

In dementing conditions, from the initial stages of poor judgment, there are increasing evidences of intellectual deterioration. The patient requires assistance in daily activities of living, such as dressing, eating, and toileting. Confusion of time occurs. Disorientation for place and person may be encountered. The setting of this progressive deterioration is attended by other evidences of neurologic dysfunction. These may include seizure phenomena, gait difficulty, or co-ordination difficulties. Usually, signs of upper motor neuron dysfunction produce spasticity and hyperreflexia. It is the accumulation of signs of neurologic involvement in addition to the mental changes which leads to proper neurologic diagnosis.

METABOLIC DERANGEMENTS

A wide spectrum of behavioral patterns may be seen in association with metabolic derangements. Three specific states will be discussed: hypoglycemia, hyponatremia, and hypokalemia.

Hypoglycemia is likely to produce the most varied mental presentations. Adolescents have presented with sudden, unexplained aggressivity and belligerence. Acute confusional states may develop in which the patient becomes disoriented for time and place. Occasionally, these behavioral alterations are a prelude to an ultimate major motor seizure when the blood sugar level plummets to sufficiently low levels. Until the hypoglycemia is recognized and pinpointed, the diagnosis can suggest a space-occupying lesion, or acute vascular episode. The most common etiology for the hypoglycemia is an underlying diabetic state in which there have been problems involving insulin dosage. Less frequent causes of hypoglycemia such as an islet cell pancreatic tumor, must be considered when a thorough workup is undertaken to explain the original hypoglycemic episode. In the child from one to four years, starvation can produce a ketogenic hypoglycemia. Such a situation can arise following surgery for removal of tonsils or adenoids where intravenous alimentation is not routinely employed. Important features of this condition are that the symptoms are immediately reversible with intravenous glucose once the hypoglycemia has been confirmed with appropriate blood sugar determinations.

Hypokalemia or hypokalemic states are usually present with asthenia and diffuse motor weakness. The patient complains of inability to walk long distances, of easy fatigability, and tends to spontaneously limit his motor expenditure. The child will stop participating in sports. The total motor output of the child is seen to change, as he shifts toward a primarily sedentary existence. The presentation is not different from that of an acute myopathic state. Once the diagnosis has been established, the symptoms will remit and improve dramatically with replacement of potassium. Common causes contributing to hypokalemia in childhood involve gastrointestinal losses from surgery or fistulas, renal disease, and prolonged usage of steroids.

Hyponatremia may present as confusional states, alterations of consciousness in which drowsiness and lethargy predominate, or a full-blown seizure diathesis. The seizures may take the form of generalized major seizures, or of multifocal variety. The development of hyponatremia in association with inappropriate antidiuretic hormone (ADH) secretion is a frequent complication encountered in children during the treatment phase of meningitis. The diagnosis can be suspected by the presence of peripheral edema, documented weight gain, hypoosmolality of serum, hyperosmolality of urine. This syndrome is readily responsive to therapeutic efforts to restore the sodium to its normal level by fluid restriction and the use of hypertonic saline when indicated.

In addition to the specific electrolytes discussed, one can encounter hypometabolic states involving vitamin deficiencies specifically with reference to the B vitamins. There are

well-known mental changes associated with pernicious ane-
mia, for example, though this disease is uncommon in childhood. The universal features common to the metabolic derangements are that they can produce a variety of behavioral
alterations, or even seizures. They can be diagnosed by appropriate blood studies, and are rapidly responsive to replacement therapy, provided their basic etiology is understood. It is essential to screen for metabolic aberrations as a
cause for unexplained bizarre behavioral states of acute
onset in the child or adolescent population.

BEHAVIORAL CHANGES ASSOCIATED WITH
THE DEAF CHILD

Recognition of deafness in infancy may be delayed until
nearly the second year of life. The failure to develop language normally is frequently the first clue of an underlying
hearing disability. The infancy period of hearing-impaired
children may be characterized by hyperactivity of a diffuse
nature. Head-banging, rocking, and other stimulatory activity may be encountered on occasion. Such children typically
evidence a delayed psychomotor development. They may
present, therefore, as children who are suspected of mental
subnormality. Another presentation may be that of an autisticlike syndrome. The infant may make poor eye contact,
relate poorly, and present general apathy. The screening of
hearing ability is, of course, an essential element of any pediatric neurologic evaluation. Because there is a high incidence
of failure to recognize deafness, it is possible for well-
informed parents to fail to discern the disability in their own
children. The presence of visual clues, including gesture,
pantomime, and facial expressions, frequently help the hear-

ing-impaired child to function, and these factors may lead to delayed recognition.

BEHAVIORAL SYNDROMES OF THE BLIND CHILD

One of the more usual behavioral characteristics of the congenitally blind child involves manneristic rubbing or manipulating of the eyes. Rocking of the body may be frequent. There is a tendency to place the fingers, usually the knuckles, into the eye sockets, and to rub in a recurrent, manneristic pattern. Some have suggested this may be an attempt for autovisual stimulation. The eye rubbing movements may or may not be attended by psychomotor delay. Associated retardation is based on the etiology of the blindness, and whether there has been a previous insult to the brain.

BEHAVIORAL PATTERNS OF RETARDATES

Manneristic behavior is also characteristic of the retarded child. This can involve head-banging, rocking, self-slapping, and even on occasions, self-mutilatory activity. One of the more dramatic experiences on visiting an institution for the retarded is the noise one hears of the rocking behavior as one approaches the wards.

DISTURBANCES OF LANGUAGE

In addition to the more usual aphasic states resulting from lesions of the dominant hemisphere, more bizarre language disturbances may be encountered which are transient. Following head trauma, for example, patients may occasionally slip into a language resembling "word salad." One adolescent who had no exposure to Latin repeated "ouchus longus, goddamnicus." The setting of developing this in the face of acute head trauma, whether of concussion or contusion, helps to define the organic basis, and allows definition from primary psychiatric causes.

Other speech disturbances involve articulatory impairment. For the patient on anticonvulsant medication for a seizure state, a subtle indication of drug toxicity is reflected in speech articulation. When the articulation loses its crispness and becomes slurred, this may be the first indication of drug toxicity. This is particularly true with hydantoins, such as Dilantin, and with barbiturates.

Where there is involvement of cerebellum or its outflow controls, an altered speech pattern may result. This can be manifest by poor modulation of tone, and a slurring of the words. This speech resembles that of someone with alcoholic intoxication. In the childhood form of Friedreich's ataxia, cerebral palsy of the ataxic variety, or acute Dilantin intoxication, this altered characteristic cerebellar speech pattern can be seen.

A child with nonspecific retardation frequently shows poor speech patterns. This may involve articulation in which pronunciation is indistinct and notable for a variety of immaturities. There is difficulty particularly with pronouncing "r" sounds, and with the sounds *f, s,* and *th.* Inability to form complete sentences is another feature. For the severely retarded child, speech may be reduced to simple grunts assisted by shaking movements of the head.

The patient affected with Gilles de la Tourette Syndrome may have, in addition to the well-known coprolalia, a variety of vocal barks and utterances which immediately suggest the diagnosis. Vocal tics are a rare, isolated phenomenon in childhood, and tend to be one manifestation of a more generalized tic disorder which can involve the eyes or head.

BIBLIOGRAPHY

Aron, A. (1972). Minimal cerebral dysfunction. *Journal of Communication Disorders* 5:142.

Craft, A., Shaw, D., and Cartlidge, N. (1972). Head injuries in children. *British Medical Journal* 4:200.

Dodge, P., and Swartz, M. (1965). Bacterial meningitis, II. Special neurologic problems, post meningitic complications and clinical pathological correlations. *New England Journal of Medicine* 272:954–960.

Goldberg, M. (1963). Hyponatremia and the inappropriate secretion of antidiuretic hormone. *American Journal of Medicine* 35:293–298.

Huttenlocher, P., Wilbourn, A., and Signore, J. (1971). Medium chain triglycerides as a therapy for intractable childhood epilepsy. *Neurology* 21:1097.

Katzman, R. (1966). Effective electrolyte disturbance of the central nervous system. *Annual Review of Medicine* 17:197.

Livingston, S. (1972). *Comprehensive Management of Epilepsy in Infancy, Childhood and Adolescence.* Springfield: Thomas.

Matson, D. (1969). Head injury—general considerations. In: *Neurosurgery of Infancy and Childhood.* Springfield: Thomas.

Mealey, J. (1968). *Pediatric Head Injuries.* Springfield: Thomas.

Menkes, J. (1974). *Textbook of Child Neurology.* Philadelphia: Lea and Febiger.

Niedermeyer, E., and Khalifeh, R. (1965). Petit mal status (spike wave stupor). *Epilepsia (Amst.)* 6:250.

Plum, F., and Posner, J. (1966). *The Diagnosis of Stupor and Coma.* Philadelphia: Davis.

Chapter 21

LEARNING DISORDERS AND MINIMAL BRAIN

DYSFUNCTION

Israel Zeifman, M. D.

DEFINITION

The absence of a coherent theory of learning (Chomsky 1975) makes it necessary that we work with models of the learning process. Such a model is the ego psychology model conceived in terms of a series of ego functions—or central nervous system (CNS) operations in a different but hopefully related language—whose operations are subject to a number of factors. These include stimulation (adequacy of range and intensity), integrity of the sensorimotor apparatus which receives the stimuli and discharges the response, and the internal motivational spectrum. The model must be able to accommodate the element of change present in the learning process despite the fixity of the ego functions.

But we are also dealing with an apparatus whose functioning is developing. Capacities which were rudimentary or nonextant at one point gradually manifest themselves and whole hierarchies of subsystems build up gradually into clinically recognizable skills. One aspect of this developmental history we have known for a long time: the effects of external events on the early development of the apparatus will be significantly greater than similar events on the already mature and functioning apparatus. The existence and importance of another aspect we are only gradually integrating: the subsystems that make up a mature skill may be varied and different from individual to individual and these differences may be a function of the rate and level of maturation of these subsystems and their integration with other existing systems. It is this model which underlies our understanding of learning disorders.

A psychoanalytic view of learning difficulties has been presented by Pearson (1952). He distinguishes direct from indirect causes of learning difficulties such as organic defects, unpleasant conditioning during the process of learning, disturbances in object relations, and inability to focus attention because of anxiety or libidinal tension. Direct causes occur when the learning process itself has been involved in neurotic conflict and the diminished capacity to learn may result from an inhibition in the use of learning, or from disturbances in the ability to "take in" or digest and assimilate the data to be learned. As well, a child may never have mastered the anxiety contained in a normal learning situation or may have disturbances in relation to reality.

Over the past twenty years there has gradually emerged the notion of a group of learning difficulties in which the psychodynamic feature, if any, is secondary to some form of deficit in the organism's learning apparatus. This group includes *minimal brain dysfunction* (MBD) and *dyslexia* as examples of *specific learning disabilities* (SLD) or simply *learning disabilities* (LD). Recognition of their frequency and importance has led to the provision of governmental funds for their diagnosis and educational management.

MBD has been defined as "a diagnostic and descriptive

category (which) refers to children of near average, average or above average intellectual capacity with certain learning and/or behavioral disabilities ranging from mild to severe, which are associated with deviations of function of the central nervous system. These deviations may manifest themselves by various combinations of impairment in perception, conceptualization, language, memory, and control of attention, impulse or motor function. These aberrations may arise from genetic variations, bio-chemical irregularities, perinatal brain insults, or other illnesses or injuries sustained during the years critical for the development and maturation of the central nervous system" (Clements 1966). LD, the educational counterpart of the above, is defined as follows: "Children with specific learning disabilities exhibit a disorder in one or more of the basic psychological processes involved in understanding or in using spoken or written language. These may be manifested in disorders of listening, thinking, talking, reading, writing, spelling or arithmetic. They include conditions which have been referred to as perceptual handicaps, brain injury, minimal brain dysfunction, dyslexia, developmental aphasia, etc. They do not include learning problems which are due primarily to visual, hearing or motor handicaps, to mental retardation, emotional disturbance or to environmental disadvantage" (Haring 1969).

Dyslexia is a term applied in adult neurology to an acquired disorder of reading which may or may not be associated with a disorder of writing. We shall use the term *developmental dyslexia* (DD) which was defined by the World Federation of Neurology in 1968 as: "A disorder manifested by difficulty in learning to read despite conventional instruction, adequate intelligence and sociocultural opportunity. It is dependent upon fundamental cognitive disabilities which are frequently of constitutional origin." In practice, this includes a difficulty in spelling. It will be noted that at least as these definitions stand MBD would be the broader term including DD.

REVIEW OF LITERATURE

Minimal Brain Dysfunction (MBD). The development of the notion of brain dysfunction has been traced to the postencephalitic picture of antisocial traits and emotional instability described sixty years ago. Kahn and Cohn in 1934 suggested the term "organic drivenness" for a syndrome of hyperkinesis and neurological disorders featuring restlessness, clumsiness, and disinhibited motor activity. Bradley in 1937 noted that overactivity responded to amphetamines. Strauss described brain-injured children as hyperactive, disinhibited and distractible, showing perseveration and increased intensity of response. The Strauss sydrome was a circular identification of behavioral characteristics with the etiological factor of brain damage, regardless of whether the latter was demonstrable. Laufer in 1957 added to this notion of an organic entity hyperkinetic impulse disorder and distinguished it from other behavior disorders because of the associated organic background factors. Despite L. Bender's 1956 view that the psychiatric disorders of brain damaged children were similar to those of other children attending psychiatric clinics, the unsupported view prevailed that hyperkinesis and brain damage were identical. Strother in 1973 listed the epidemiological studies of perinatal insults (Pasamanick, Towbin, and others) supporting the view of minimal brain damage. The term brain dysfunction was introduced to signify that the abnormality, either behavioral or cognitive, is only sometimes associated with actual brain disease or damage. The Task Force in 1966 (Clements) which adopted the term "dysfunction" listed ninety-nine signs and symptoms exhibited by children in this category and recommended that an effort be made to identify more homogeneous subcategories.

Developmental Dyslexia (DD). "Congenital word blindness" was coined by Morgan in 1896 to describe a fourteen-year-old who could not read but was otherwise bright, made a good school adjustment, and showed no visual disturbance. Hinshelwood in a monograph on the subject in 1917 described several cases. He agreed with Morgan's suggestion of a defect in the development of the left angular gyrus and noted a hereditary tendency existing in the family of these cases. He was concerned about the educational approach to these children, mentioned that the "look say" method of reading teaching was especially difficult for these children and emphasized that they usually could be taught to read with sufficient time and patience. He believed the disorder to be relatively rare and needed to be distinguished from common reading delays due to environmental circumstances or associated with physiological variations of acquisition of reading. He referred to these milder reading disturbances as "congenital dyslexia." Orton (1937) believed congenital word blindness was a common disorder of children. He described the accompanying writing disturbance as characterized by reversals of words, rotations of letters, mirror writing, and spelling problems. He also stressed the frequency of speech problems such as stuttering. He believed the essential element in the reading impairment was a defect in recognition and recall of letter orientation and letter sequencing in words and suggested "strephosymbolia" as a term to replace congenital word blindness. The entire syndrome was due, he suggested, to failure of hemispheric lateralization and should be regarded as not due to a specific lesion but rather to a maturational disorder based upon delayed cerebral development. Orton's work was of great importance in influencing his students to strive toward the development of improved teaching methods for backward readers and in emphasizing the importance of distinguishing this problem from brain damage or mental retardation syndrome.

The term dyslexia, while it does not imply any specific etiology, has come to mean a learning or cognitive disorder of constitutional origin as opposed to those that are environmentally determined. In Critchley's view, developmental dyslexia is due to an immaturity of cerebral functions and he considers the basic disturbance a disorder of symbolic processes. He generally believes that the strong familial predilection and the characteristic disturbance of the use of symbols point to a constitutional disorder in children. Duane (1977), however, states that "despite the clustering of associated cortical (parietal) symptoms and signs in many of these children, there is sufficient heterogeneity in the clinical expression to weaken the argument that it is a pure syndrome."

INCIDENCE

The incidence of MBD in school populations has been variously estimated at from 1–20 percent of school children between five and twelve years of age. A 1970 national survey using reports by school principals showed 3 percent of SLD. A USPHS research study carried out in a local population found 15 percent of "underachievers" of whom 7.5 percent fell into the group of LD. Separating the prevalence of DD from MBD-SLD is even more problematic since frequently reading evaluations are used to screen cases of MBD. The incidence of MBD in the adult population is not known. Rutter's statistics indicate that the frequency of psychiatric disorders in children having specific reading retardation is three times that of the control child.

The sex distribution is striking: from three to six times more frequent in boys. This frequency holds for MBD and DD.

ETIOLOGY

Historically MBD, as a deviation of CNS function, was evoked to broaden the concept of the brain-damaged child to include less severely affected children. What is the evidence of CNS involvement? The evidence rests on: (1) borderline disturbances of neurological functions ("soft signs"); (2) EEG; (3) evidence of perceptual deficits as determined by psychological tests; and (4) history.

Schain (1977) points out that the difficulty interpreting "soft signs" arises from the lack of normative data on these signs and the subjects' attentional and mental problems which render evaluation unreliable. Rutter (1970), noting that the reliable soft sign findings were those consistent with a picture of developmental lag (synkinesis, poor right-left discrimination, perceptual deficits), argued for a constitutional trait rather than a morbid condition of the nervous system.

As for EEG findings, Rutter's studies of MBD children (1970) have revealed up to 50 percent incidence of abnormalities. Schain feels that "the presence of EEG abnormalities in children with learning disorders is not a guide to the presence of MBD . . . at the present level of knowledge . . . The wide range of EEG variations in childhood must be kept in mind."

The perceptual deficits demonstrated by psychological tests are conceptualized as resulting from dysfunction of central processing affecting either auditory or visual processing. But it has been argued that the information processing model assumed in this view, in which psychological tests objectify the deficits in the perceptual processing system, would be subject to powerful distorting factors such as emotional disturbance in the child and cultural phenomena affecting test performance. Furthermore, there are variations in the acquisition of perceptual skills just as there are of motor skills and a wide variation in their acquisition or a maturational lag in their development might lead, for example, to delay in certain symbol formation capacities, e.g., in the recognition of words as symbols. If the primary difficulty in the hyperactive child with perceptual deficits is the attention disturbance, the latter may be the source of the LD and the inadquate performance in perceptual skills.

The evidence for minimal neurological damage not extensive enough to result in gross neurological deficits but sufficient to produce language, perceptual, and motor disturbances, is often based on a history of prematurity or low birth weight, perinatal injury, lead poisoning, meningitis or encephalitis. It should be remembered that the presence of any of these factors indicates that the child is at risk for neurological sequelae. There is often a history of delayed motor and language development. In a retrospective study of MBD, seizures in infancy and early childhood were reported in 15 percent, and half of these were of febrile origin. But the fact remains that such historical data do not necessarily establish the cause of LD.

There is no obvious cause in 50 percent of the cases diagnosed as MBD and it is this group that gives additional support to the idea of a developmental immaturity as the primary difficulty. Such a theory is further supported by the waning of the "soft signs" and hyperactivity with increasing age. The hypothesis of delayed maturation has the additional advantage that it encourages intervention and the possibility of improvement of functioning.

Orton first proposed that the cause of DD was an impairment in the development of cerebral dominance controlling lateralized functions. He suggested that the usual course of language development proceeded from bilateral language representation to suppression of the right hemisphere. The defective lateralization in dyslexia results in the competing mirror images within the CNS which he felt explained the clinical observations of directional errors in reading and writing, etc. Support was also sought in the frequency of left handedness, ambidexterity and mixed laterality in the dyslexic population. Although the incidence of left-handedness is higher in the dyslexic population, Belmont and Birch demonstrated that there was no specific causality between mixed laterality and reading retardation, when they found that the incidence of reading retardation in a group selected for mixed laterality was no higher than in a uniformly lateralized population. Kinsbourne has summarized this relation between lateralization of handedness and LD as follows: "Some children who are late to manifest consistent handedness also show transient cognitive immaturities that result in school problems, but the relationship is too inconstant to be clinically useful in individual diagnosis." The question of lateralization of function or its failure as the mechanism or cause of cognitive disturbances (including DD) continues to be a lively issue.

Wender (1973) has proposed a biochemical hypothesis for

at least some of the MBD group. His model is organized around two primary deficits, in arousal (the subjects are underaroused and respond with defective attention focusing activity) and in a diminished capacity for positive and negative affect (the subjects have a diminished ability to experience pain and pleasure, hence to learn, etc.). The specific physiological basis of the abnormalities is thought to be a functional underactivity of one or more of the monoaminergic systems. Wender is aware of the danger of circularity in deriving a pathogenic mechanism from a treatment response but the temptation of using the MBD stimulant responder* group as a key argument in favor of a biochemical defect is too great. He would also support the theory of a biochemical origin by invoking the evidence of genetic transmission of MBD. Unfortunately most of this evidence of family clustering of MBD is derived from DD studies and in the latter classification, in those subjects where no attentional deficit can be diagnosed, the use of stimulant medication is of no particular use.

The evidence of genetic factors in MBD is essentially derived from the studies of specific reading retardation or DD and again underscores the heterogeneity of the MBD classification. Hallgren's study in 1950 found that 88 percent of the families of 112 primary cases of specific dyslexia contained one or more secondary cases as determined by test procedures or questionnaires. Finucci in a 1976 study of a DD population found 45 percent of first degree relatives were affected by some manifestations of reading disability: the predominance of male subjects was confirmed but no single mode of genetic transmission was evident. Twin stud-

---

*Stimulant responder refers to that group of the MBD population who show a positive behavioral response to a test dose of amphetamine or amphetaminelike medication.

ies of reading disability further support a genetic hereditary factor.

DIAGNOSTIC CONSIDERATIONS

The child psychiatrist is often consulted about a child with a learning disorder who, despite normal intelligence, is underachieving. The physician's task will consist of: (1) confirming the reality of the child's normal intelligence and his underachievement; (2) obtaining assessments of the child's performance in terms of his cognitive and attentional integrities, his neurological and psychiatric status, and any family history of learning disturbances. Such an evaluation must inevitably have a collaborative quality since the areas of assessment are specialized and each assessment produces valuable information for the other evaluations. For example, the cognitive assessment by the Wechsler Intelligence Scale for Children (WISC) would be of significance not only to the educator but also to the neurologist and psychiatrist. It would also provide significant data for planning remedial strategies for cognitive functioning. How much of this assessment the child psychiatrist will carry out by himself will depend upon his training and interest but in no sense can the evaluation be considered complete without considering all the dimensions of the situation. This is so because there are as yet no pathognomonic diagnostic features of these disorders. We are obliged then to confirm the existence of some learning backwardness, pinpoint its nature as best we can, determine whether it is worthy of intervention or not, and decide upon an appropriate form of intervention.

ASSESSMENTS

Cognitive or Central Processing Difficulty. The most frequently used basic evaluative tool will be the WISC. A discrepancy beyond five to ten points in the Verbal and Performance parts and a scatter in the subtests will be suggestive of the direction of the cognitive limitations. The verbal subtests (information, comprehension, arithmetic, similarities, vocabulary, and digit span) use the auditory modality and are directed towards assessing the child's ability to understand and use language. The performance subtests (picture completion, picture arrangement, block design, object assembly, and coding) use the visual modality and are directed towards visual-perceptive skills, though obviously there is a verbal-auditory component present in its administration.

Two WISC subgroup clusters have frequently been noted:

1. A Performance > Verbal in a male with a family history of language disturbance, a history of delayed language development and reading, and spelling mistakes is suggestive of difficulties connecting word symbols to letter sounds. Digit span (audioverbal) and coding (visuomotor) subtests are low. This group is low in rote repetitive skills, especially those requiring maintenance of sequences or memorizing rote series. They also fail to copy well. This cluster has been called "Specific Language Disability" (Denckla 1972).

2. A Verbal > Performance, with important deficits in block design, object assembly, and arithmetic subtests is clustered with confused right-left commands in relation to self and in space (usually discriminated by age seven) and failure in tests of "finger order sense." This "specifice visuospatial disability" (Denckla 1972), which may be accounted for by the difficulty in making use of information about relative positions in space, manifests itself with problems in remembering sequences in arithmetic manipulations which involve

relative position of digits. In addition to arithmetic problems this group shows poor written work and makes mistakes in letter sequences rather than letter choices, but reading as decoding is average or better.

For the preliminary screening of a reading problem a test such as the Gray Oral Paragraphs may be used. A more thorough reading analysis would provide in addition to grade equivalent, scores for rate, accuracy and comprehension in both oral and silent reading and some indication of the child's learning ability. Such an expert educator's assessment would also include scores for listening, comprehension, sight vocabulary, visual memory of word forms, phonic analysis of word elements, knowledge of auditory blending, handwriting, and spelling. It is evident that such an assessment would provide diagnostic material for assessing the child's behavior and emotional response while engaged in reading.

The Benton Visual Memory Test correlates with reading and assesses visual memory: memory of form and spatial attitude (position and rotation) as well as sequences of the stimuli. (A design is exposed for ten seconds and subsequently four designs, including the one that has been exposed are shown. The subject is expected to indicate the original design from the group.)

The Bender Gestalt Visual Motor Test is classically part of the test battery for LD and MBD. Its specificity for brain damage has been questioned by Shaffer and it has been suggested by P. Ackerman that the immature Bender protocols reflect more general neurological and/or mental immaturity than visual motor perception deficit. Its value for assessing cognitive functioning is enhanced if one watches how a child produces the designs (compulsiveness, impulsiveness). Some of the criteria in evaluation are: primitive and fluid figures, verticalization, closure of open figures, and rounding of square or squaring of round figures.

The assessment of auditory perception involves the evaluation of speech and hearing in various kinds of communicative situations. Auditory perception has been analysed into various functions, for example, auditory discrimination, processing, retrieving, sequencing of spoken language, etc. Auditory perceptual difficulties are apparent when a child cannot integrate auditory messages even with normal hearing and this can be roughly tested by observing the child's response to a series of commands or asking him to repeat a series of digits or a sentence one has given him. While auditory memory and some language processing features can be screened this way, the physician will seek the evaluative skills of the speech and hearing specialist to pinpoint speech and hearing deficits. The Wepman Test of auditory discrimination assesses auditory memory and the ability to distinguish between phonemes. The early diagnosis of auditory perceptual difficulties is especially important for language development and remediation possibilities.

Language perception in the young child is assessed with the Peabody Picture Vocabulary Test. (Four pictures are shown and a single word describing one of the four is given. The child is asked to point to the picture which represents the word.) Language expression can be assessed in an older child by asking him to tell about a game. The auditory sequencing subtest of the Illinois Test of Psycholinguistic Abilities (ITPA) provides a test for language expression. Deficits in auditory discrimination, language processing, reception, and motor expression correlate with high risk for reading disability.

Some of the errors made by children in reading, which while not specifically characteristic of DD, contribute to the impression of cognitive disorder in this group of poor readers are: an inability to pronounce an unfamiliar word with a tendency to guess wildly at its phonic structure; a failure to realize the difference between words which are somewhat similar in spelling or sound (ON-NO, PUB-BUD); a failure to detect the difference in auditory properties of words or letters; failure to read with complete understanding; interpolation of inappropriate phonemes (TRICK for TICK); and substitution of one word for another (WAS for LIVED, THE for AN). Writing and spelling difficulties may be associated with the reading disability and these can be uncovered by having the child write spontaneously or to dictation. Some of the characteristic defects in the writing are: a malalignment; intrusion of block capitals into the middle of a word; omission or repetition of words and letters; and rotation of letters.

Attentional Disturbances and Behavioral Difficulties. This symptom cluster includes a large number of overlapping descriptive terms for behaviors which are assessed clinically: hyperactivity, distractability, short attention span, impulsivity, perseveration, perceptual-motor deficits. Attempts at laboratory evaluation have sometimes failed to isolate the symptom while other laboratory evaluations have suggested correlation with deficient intersensory integration and specific deficits of auditory and visual perception. Even hyperactivity is known to be sometimes difficult to demonstrate in a one-to-one setting in the consultation room. The literature on attention in LD has recently been reviewed (Tarver 1974) and the neurophysiological literature on attention which has received renewed interest has produced evidence for three subsystems: arousal, activation, and effort (Pribram 1975). The clinical phenomena of deficiencies in vigilance, attention, concentration, maintenance of a set of expectations, distractedness, and forgetting would seem to correlate nicely with the notion of varied sybsystems of attention. But the study of such correlations is only beginning.

Of the tests already mentioned, Digit-Span and Arithmetic have been found to differentiate best children with LD from controls. Piaget's concept of decentration seems particularly apt to the development of attention in relation to cognition. According to him the young child's perception is centered on the dominant aspects of the visual field. It becomes increasingly decentered and free from domination by field effects, enabling the child to mentally manipulate perceptual configurations as development proceeds. In LD there is a consistent deficiency on tests of embeddedness and subjects are more dominated than controls by stimulus features of the task.

CNS Neurological Signs. Those neurological signs which concern us here are not the long tract signs indicative of brain damage but those sensori-motor phenomena which normally are transiently present during development. These signs are found in the younger age groups, but are rare in adolescents. They are pathological when they persist beyond the age of normal occurrence, though the limits of their manifestation have not been rigorously established.

These "special" neurological signs are concerned with motor functioning and in a general way they reveal the smoothness or integration of complex muscular movements performed in the increasingly complex adaptive movements acquired in the course of development. Such a developmental series can be outlined from an appreciation of the child as awkward, to assessing his gait, running, skipping, following verbal directions, modulating of motion, and writing. Every examiner develops his own test items and what is crucial is that he have a sense of the range of appropriate functioning of the item he is evaluating. Some of the motor integrations elicited are: asking the child to hop; skip; walk backward; walk with tandem steps along a straight line; balance an object; throw, catch or bounce a ball; touch fingers-to-thumb; alternate movements of the hands; tap index finger on thumb, each hand. The observer will also note the associated movements occuring with these tests and evaluate the synkinesis as well as the nonsymmetrical overflow of movement. Right-left confusion may be elicited in reference to the child's own body and to the examiner. Confusion of spatial direction may be further elicited by having the child execute spatial commands: up and down, right, left, on, under, below, behind, and beyond. Impaired temporal notions may be elicited by having the child imitate a simple rhythm, sequential recitation of months, days of the week; by exploring the use of time adverbs, past and present, now and then, yesterday.

Observing the child writing will be a valuable aid in assessing the child's integration of language and fine motor control. The focus will be on the facility or difficulty of the act: for example, hesitancy in upward or downward swings; where on the connecting swings new letters are started; disjointed letters; poor spacing between letters or words, etc.

While anxiety may influence the productions elicited in these tasks, theoretically, emotional states are not the cause of these productions in a direct specific sense. However, it is possible that the frustrations provoked by failed motor integrations may be the nuclei for developing distortions of psychic integrations. This is important because the fate of these neurological signs is largely to disappear with age but the psychic integration it provoked may pursue an independent course.

The so-called pure DD will have very few positive neurological signs in addition to the cognitive difficulties. The most common MBD case will have neurological signs in addition to cognitive disturbance and an attentional disorder. The other end of the MBD spectrum will be the MBD child with almost pure attentional disorder and few neurological or cognitive signs. Given the variability of the neurological signs from one child to the next, their transience and consequent nondiagnostic value, it may be asked in what way are they useful. It has been suggested that the neurological data help to identify the problem involved as more serious than just a school failure; that this data give the physician a chance to gauge the child's progress and maturation over the years; and finally, it permits the physician to rule out more severe organic disease. Supportive of the first point in this argument is the finding of P. Ackerman that neurophysiological immaturity (NI) was the statistically most significant finding in LD as compared to normal achievers in elementary school boys: 66 percent in LD compared to 10 percent in normals. Incidence of hyperactivity was 60 percent in LD compared to 0 percent in normals.

Psychiatric Evaluation. The aim of this assessment is to establish a picture of the whole child from the multiple viewpoints we are accustomed to in child psychiatry. Such an assessment must involve observation and interview with the child. It will also include family background and history, teacher and school reports, and registering of the possibly significant environmental influences. The child's personality can be assessed within A. Freud's developmental framework: object relations, defensive organization, reality testing, regression and fixation points, nature of conflicts, capacity to tolerate frustration, sublimation potential, attitude to anxiety, and balance between progressive and regressive developmental forces in the child.

Within this overall assessment the presenting complaint of LD will lead to a focus on certain areas relevant to the development of learning (Weil 1977a):

1. The mother-child relationship and its vicissitudes: the quality of maternal investment in the child; the existence of cognitive deprivation; the development of an early sadomasochistic pattern.

2. Neurotic development: the existence of unconscious conflicts leading to symptoms (i.e., phobic or obsessive-compulsive trends) or inhibitions which interfere with the deployment of interest and energy towards learning. Weil (1977a) has emphatically stated, "Neurosis does not create reversal of letters and words. However, if a child has such a maturational weakness, tending to reversals and poor reading, neurotic conflicts may bring it out much more."

3. Disturbances relating to the *neurophysiological immaturities* (NI): There is no specific personality picture correlated with such immaturities. It will be necessary to determine whether the presenting situation is the first occurence of the cognitive or social failure or whether there have been long-standing difficulties in motility and language development which have been ignored. Weil (1977a) has described several disturbance patterns in relation to NI. The occurence of these symptom complexes is often a consequence of parental interaction with the child.

(*a*) Children with motor awkwardness or spatial orientation difficulties show a greater dependency on the mother. This makes them vulnerable to the development of phobic or later obsessive-compulsive trends.

(*b*) Early sadomasochistic interaction with the mother may occur as a result of exaggerated childhood tendencies (impulsive, hyperactive, aggressive).

(c) A self-image of badness may occur in a good environment from the child's internalizing the parent's injunctions, without being able to live up to them.

(d) Reining in of aggression may lead to its emergence in profuse fantasy or to projection outward in phobic elaboration. Temper tantrums and scenes may develop. There may be a paranoid coloring. Further frustration may lead on to an early stage of delinquent development.

Not infrequently connected with NI in children with high verbal IQ who fail in school performance are a spectrum of difficulties which A. Freud has situated in the final stages of the developmental line from play to work. There is a failure to develop the prerequisites of the right attitude to work: a failure to control and modify the pregenital drive components in the activity; incomplete functioning according to the reality principle; inability to accept pleasure as an ultimate result of the activity.

The assessment will attempt to establish the strength of the forces contributing to the LD. Strong neurotic tendencies coupled with very mild NI would suggest psychotherapeutic approaches. It would be expected that the NI would be worked out through the spontaneous development of compensating strategies and the natural waning of the immaturity. The psychiatrist's task is establishing the existence of significant neurotic features, constitutional factors, family and environmental pressures contributing to or grafted onto the NI. The child's difficulty in accepting a recommendation for remediation of a LD must also be considered a dimension of the psychiatrist's evaluation.

Differential Diagnosis. By definition the causal connections of the features of the MBD syndrome—cognitive, attentional, CNS, psychiatric—are hypothetical at best and frequently obscure. Hence, the importance of recognizing other factors that may be causally connected to features making up the MBD syndrome and yielding a picture which may or may not be MBD or may be MBD plus a known contributing cause:

1. Such a diagnostic dilemma is common with children from low socioeconomic backgrounds (Cohen 1976). Statistically such backgrounds correlate with increased risk for intrinsic psychological and neurological impairment, yet the behavior and scholastic problems may stem from any or all of the following: inadequate family care, maladaptation to school, and educational mislabeling. Nor are such cases so rare from the most advantaged socioeconomic groups.

2. Transient phenomena affecting the child's cognition and attention, i.e., parental divorce, etc.

3. Parental or school demands exceeding the child's motivational level.

4. Known organic entities: meningitis, lead ingestion, etc.

TREATMENT

Given the variability of the manifestations of the MBD syndrome and of the variable intensity of the manifestations in each case, the treatment, ideally, will be individually tailored. The three principle syndrome complexes each has its basic treatment modality: cognitive deficits by special education; attentional disorder by medication and/or special management designed to diminish stimuli; psychiatric disorder by psychotherapy. In practice treatment will consist of some combination of these modalities. Cantwell's review (1977) of treatment demonstrates the lack, inadequacy, or contradictory nature of outcome studies of MBD treatment modalities. Consequently, treatment judgment will have to be based on clinical experience. This experience leads to the following guides to treatment:

1. The treatment of an MBD child should be conceived of as a long-term relationship with the family and child, regardless of how loosely the relationship is conceived, requiring periodic monitoring.

2. Communication with the parents and with the child, including a frank recognition of the NI, is an essential step. Involvement of parents and family in the treatment is important and the form of this involvement will depend upon the treatment modalities used (Cantwell 1977).

3. Special education remediation is often a slow process and when associated with an attentional disorder the latter may respond to stimulant medication. The cognitive processing problem is only secondarily affected by the medication and its remediation continues at its own rate.

4. The attentional disorder, if it is severe enough, may require medication: amphetamine, methylphenidate, magnesium pemoline and, in some cases, a phenothiazine.

Since identification of responders, dose, side effects, duration of drug administration and effects of long-term use (dysphoria, physical growth effects) are the subject of current investigation, close monitoring of the child and con tact with parents and school is a desideratum of drug administration. In older children the attentional disorder will tend to augment the personality disorder which has developed and the latter may require psychiatric management.

5. Psychotherapeutic treatment of whatever form will not remediate the cognitive processing disturbance which, if it is of some significance, e.g., has lead to or threatens school failure, should also receive appropriate educational remediation. Failure to provide special educational remediation may foredoom the psychotherapy.

framework. This would be very seductive to the analyst, especially if the patient, as is often the case in mild NI, has been capable of developing strong compensatory substitute functioning. But is it possible that some of the difficulties encountered in the treatment of adult character disorders stem from unrecognized deficits that have become integrated in the course of development? One sometimes encounters "borderline" patients who despite years of "good" treatment seem stubbornly ensnared in a stance of protest leading them to live their lives in much disorder. Perhaps reconstruction recognizing the really impossible demands they have internalized while they struggled as children with NI would be a helpful avenue to explore.

SUMMARY

The learning disorders focused on are the minimal brain dysfunction syndrome with its specific learning disabilities, including developmental dyslexia. The etiology, diagnosis, and treatment are reviewed from a clinical child psychiatric point of view. The importance in our present state of knowledge of expressing the diagnosis in behavioral terms is stressed. The rarity of psychoanalytic recognition of the syndrome is noted.

BIBLIOGRAPHY

Cantwell, D. (1977). Psychopharmacological treatment of the MBD syndrome. In *Psychopharmacology in Childhood and Adolescence,* ed. J. Wiener, pp. 119–148. New York: Basic Books.

Chomsky, N. (1975). *Reflections on Language.* New York: Pantheon. Fundamental issues for learning theory from a rational point of view.

Clements, S. (1966). *Minimal Brain Dysfunction in Childhood: Terminology and Identification.* Washington: Public Health Service Publication Number 1415.

Cohen, D. (1976). Diagnostic process in child psychiatry. *Psychiatric Annals* 6:29–56. A good review article with extensive bibliography.

de Hirsch, K. (1975). Language deficits in children with developmental lags. *Psychoanalytic Study of the Child* 30:95–126. Review by a pioneer in childhood language disabilities who is sensitive to psychodynamic factors.

Denckla, M. (1972). Clinical syndromes in learning disabilities. *Journal of Learning Disabilities* 5:401–406.

Duane, D. (1977). Perspectives of dyslexia. *Psychiatric Annals* 7:17–32.

Haring, N., and Miller, C. (1969). *Minimal Brain Dysfunction in Children, National Project on Learning Disabilities in Children.* Washington: Public Health Service Publication Number 2015.

Orton, S. (1937). *Reading, Writing and Speech Problems in Children.* New York: Norton.

Pearson, G. (1952). Survey of learning difficulties in children. *Psychoanalytic Study of the Child* 7:322–386.

Peters, J., Davis, J., Goolsby, C., and Clements, S. (1973). *Physician's Handbook, Screening for MBD.* Ciba.

Pribram, K., and McGuinness, D. (1975). Arousal, activation and effort in the control of attention. *Psychological Review* 82:116–149.

Rutter, M., Graham, P. and Yule, W. (1970). *A Neuropsychiatric Study in Childhood.* Philadelphia: Lippincott.

Schain, R. (1977). *Neurology of Childhood Learning Disorders,* 2nd ed. Baltimore: Williams and Wilkins.

Tarver, S., and Hallahan, D. (1974). Attention deficits in children with learning disabilities. *Journal of Learning Disabilities* 7:560–569.

Weil, A. (1977a). Learning disturbances with special consideration of dyslexia. Issues Child Mental Health 5:52–66.

———— (1977b). Maturational variations and genetic-dynamic issues. Paper presented at the Brill Memorial Lecture, New York Psychoanalytic Institute, November. Child analyst author who has striven innovatively with the problems posed by developmental deviations.

Wender, P. (1973). Some speculations concerning a possible biochemical basis of MBD. *Annals of New York Academy of Sciences* 205:18–28.

Chapter 22

HYPERKINETIC SYNDROME

Arnold R. Cohen, M.D.

DEFINITION

The hyperkinetic syndrome of childhood is characterized by overactivity, distractibility, poor attention span, emotional lability, and frequently by learning difficulty. The syndrome of hyperkinesis must be distinguished from the symptom of hyperactivity or overactivity. What appears to be overactivity occurs normally during the earlier years of childhood and it occurs pathologically in a large number of childhood disorders. In the past there has been confusion in the child psychiatric literature because hyperkinetic syndrome has been occasionally considered to be synonymous with the symptom of hyperactivity or with the syndrome of minimal brain dysfunction.

Minimal brain dysfunction refers to a pathophysiological entity of childhood in which there is impairment of perception, cognition, conceptualization, language, or motor functions. There is demonstrable deviation of function of the central nervous system. Within this group of children there are many who manifest behavioral signs of overactivity and of poor attention span. Because of this association, the presence of brain dysfunction has often been inferred in behaviorally disturbed hyperactive children even in the absence of demonstrable brain dysfunction. But there are also many children who have evidence of minor central nervous system deviation who do not have evidence of hyperactivity. Hyperkinetic syndrome and minimal brain dysfunction syndrome clearly overlap. It is possible that there are several specific disorders within these groups each with different etiologies that manifest in similar, often overlapping ways.

REVIEW OF LITERATURE

The literature on the hyperkinetic syndrome is enormous and is growing larger at a rapid rate. Reviews of the syndrome and of its treatment appear with great frequency. The most complete of recent reviews are in the form of monographs. Cantwell (1975) reviews the literature from the "medical model" point of view. Wender (1971) focuses on brain dysfunction as the etiological cause of hyperkinesis. Safer and Allen (1976) review the clinical diagnosis of the hyperkinetic syndrome, its differential diagnosis, and its treatment with pharmacotherapy as well as with behavioral therapy. Ross and Ross (1976) exhaustively review the concept of hyperkinesis, its physiology, etiology, pharmacotherapy, psychology, behavioral management, and educational intervention.

Our earliest modern awareness of the hyperkinetic syndrome began in the early twentieth century with Still's observation of hyperactivity and impulsive behavior in brain-injured children. The association of brain injury and hyperactivity was supported by reports of the development of a hyperactivity syndrome in children who had recovered from encephalitis after the great influenza epidemic of 1918. It was in 1937 that Bradley reported the positive effects of Benzedrine on the behavior of hyperactive postencephalitic children. Later, observations of impulsive hyperactive behavior in children without demonstrable brain pathology led to the idea that brain damage could be inferred from the behavioral signs alone and this then led to the concept of minimal brain damage.

In the ensuing years, further evidence of minimal brain impairment as an etiology for hyperactive behavior accumulated. Animal studies and epidemiological studies of anoxic infants solidified this point of view. Bradley's observations which went relatively unnoticed reemerged in the 1960s. Stimulant medications, in particular dextro-amphetamine and methylphenidate gained wide acceptance as the appropriate treatment for hyperkinetic syndrome. Some recommended medication alone without psychotherapy as appropriate treatment for the syndrome, a view that gained some acceptance. Most recently, attempts at defining proper educational environments and appropriate forms of behavior modification for these children have also begun to appear.

In the late 1960s follow-up studies began to appear: Menkes, Rowe, and Menkes (1967); Mendelsohn, Johnson, and Stewart (1971); and Ackerman, Dykman, and Peters (1977). These studies suggested that the syndrome was not necessarily outgrown as had been previously thought. Nor was the prognosis always positive. Indeed, antisocial behavior was found to be a frequent problem for adolescents who had a history of hyperkinetic syndrome in childhood. Although the majority of youngsters did well at outcome, significant numbers had low self-esteem, continued learning difficulty and signs of restlessness and rebellious behavior.

Discouragingly, at follow-up children who had treatment were not demonstrably different than those who had not been treated.

In the past several years there has been a shift from the concept of brain damage to the concept of brain dysfunction, but at the same time it has also become clear that there are a great number of children without any evidence of brain pathology who are overactive and impulsive. Indeed, only a small number of these children have demonstrable brain pathology. Although neurophysiological immaturity or dysfunction continues to be the most commonly accepted etiology for hyperkinetic syndrome, many now think of the syndrome as the cumulative result of the interaction of an immature or deviant physiological substructure with contributing environmental factors.

INCIDENCE

The hyperkinetic syndrome is quite common. The estimates of its prevalence in our society range from about 4 percent to about 10 percent of the grade school population. The incidence of the disorder depends upon the area of the country studied, population surveyed, and, of course, the diagnostic criteria of the investigators. Hyperactivity as a symptom is much more common than hyperkinesis as a syndrome. Overactivity is among the most common reasons for referral to child guidance clinics and is among the most common complaints of parents about their children in general. Boys seem to be affected by the hyperkinetic syndrome and by the hyperactivity symptom two to three times as often as are girls. The symptom of overactivity diminishes towards puberty, but evidence of the syndrome continues into adolescence in most cases.

ETIOLOGY

Genetic, organic, and psychogenic etiological factors are important in the hyperkinetic syndrome and there is good evidence that all three interact or contribute to its expression.

Family studies suggest that hyperkinetic syndrome is often a familial disorder. The adoption studies done thus far point to genetic factors as a major etiological concern. Not only is the hyperkinetic syndrome often familial, but parents in affected families are more likely to suffer from alcoholism, hysteria, and antisocial behavior than are the parents of normal control children. This is important because these three adult syndromes are often found at outcome in follow-up studies of hyperkinetic children. It is thought that a polygenetic mode of inheritance is likely to be the form of genetic transmission. Genetic mechanisms may account for one subgroup of hyperactive children; other etiologies are also probable. Brain damage from birth trauma, or prenatal or postnatal illness have all been offered as causes of hyperactivity and, indeed, a positive history of these early traumas is more likely to be found in a hyperkinetic population than in a normal population. Still, some children with overt brain disease have no evidence of hyperkinesis and a minority of hyperactive children have strong evidence of brain damage. However, if one studies the hyperkinetic population alone there is a higher than normal prevalence of neurological soft signs and electroencephalographic (EEG) abnormalities.

Other organic causes for hyperkinetic syndrome may include subclinical lead intoxication or other toxic substances not yet identified. Feingold has recently suggested that food coloring and other food additives may cause hyperactivity by some as yet unknown allergic mechanism. He has reported that about one-half of his hyperkinetic children were able to discontinue their stimulant medication and function well when given an additive-free diet. These findings have been questioned but the additive-free diet does seem to benefit a small number of hyperkinetic children.

Brain dysfunction and maturational immaturity have become important areas for research into the etiology of hyperkinetic disorder. Wender (1971) first proposed that hyperactivity was a result of a disequilibrium between excitatory and inhibitory systems within the reticular activating system. He assumed that the inhibitory system was monoaminergic and for some reason it was understimulated. He proposed that the excitatory system was not sufficiently inhibited because of this and that random overactivity resulted.

Satterfield (1972) showed that hyperkinetic children had low central nervous system arousal levels which were normalized by the use of stimulant medication. This and other data led Satterfield to infer that hyperkinetic children had decreased activity in some central nervous system pathways. This neuronal hypoactivity in turn diminished inhibitory control of attentional behavior and impulsivity. He proposed that the major defect in the hyperkinetic disorder was the inability to maintain attention, the overactivity being secondary. Margolin (1978) reviewed the literature on the hyperkinetic syndrome and brain monoamines. The data available suggest that hyperkinesis is a disorder of attention as Satterfield has felt and that the attentional deficit is related to deficient brain monoamine metabolism. At this time it seems that dopamine hypoactivity is a probable factor in the pathophysiology of the hyperkinetic syndrome.

Hyperkinetic children with their attentional problems tend to fail at tasks requiring concentration. This leads to school and social failure and ultimately to a loss of self-esteem. Unable to succeed at tasks requiring attention, reflection and concentration, these children may turn to impulsive behavior for gratification. This may then reinforce their physiological predisposition to impulsivity and inattention. This hypothesis may account for some of the antisocial, antiauthority, impulsive behavior seen in many of these children as they grow up. Several studies show that a significant number of adolescents who had hyperkinesis as children continue to have problems with attentionality, learning, and antisocial behavior in adolescence. There is also evidence to suggest that socioeconomic variables influence prevalence and outcome of the disorder, with hyperkinetic children from lower socioeconomic class being much more likely to show antisocial and impulsive behavior later in life than those from higher socioeconomic class.

DIAGNOSTIC CONSIDERATIONS

The diagnosis of the hyperkinetic syndrome is a clinical one. The presence of *overactivity, distractibility, excitability,* and *impulsivity* in a child lead one to the diagnosis. Difficulty in learning also heightens one's clinical suspicion. In addition, a fair number of these children are enuretic as well. Hyperkinetic children appear immature and not well organized. They do most poorly in group situations where multiple extraneous stimuli compete for their attention.

Hyperkinetic children must be distinguished from anxious children who also may be overactive and distracted. These children are usually better organized and more mature. They are often aware of their anxiety, and experience their symptoms in a dysphoric manner. Other children who may resemble hyperkinetic children are the youngsters classified in the category of unsocialized aggressive reaction. These children sometimes appear pseudo-mature and apparently well organized. There is usually the presence of overt hostility and aggression. They seem willful in their misbehavior and their histories are replete with examples of sociocultural deprivation.

The hyperkinetic youngster may have a history of similar disorder in the extended family or in the siblings. There may also be a history of prenatal or neonatal difficulty, developmental irregularity, or early signs of overactivity. Mothers may complain that the youngster was colicky, fidgety, fretful, and had sleeping difficulty from early infancy onward. Other mothers report that they were unaware of any differentness in their youngster at all. Many parents were aware that the youngster seemed overactive, but did not place importance on this until the child entered school. The mother may report that her youngster had always been clumsy, was constantly falling, or was unable to perform age-appropriate motor tasks.

Although the diagnosis of hyperkinetic syndrome is a clinical one, the presence of neurological soft signs may be confirmatory. Psychological testing for graphomotor, visual motor and other organic deficits is useful. EEG's are frequently positive with nonspecific changes, but like the other neurological findings, are not necessary for the diagnosis. Parent and teacher questionnaires are helpful in identifying these children but the four cardinal features continue to be the necessary criteria for diagnosis.

Many clinicians report that these youngsters appear little different than normal children in the one-to-one interview situation. Some hyperkinetic children do exhibit their symptoms in the office interview. In addition, clinical assessment is necessary to rule out the possibility of neurotic anxiety, unsocialized aggressive reaction, and childhood schizophrenia. Finally, although uncommon, there are medical conditions which are characterized by hyperactivity. A pediatric evaluation should be performed to rule out these possibilities. These disorders include hyperthyroidism, lead poisoning, deafness and blindness, acute toxic diseases, and chronic brain syndromes.

TREATMENT

The most important part of the treatment consists of an explanation of the disorder to the child and his family. Although individual psychotherapy may or may not be warranted, family sessions around the family's inability to deal with the child's hyperactivity and possible interventions in the behavior are necessary. The goals should be to help diminish the family's intolerance to the overactivity, to help the family develop tasks that are within the child's limited attentional ability, and finally to help structure programs to modify the hyperactivity itself (Ross and Ross 1976). When other psychiatric symptoms complicate the hyperkinetic syndrome, individual psychotherapy should also be offered.

When environmental manipulation, family counseling, and other attempts at interventions fail to diminish the hyperkinetic youngster's difficulties, central nervous system stimulant medication must be considered. About two-thirds of children who suffer from hyperkinetic syndrome improve either greatly or moderately when placed on stimulant medication. The response is sometimes dramatic and often within the first day of treatment. In medication-responsive children, there is a marked increase in attention span and the children appear less overactive. There also seems to be an improvement in visual motor performance and in learning. The improvement in learning may be state-dependent and may not be well maintained in the non-drug state.

The poorest response to stimulant drug treatments occurs in hyperkinetic children with grossly disturbed family constellations. Satterfield has found that the response to medication is best and most predictable in children with low skin conductance, abnormal EEG, and four or more neurological "soft signs." However, medication may be helpful in any child with a clinical picture of hyperkinetic syndrome. The absence of neurological findings should not preclude a trial of medication.

Side effects of stimulant drugs include insomnia, anorexia, and gastrointestinal side effects as well as some depression. At higher dose levels there can be an increase in overactivity and in anxiety. Diminished growth and weight gain have been reported in children treated with stimulant medication. Dextroamphetamine is supposedly worse in this respect than methylphenidate. Compensatory growth spurts have also been reported, some authors concluding that drug holidays are sufficient to normalize growth and weight gain. More recent investigations conclude that lack of weight gain and lack of growth is not an important clinical consideration and that methylphenidate does not interfere in any significant way with growth. Although drug holidays are suggested by some authors, others argue that a need for stabilized inner environment necessitates keeping the youngster on as even a dose of medication as is possible throughout the day and throughout the week.

Recently magnesium pemoline, a weaker central nervous system stimulant, has been shown to be effective in the treatment of hyperkinetic syndrome. It has an advantage over methylphenidate in that it remains active in the body for a longer period of time and can be given in single daily doses.

Supposedly the onset of action is gradual and the child may need to be on medication for several days before medication effect can be noted.

Some children initially considered hyperkinetic do not respond well to medication and others become precipitously worse. Children who are suffering from neurotic anxiety and from borderline psychosis tend to become more disorganized and anxious. Frank psychosis may emerge in the borderline youngster. These adverse effects are readily reversible with discontinuance of medication. These adverse effects must also be distinguished from the effects of overmedication in responsive children.

The stimulant medications are usually given in divided doses in the early morning and at noon. The usual starting dose is 5 mg twice a day of methylphenidate or 2.5 mg of dextroamphetamine twice a day. The dose is then titrated upward to a point where there is maximum therapeutic effect without adverse or side effect. This dose may range up to 40 to 60 mg of methylphenidate or about half that amount of dextroamphetamine. Pemoline is usually given in the morning with a starting dose of 37.5 mg, which may be gradually increased by 18.75 mg at one week intervals, with the maintenance dose often ranging between 56.25 and 75 mg.

Imipramine has been reported to be useful in the treatment of hyperkinetic disorder. The percentage of children who improve on imipramine is almost as high as that for stimulant medication. Some clinicians feel that the improvement seen with imipramine is not as well maintained as the improvement seen with stimulant medication. It appears, though, that tricyclic antidepressants do have a place in the treatment of hyperkinetic syndrome, particularly if enuresis is also present or if stimulant medication has not been effective. Tricyclic antidepressants can be quite dangerous in children at higher than recommended doses. Cardiac arrhythmias, as well as seizures, have been reported and the dose given should not exceed 4 mg per kilogram of body weight.

When stimulant medication and other treatment is not effective, small doses of phenothiazine may be given a therapeutic trial. The major tranquilizers nonspecifically slow down hyperkinetic children but in higher doses interfere further with cognitive function. Benadryl has also been suggested as a useful medication for the treatment of hyperkinesis, especially in children under the age of ten. There are anecdotal clinical reports of its effectiveness but controlled studies have not been done. Lithium and diphenylhydantoin have been reported as helpful in some youngsters with episodic hyperactivity but do not seem to have a major place in the therapy of hyperkinetic children at this time. There have also been reports attesting to the efficacy of caffeine but it does not appear to be of significant value.

Stimulant drug treatment of hyperkinetic children is usually continued till there are signs of abatement of the overt overactivity. Occasional drug holidays may be useful to see if there has been underlying clinical improvement. In the past it has been suggested that medication should be discontinued by adolescence. However, there are several reports that indicate that stimulant medication may still be useful in adolescents with a history of hyperkinetic syndrome. Stimulant medication may be safely given to these youngsters as long as there is no sign of euphoria. In fact, in follow-up studies, stimulant medication abuse has not occurred in these youngsters, probably because it does not promote euphoria in them.

DISCUSSION

The literature reviewed on the hyperkinetic syndrome strongly emphasizes organic and physiological disturbances. Emotionally caused hyperactivity and immaturity have been excluded from consideration in this syndrome. Our clinical experience has not always allowed us to differentiate physiological and environmental causes for hyperkinesis. We often see hyperactive children who have psychiatric histories that would suggest behavioral problems, and these are not easily categorizable as neurotic or unsocialized aggressive children. This has led us to postulate that there are all degrees of hyperkinetic temperament. The hyperactivity may or may not be clinically important unless psychological factors have tipped the scales towards maladaptive behavior, or unless the physiological deficits are pronounced.

Although some follow-up studies do not find that stimulant medication alters the child's long term prognosis, we believe that medication has a definite place in treatment. Stimulant medication, as it increases attention span, reduces frustration and failure at home and in school. This should enhance self-esteem, decrease family conflict and increase the likelihood of better emotional functioning in the long run. Therefore we use medication in the treatment of some hyperkinetic children but only as one part of the total treatment plan.

SUMMARY

The hyperkinetic syndrome is a behavioral syndrome of childhood in which there is a defect in the ability to maintain purposeful attention. Children affected with this disorder demonstrate overactivity, distractibility, poor attention span and excitability. Learning difficulties are common, signs of minimal brain dysfunction occur in the majority of these children and nocturnal enuresis occurs in some. Antisocial behavior traits are also more likely to occur in hyperkinetic children especially as they grow older. Hyperkinetic syndrome is a common disorder of childhood. It is found predominantly in school age boys and occurs in about 5 percent of the general population. It is found more commonly in the lower socioeconomic population groups.

The primary deficit in hyperkinetic children is the inability to maintain purposeful attention. This may be due to dopaminergic neuronal hypoactivity in certain parts of the brain. Impulsivity, poor attention span and excitability result from this deficit. The children become frustrated at their academic and social failure and poor self-esteem ensues. This model suggests a biological-environmental interaction to explain the full symptom picture of hyperkinesis. Genetic predisposition, birth trauma, brain injury, toxic ingestion, and environmental input have all been advanced as underlying causes for hyperkinetic syndrome.

Treatment consists of a combination of medication, education, and family counselling. Behavior modification and special educational techniques are important aspects of the treatment. Individual psychotherapy may be useful for coexistent psychiatric problems. Stimulant medication has long been the medical treatment of choice. Stimulant drugs (and to a lesser extent tricyclic antidepressants) increase the attentional behavior in children diagnosed as hyperactive.

BIBLIOGRAPHY

Ackerman, P., Dykman, R.A., Peters, J. (1977). Teenage status of hyperactive and non-hyperactive learning disabled boys. *American Journal of Orthopsychiatry* 47:577–596.

Cantwell, D., ed. (1975). *The Hyperactive Child.* New York: Spectrum. A clear and complete selection of papers that describe the clinical syndrome, its physiology and treatment.

Margolin, D. (1978). The hyperkinetic child syndrome and brain monoamines: pharmacology and therapeutic implications. *Journal of Clinical Psychiatry* 39:120–130.

Mendelson, W., Johnson, N., Stewart, M. (1971). Hyperactive children as teenagers: a follow-up study. *Journal of Nervous and Mental Diseases* 153:273–279.

Menkes, M., Rowe, J. and Menkes, J. (1967). A twenty-five year follow-up study on the hyperkinetic child with minimal brain dysfunction. *Pediatrics* 39:393–399. This first long-term follow-up study is still important because all the children had evidence of MBD as well as hyperactivity.

Ross, M., and Ross, S. (1976). *Hyperactivity: Research, Theory and Action.* New York: Wiley-Interscience. The most complete review of the hyperactivity syndrome with particular emphasis on management. Extensive bibliography. Highly recommended.

Safer, D., and Allen, R. (1976). *Hyperactive Children.* Baltimore: University Park Press. This book provides a good review of the syndrome. The emphasis in treatment is on stimulant medication and behavior modification.

Satterfield, J., Cantwell, D., Lesser, L., and Podosin, R. (1972). Physiological studies of the hyperkinetic child: I. *American Journal of Psychiatry* 128:1418–1424.

Wender, P. (1971). *Minimal Brain Dysfunction in Children.* New York: Wiley-Interscience. This book is of particular value in its attempts to set up theoretical ways of conceptualizing the emotional and physiological aspects of hyperactivity syndrome.

Chapter 23

TIC DISORDERS

Elaine S. Shapiro, Ph.D.

Arthur K. Shapiro, M.D.

DEFINITION OF SYNDROME

Tics are involuntary movements or utterances involving contractions of functionally related groups of skeletal muscles in one or more parts of the body. These symptoms are brief, frequent, rapid, sudden, unexpected, repetitive, purposeless, inappropriate, stereotypic, irresistible, and of variable intensity. They occur at irregular intervals, and usually involve a number of muscles in their normal synergistic relationships. Symptoms may be stable over time, decrease during nonanxious distraction or concentration, disappear during sleep, and increase with tension. Tics can be voluntarily suppressed for a variable period of time, but the effort causes an increase in tension and the symptoms must later be discharged.

There are at least three tic conditions which should be differentiated. The differential diagnosis will be discussed in the section on Diagnostic Considerations. It is probable that these tic conditions represent a continuum going from the mild transient tic of childhood to the most complex, severe multiple tics of Gilles de la Tourette syndrome.

REVIEW OF LITERATURE

Authors in the past did not differentiate among tics, dystonias, choreas, habits such as nail-biting, writer's cramp, enuresis, compulsions and so on. Complex multiple tics with vocalization were described but thought to be a suborder of the choreas. Charcot attempted to differentiate between a single tic and a more severe, morbid type. The single tic was characterized by a facial grimace accompanied by a slight movement of the arms or fingers and a monosyllabic exclamation. Charcot called these single tic infirmities because they did not severely impair an individual's functioning. The more complex multiple tics were described and delineated by Charcot's resident, Gilles de la Tourette, in 1884 and 1885, and the illness was named after him in recognition of his clinical description of the syndrome. In the early period between 1825 and 1900, tics were thought to be the result of degenerative hereditary antecedants, and family backgrounds were frequently characterized as alcoholic, epileptic, and so on. Tics in family members were noted occasionally but not considered important.

Meige and Feindel published an important treatise on tics in 1907 which became the classic reference for about 70 years. The etiological emphasis changed from hereditary factors to the mental or psychological state of the individual. Although Meige and Feindel referred to ticqueurs as predisposed individuals, they were described as emotionally unstable and infantile. Gilles de la Tourette syndrome was thought to be a separate entity, a progressive illness with coprolalia and sometimes echolalia which might culminate in insanity.

The erroneous belief that tics were caused by psychological factors and had a morbid prognosis was an unfortunate development. The emphasis on a psychological etiology was further elaborated by psychoanalytic writers in the 1920s who concentrated on the deeply hidden or unconscious conflicts of patients.

Freud did not write specifically about Tourette syndrome except to briefly comment on coprolalia in 1899. Coprolalia was explained as the defense against the impulse to curse which then results in cursing. According to Ferenczi, Freud felt there was an organic basis to the illness.

Ferenczi in 1921 was the first to deal with the conflictual, erotic, and instinctual life of the patients. Ferenczi considered tics to be a narcissistic disorder. Stereotypic tics were characterized as equivalents of onanism.

Abraham disagreed with Ferenczi and emphasized the anal-sadistic conflicts, classifying tics as conversion symptoms more resembling catatonia than hysteria.

The major psychoanalytic work on tics was by Mahler and her colleagues over the period 1943–1949. Mahler (1949) described tics as the expression of an internal conflict between gratification of and defenses against instinctual impulses attributed to parental restriction of motor restlessness in their constitutionally predisposed children.

In the last twenty years, other psychological theories have been advanced to explain the etiology of tics and Tourette syndrome. These have included family tensions (Bruch and Thum; Dunlap), overdemanding parents (Kanner), and overlearned normal movements (Yates).

A burgeoning of interest in tics and Tourette syndrome began in the 1950s characterized by the collection and study of a large number of patients (Zausmer, Pasamanick, Torup, Kelman, Fernando, Corbett). Some authors were committed to an organic and others to a psychogenic etiology. Zausmer, for example, believed that the crucial psychological factor was the disturbed and anxiety-producing mother-child relationship. Pasamanick, however, was impressed with the evidence that cerebral injury was implicated in the etiology of tics. He noted the increased frequency of hyperactivity among children with tics, the relationship of tics to epidemic encephalitis and that more males than females had tics.

The introduction of psychopharmacological drugs in the 1950s led to the successful use of haloperidol for tics and Tourette syndrome as reported in 1961 by Seignot and also Caprini and Melotti. Challas and Brauer (1963) as well as Shapiro and Shapiro (1968) also reported on the effectiveness of haloperidol. A renewed interest in the organic basis of these disorders was further stimulated by important neurochemical discoveries such as the relationship of the neurotransmitter dopamine to the basal ganglia. These led to new theoretical constructs and experimental clinical studies in Parkinsonism and other movement disorders.

The recent use of behavioral techniques for the treatment of psychological disorders stimulated unsubstantiated claims about the effectiveness of behavioral treatment of tics and Tourette syndrome which were based on the erroneous belief that involuntary neurological symptoms could be learned and unlearned.

INCIDENCE

The frequency of tics in children has been reported as 5 percent (Pringle 1967), 12 percent (Lapouse and Monk 1964) and 23.6 percent (Boncour in 1910).

The prevalence of Tourette syndrome is difficult to estimate because of frequent misdiagnosis. A registry started by Abuzzahab and Anderson (1973) culled 430 cases from the world's literature. Shapiro et al. (1978) studied 392 patients between 1965 and 1977 and since then have recorded a total of more than 600 cases.

The reported distribution by sex varies as well. Lapouse and Monk reported more boys than girls in the nine to twelve year age group, but in the overall sample of age six to twelve, there was an even distribution of boys and girls. Torup (1962) studied 237 children with tics and found the boy:girl ratio to be 3:1. Pringle (1967) studied 11,000 seven-year-olds in England and found evidence of tics in 5.9 percent of boys and 3.8 percent of girls. Shapiro et al. (1978) found the ratio to be 3:1, with boys predominating, in a study of 145 patients with Tourette syndrome.

ETIOLOGY

Tics have traditionally and, we believe, erroneously, been attributed to underlying tension or anxiety in the child stemming from an unconscious conflict or in response to parental or family pressures, symbolically expressed as a tic. Specific psychodynamic formulations were elaborated by Ferenczi, Abraham, Klein, Mahler and her co-workers, and Gerard.

Shapiro et al. (1978), based on their clinical experience and a review of the literature, found insufficient clinical and experimental data to support a psychological etiology for tics or Tourette syndrome. Although psychological and environmental factors can influence (increase or decrease) symptomatology, these factors cannot be considered proof of psychogenesis. The authors tested the widespread psychodynamic formulation which interpreted tics and other symptoms of Tourette syndrome as the symbolic expression of a massive, unconscious conflict about the expression of hostility and aggression, that resulted in reaction formation, obsessions, compulsions, symptom substitution, and ultimately revealed an underlying psychotic process. They found that psychopathological states such as hysteria, inhibition of aggression, obsessive-compulsive traits, schizophrenia or other psychoses did not characterize patients with Tourette syndrome more than a matched outpatient psychiatric sample.

Other authors have stressed that tics are the result of an interaction between psychological factors and organic factors (Lucas, 1967; Abuzzahab and Anderson, 1973). Postulating a dual etiology seems unparsimonious to the present authors. We postulate that both tics and Tourette syndrome are caused by a primary organic disease of the central nervous system. While it is recognized that the evidence is inconclusive because a specific lesion has not been demonstrated, we believe that the circumstantial evidence supports an organic etiology for tics. The evidence includes the following findings. The higher male to female ratio is similar to the sex ratio found in other organic conditions such as infant mortality, MBD, dystonia muscularum deformans, childhood autism, and other probably organic illnesses. The higher than expected frequency of organic stigmata in patients suggests an organic etiology: factors such as 42 percent of patients with organic signs on the Bender-Gestalt test, 68 percent with overall ratings of organicity on psychological testing, 22.8 percent with left handedness or ambidexterity, 57.1 percent with soft signs of neurological abnormality, 46.8 percent (about 25 percent of adults and 71 percent of children) with EEG abnormalities, and 57.9 percent with signs or symptoms of MBD. Many of these abnormalities are similar to those found in children with signs and symptoms of MBD. The sex ratio is similar and a number of patients in both groups become asymptomatic with maturational development. The low prevalence of Tourette syndrome in the population suggests a specific physiological factor since most people do not respond to psychological, social or cultural stress with Tourette syndrome.

The differential and greater success of treatment with a class of drugs having similar biochemical characteristics (antipsychotic drugs which are strong dopamine blockers such as haloperidol and pimozide) supports an organic etiology.

Genetic factors in tics and Tourette syndrome are strongly implicated in some families. Torup (1962) reported that in a random sample of forty-two children without tics in a pediatric clinic, ten had a family member with tics. Of eight children with tics, four had a family member with tics. In three retrospective studies of 513 patients with tics (Zausmer, Torup, Corbett et al.), 24.8 percent to 29.4 percent had a family member with tics.

Shapiro et al. (1978) reported 34.5 percent of 139 patients with Tourette syndrome had a history of tics in various family members. Tourette syndrome itself has been found in 30 of about 500 families by us. Eldridge et al (1977) report a high percentage of motor or vocal tics or both in families of Tourette patients.

DIAGNOSTIC CONSIDERATIONS

Acute transient tic disorder of childhood is the most common tic condition in children. The symptoms are usually referred to as "habit tic" by pediatricians, and parents are advised not to pay attention to them as they will go away. The onset is during childhood or early adolescence and the duration of the tic symptoms is at least one month but not more than one year. The most common movement is an eye blink or a facial tic. However, the whole head, torso or limbs may be involved. In some individuals, one or more tics may be performed simultaneously, sequentially or at different times. In rare cases, vocal tics may be present. The symptoms can be voluntarily suppressed for minutes to hours and the intensity can vary over weeks or months.

Subacute tic of childhood or adolescence begins in childhood or early adolescence and is characterized by one or more motor movements or vocal tics which persist longer than one year but remit by or during adolescence. In some individuals more extensive symptomatology, involving multiple changing and fluctuating involuntary motor movements, noises or words, may occur. The symptoms and clinical course are indistinguishable from Tourette syndrome (the third tic condition) except for duration.

If the symptoms do not remit by or during adolescence and persist throughout life, the disorder is diagnosed as Tourette syndrome.

Chronic multiple tic or Tourette syndrome has its onset between two and fifteen years, similar to the age of onset for *transient tic disorder* and *subacute tic disorder*. The motor tics usually involve the head and frequently other parts of the body, torso, upper and lower limbs. Vocal tics are always present and may be multiple. They include various complicated sounds, words, or coprolalia (involuntary utterance of vulgar or obscene words), the last occurring in 60 percent of the cases. Other possible associated features of this disorder are echolalia (repetition of another's last words or phrases), palilalia (repetition of one's own last words or phrases), echokineseis (imitation of the movements of others), and mental coprolalia (thinking about curse words). The movements can be voluntarily suppressed for minutes to hours. The number, type, and intensity of symptoms varies over weeks or months and the illness is characterized by a fluctuating, waxing and waning, clinical course.

Typically the first symptom is a single motor tic, most frequently an eye blink. Initial symptoms also include tongue protrusion, squatting, sniffing, hopping, skipping, throat clearing, stuttering, sounds, words or coprolalia. In many patients the initial symptoms are multiple and include combinations of motor and vocal tics. New symptoms are added to, or replace, old symptoms over months or years. Tourette syndrome, unlike *subacute tic,* is chronic and lifelong.

TREATMENT

INDICATIONS

Given the self-limited nature of transient tics of childhood, treatment is usually not recommended. Parents are advised to continue to observe the tics. If the tics increase or become severe, the child should be reevaluated to see if treatment is warranted. Treatment is indicated for children with subacute tics or with Tourette syndrome when the symptoms cause psychosocial difficulty with peers, teachers, or others.

PSYCHOLOGICAL TREATMENT

Many physicians and investigators feel the tic symptoms are an expression of underlying psychological problems and recommend some form of psychological treatment. Shapiro et al. (1978) reviewed the effectiveness of psychological treatments for tics and Tourette syndrome. The treatments included psychoanalysis, psychotherapy, family therapy, hypnotherapy, isolation, sleep therapy, behavior therapy, and so on. The average improvement for all psychological modalities after six months was 9.2 percent. Psychotherapy, compared with other psychological modalities, had an average improvement rate of 12 percent. This improvement rate might be considered the rate of spontaneous improvement. Psychological treatment including psychotherapy was clearly ineffective as a primary treatment for tics and Tourette syndrome. Further, our studies have not been able to support the notion that psychological conflicts cause tics or Tourette syndrome. These disorders, in our opinion, have an organic or neurological etiology. Psychological treatment, as a primary treatment for tic symptoms, therefore is both ineffective and inappropriate. Psychotherapy may be indicated for emotional problems consequent to having tics or Tourette syndrome. Psychotherapy may also be indicated to manage behavior associated with learning disabilities or MBD, both conditions frequently also present in children with tics.

MEDICATION

The advent of psychochemotherapy in the 1950s led physicians to use most of the available drugs to treat tics and Tourette syndrome. The drugs included all of the sedatives, antianxiety drugs, anticonvulsants, antipsychotics, and antidepressants. Interest in haloperidol to treat tics and Tourette syndrome was stimulated by early reports of its successful use by Seignot, Caprini and Melotti, Challas and Brauer (1963), and Shapiro and Shapiro (1968).

Shapiro et al. (1978) reviewed the effectiveness of medication to treat tics and Tourette syndrome. Haloperidol, a butyrophenone type of antipsychotic medication, based on the result of this survey, is clearly the best treatment for tics and Tourette syndrome. The percent improvement for all patients on haloperidol was 89 percent compared to 48 percent for all other antipsychotic medications and 20 percent for other chemotherapeutic agents.

The effectiveness of haloperidol was further confirmed in the follow-up study by Shapiro et al. of eighty patients with Tourette syndrome, an average of 2.9 years after initial evaluation. Fifty-nine patients on haloperidol alone had an average decrease in symptoms of 80 percent. The longer patients were on medication, the greater the rate of improvement. Between seven and twelve months, the rate of improvement varied between 75 and 85 percent; between thirteen and forty-eight months, 80 to 89.9 percent; and between forty-nine and one hundred-three months, 90.5 to 99 percent. The dosage of haloperidol varies for each patient and it is generally advised that the dosage be titrated in very small increments every fifth day until adequate clinical response is achieved. To minimize extrapyramidal side effects, benztropine mesylate should be used. This regimen may avoid discouragement from the side effects that may occur in some patients. The major side effects of the medication are motor lethargy and motor restlessness which contribute to the difficulty in management of patients. It takes from three to six months for the dosage, effectiveness and side effects to become stabilized. Drug management, comprehensively described by Shapiro et al. (1978), should be handled by a physician skilled in the use of psychotropic medication. Although haloperidol is not approved by the FDA for use in children under twelve, with a signed and informed consent of the parents it can be used in the treatment of Tourette syndrome in this age group.

SUMMARY

Tics occur in approximately 5 to 23 percent of the population. The age of onset is between two and fifteen years with an average age of onset of seven years. More boys than girls are usually affected and the sex ratio is approximately 3:1.

Three major categories have been described. *Transient tic of childhood* characteristically has one or more simple motor tics and usually remits in one month to one year. Since the remission is usually spontaneous, treatment is not recommended.

The *subacute tic of childhood or adolescence* is indistinguishable from Tourette syndrome except that the symptoms remit before or during adolescence, whereas Tourette syndrome is chronic and lifelong. Treatment is indicated if the symptoms provoke ridicule and rejection from peers, neighbors, teachers, and even casual observers that may lead to psychosocial problems.

Chronic multiple tic or Tourette syndrome, a chronic and lifelong condition, is characterized by multiple motor and vocal tics, including coprolalia in about 60 percent of the cases and echo phenomena in about 35 percent. The symptomatology is often viewed as bizarre, disruptive, and frightening and early diagnosis and treatment are urgent if the child is to avoid the secondary psychosocial effects of this illness.

The clinical data indicate that haloperidol is the treatment of choice and that psychotherapy, behavior therapy, hypnosis, and other psychological modalities are ineffective treatments for tics and Tourette syndrome.

BIBLIOGRAPHY

Abuzzahab, F., and Anderson, F. (1973). Gilles de la Tourette's syndrome: international registry. *Minnesota Medicine* 56:492–496. The first article recording numbers of Tourette syndrome cases.

Challas, G., and Brauer, W. (1963). Tourette's disease: relief of symptoms with R1625. *American Journal of Psychiatry* 120:283–284. The first reported use of haloperidol for Tourette syndrome in the United States.

Eldridge, R., Sweet, R., Lake, C., Ziegler, M., and Shapiro, A. (1977). Gilles de la Tourette syndrome: clinical, genetic, psychological and biochemical aspects of 21 selected families. *Neurology* 27:115–124.

Lapouse, R., and Monk, M. (1964). Behavior deviations in a representative sample of children: variation by sex, age, race, social class, and family size. *American Journal of Orthopsychiatry* 34:436–446. Excellent epidemiological study.

Lucas, A. (1967). Gilles de la Tourette's disease in children: treatment with haloperidol. *American Journal of Psychiatry* 124:146–149.

Mahler, M. (1949). Psychoanalytic evaluation of tic in psychopathology of children: symptomatic tic and tic syndrome. *Psychoanalytic Study of the Child* 4/5:279–310.

Pringle, M., Butler, N., and Davie, R. (1967). *11,000 Seven Year Olds.* London: National Bureau for Cooperation in Child Care.

Shapiro, A., and Shapiro, E. (1968). Treatment of Gilles de la Tourette's syndrome with haloperidol. *British Journal of Psychiatry* 114:345–350.

Shapiro, A., Shapiro, E., Bruun, R., and Sweet, R. (1978). *Gilles de la Tourette Syndrome.* New York: Raven Press. A definitive volume on Tourette syndrome.

Torup, E. (1962). A follow-up study of children with tics. *Acta Pediatrica* 51:261–268.

Chapter 24

MENTAL RETARDATION

Stanley Turecki, M.D.

DEFINITION AND CLASSIFICATION

Mental retardation does not constitute a single diagnostic entity. Rather, the term refers to a group of individuals who, by virtue of impairments in their intellectual functioning and behavior, are handicapped in coping with their social environment. It is a complex and multidimensional problem which cannot be viewed from any single perspective, be it medical, educational, psychological, or social. Mental retardation is best understood not as an abnormality in the accepted clinical sense but as a developmental pathway which represents a variation of human functioning and behavior, and which should only be defined in broad terms. One widely accepted definition is offered by the American Association on Mental Deficiency (1973): "Mental retardation refers to significantly subaverage general intellectual functioning existing concurrently with deficits in adaptive behavior and manifested during the developmental period." This definition, like the one currently used by the American Psychiatric Association (1968) stresses the low measured intelligence (two or more standard deviations from the mean), the problems experienced by the individual in his efforts to adapt to his environment, and the developmental origin of the retardation (upper age limit of eighteen years), without attempting to address more specifically the questions of etiology or prognosis.

Based on this behavioral definition, the level of mental retardation can be classified on two dimensions. Intellectual functioning is measured by standardized tests, such as the Wechsler Intelligence Scale. The mean or average intelligence quotient is 100, and a standard deviation is 15 points. An IQ score of above 85 is regarded as normal. Borderline intelligence (IQ 70–84) is no longer classified as mental retardation. The four levels of retardation are Mild (IQ 55–69), Moderate (IQ 40–54), Severe (IQ 25–39), and Profound (IQ below 24). Deficits in adaptive behavior, the other necessary dimension for the identification of an individual as retarded, are generally much harder to define and categorize. Rating scales for measurement of adaptive behavior are available but poorly developed and less reliable than standardized intelligence tests. They should be used in conjunction with clinical observation and all available sources of information regarding everyday behavior. As with intellectual functioning, deficits in adaptive behavior are categorized according to four levels, in terms of an individual's ability to maintain himself independently and to meet the standards of social responsibility appropriate to his age and cultural group. The two dimensions of the behavioral classification may be combined in a table which identifies the developmental characteristics of the mentally retarded at various ages (Cytryn and Lourie 1975, p. 1161).

The biomedical approach to classification attempts to separate clinical subcategories of mental retardation according to etiology. The emphasis is on specifying an underlying disorder which is presumed to have caused the retardation. Such an approach is presented in the *Diagnostic and Statistical Manual (DSM-II)* of the American Psychiatric Association (1968). Its clinical usefulness is limited and it will probably be replaced in DSM-III by a multiaxial system of diagnosis and classification.

REVIEW OF LITERATURE

An extensive literature exists on the subject, drawn from the fields of psychiatry, psychology, special education, pediatrics, neurology, and sociology. The references listed in the bibliography provide a sampling of writings of particular interest to the psychiatrist. Selective annotation is offered as a guide.

INCIDENCE

It is estimated that 3 percent of the population of the United States—some six million people—are mentally retarded. The prevalence varies according to the age group. In early childhood it is only 1 percent because only the more severe forms are identified on routine examination. It is highest during the school years when the intellectual and social performance of the retarded sets them apart from other children. In adulthood the prevalence again drops to 1 percent, when many retarded individuals blend into the general population. The overwhelming majority, 85 percent of retarded people, are mildly retarded without significant organic pathology.

The prevalence of psychiatric disorder in the retarded is controversial. One view is that none are "simply retarded" (Webster; see Menolascino 1970) and at best show deviant personality development. This could, however, be seen as reflecting the deficits in adaptive behavior and thus as part of the mental retardation syndrome. The generally accepted view (Rutter 1975) is that mentally retarded children are much more likely than other children to develop emotional and behavioral disturbances, the incidence being put at around 35 percent. However, especially among the mildly retarded, the type of disorder is not distinctive. Childhood psychosis and the manifestations of organic brain syndrome are seen more commonly in the more severe forms of retardation.

ETIOLOGY AND DYNAMICS

There are some two hundred listed biological causes of mental retardation. Virtually any condition associated with developmental defect of the central nervous system can result in retardation. The insult may be genetically determined, congenital, or result from infectious, traumatic or toxic influences during the prenatal, perinatal, or postnatal periods. Comprehensive listings of the biomedical causes are readily available (see bibliography). Although these diseases have been extensively studied, e.g., Down's syndrome, inborn errors of metabolism, etc., they are responsible for only a small percentage of cases, usually among the more severely retarded. In the vast majority of the mildly retarded sociocultural factors are of paramount importance. The absence of known organic etiological factors and the frequent coexistence of retardation among members of the same family have

led to the use of the term "familial mental retardation."
Controversy exists as to the relative importance of genetic
factors versus environmental influences in this group with
modern opinion favoring the latter.

Mental retardation is such a broad concept that it is difficult to generalize about the psychodynamics. With this reser-
vation in mind the dynamics, particularly of the mildly retarded child, are best understood by viewing him as
developmentally arrested, vulnerable to discordance in his
significant relationships, and consequently at risk for regression and psychopathology. The deviant developmental pathway is evident in delayed or arrested patterns of maturation.
Retarded children are physiologically immature with primitive sensory and perceptual experiences reinforced by their
prolonged infancy. Milestones are delayed. Passivity, simplic-
ity of emotional and intellectual life, resistance to change,
and a limited capacity for abstraction and problem solving
are all characteristic. Personality development is also
affected. One finds prolonged dependency, an exaggerated
need for attachments, preservation of early determined patterns of object relatedness, considerable difficulties with
separation-individuation, and a generally immature personality configuration. Even under the best of circumstances a
retarded child places considerable strain on his family and in
particular on the mother-child relationship. Guilt, confusion,
disappointment, denial, unrealistic expectations, and some
degree of rejection are commonly seen in parents of retarded
children, especially when their own self-esteem is low or
when the general family equilibrium is precarious. As he
grows older the retarded child is increasingly exposed to
environmental demands for performance beyond his capacity. He falls further and further behind his peers, and is
frequently exposed to ridicule and scorn. Emotional devel-

opment is therefore not only delayed but fraught with hazard. The constitutional handicaps and interpersonal stresses result in poor ego defenses, and therefore in a chronic sense of failure, impaired self-image, frequent anxiety, and a generally poor adjustment with increased risk for psychopathology.

DIAGNOSTIC CONSIDERATIONS

"Mental retardation" is not a diagnosis. A careful, individual multidisciplinary investigation is always needed in order to arrive at a diagnostic statement meaningful to prognosis and therapeutic strategy. The medical and neurological work-ups are addressed to issues of etiology and identification of associated handicaps, particularly the manifestations of brain disease. Karyotyping, urine and blood studies, x-ray of the skull, and EEG are examples of specialized medical procedures. Evaluations of speech, hearing, and eyesight are requested when deficits in these areas are suspected. Psychological tests provide a standardized measure of intellectual functioning. However, an awareness of their drawbacks (e.g., only present functioning is measured, cultural bias) should lead to caution in interpreting the results. A psychoeducational profile is needed on every school-age child.

The psychiatrist, as a member of the multidisciplinary team, uses the above information to supplement his own unique contribution, the evaluation of the mentally retarded child as an individual dynamically interacting with his environment. A careful, comprehensive evaluation is needed, including assessment of the developmental level, social and adaptive behavior, individual psychodynamics, and both familial and extrafamilial environment. The direct examination of the mildly retarded child is similar in format to that of other children and relies primarily on verbal communication. With more severely handicapped children observation is more important. The end result is both a formal psychiatric diagnosis and a developmental profile of the child which identifies areas of strength as well as points of arrest or regression.

The differential diagnosis of mental retardation includes sensory handicaps such as deafness and blindness, brain syndromes with isolated handicaps, especially aphasia, and specific learning disability which if undiagnosed can superficially look like retardation. Children from culturally deprived homes may present with apparent retardation which is reversible with appropriate early stimulation. The most complex problem arises in attempting to differentiate the more severe forms of retardation from autism, brain damage, and the pseudo-defective type of childhood schizophrenia. All these children show bizarre and stereotyped behavior and function at a retarded level. From a prognostic point of view, distinguishing between them is unnecessary and the term "atypical child" avoids the need for such distinction.

TREATMENT

A variety of therapeutic interventions can have a significant impact on the development of the retarded child. They should always be related to the special needs of the retarded for considerable external stimulation, routines, structure, and relatedness to the meaningful persons in their lives. They all aim at minimizing the physical, emotional, social and intellectual disabilities of the retarded, and require careful individualized planning. Whenever possible the younger child should attend a regular nursery, although the more severely handicapped may have to be grouped. Special educational, vocational, and recreational programs are usually needed as he grows older. Correction or amelioration of associated handicaps is achieved through special interventions such as speech therapy, physical therapy, surgical procedures, and prescription of hearing aids or eyeglasses. Residential care should not be equated with chronic institutional placement which is only appropriate for a small number of the severely and profoundly retarded. The trend in recent years has been to development of supportive services for the retarded in the community. In this context, periods of short-term or intermediate placement away from home, in small, well-staffed, carefully organized facilities can be extremely valuable. Active parent organizations have played an important role in the development of a variety of much-needed programs devoted to keeping the retarded in the mainstream of life.

Psychiatric and related interventions are often needed. Parental guidance is of paramount importance. The period after the initial identification of a child as retarded is crucial. Initial grief reactions and subsequent rejection are common. Parents have to be helped through these early stages to the development of an accepting hopeful attitude, which in turn creates an optimum emotional climate for the child. In addition, a concrete, individualized program of counseling is formulated to educate parents as to the expected development of their retarded child so that their functioning and expectations can be appropriately modified. Direct interventions for the retarded child with emotional or behavioral difficulties are no different in principle from those used with other troubled children. Psychotherapy is of definite value. A mildly retarded child is very responsive to the therapeutic relationship, and can even express and deal with conflicts when he trusts the therapist. Play techniques are especially useful. The indications for psychotropic medication use and the choice of drug are the same as for other children and relate to the target symptoms. Tranquilizers, antidepressants, and stimulants all have a place. Barbiturates should be avoided. The mildly retarded child responds well to group therapy, and can often be placed in a heterogeneous group. Behavior modification techniques are of proven value for the more severely retarded, and are also useful with mildly retarded children who display maladaptive behavior. A good general principle applying to all direct psychiatric treatment is that of short-term interventions related to specific periods of developmental or interpersonal stress. Finally the psychiatrist can be very helpful in the role of consultant to special educational, residential, and community programs for the retarded.

DISCUSSION

Mental retardation is as much a part of a social process as it is a clinical entity. The identification of a child as retarded can unfortunately result in automatic labeling and make him subject to the expression of prejudice, stigmatization, and social control. Such general labeling is, of course, totally unwarranted and should be strongly resisted at every opportunity by all involved professionals. The mentally retarded are no more a homogeneous group of individuals than are the disturbed. Some 85% are mildly retarded and have much more in common with children of normal intelligence than with the severely retarded. Intelligence itself is not fixed and immutable. With appropriate, carefully planned, individualized interventions such children can be helped to achieve considerably improved or even normal intellectual functioning. The vast majority have the potential to live in the community with some measure of success and pleasure.

The psychiatric profession's involvement with the mentally retarded diminished during the era of psychoanalytic influence. Fortunately this trend has been reversed in the past decade. Even so, only a very small number of psychiatrists work directly with the retarded, and a system of prejudicial exclusion from psychiatric services is still operative, although less so than in the past. A realistic, yet hopeful and dynamic approach to the problems of the retarded is needed. Their deviant development, frequently associated with other handicaps, places particular importance on continuity of multidisciplinary care with programs planned from infancy through adulthood. A vigilant emphasis on continuous reevaluation addresses the issues of the heterogeneity and individuality of retarded children.

SUMMARY

Mental retardation is defined and classified according to dimensions of both intellectual functioning and social behavior. The prevalence is estimated at 3% of the general population. The etiology is multidetermined and the dynamics relate to the interaction between the developmentally arrested individual and his environment. Careful individual assessment is needed in order to formulate a plan of intervention. Both diagnosis and treatment rely on a multidisciplinary approach with an important role for the psychiatrist. The retarded are often discriminated against by society. Such attitudes should be strongly resisted by all professionals devoted to their care.

BIBLIOGRAPHY

American Academy of Child Psychiatry (1977). Mental retardation. *Journal of the American Academy of Child Psychiatry* 16:1–88. This special section consists of a collection of articles, with extensive references, for the psychiatrist occasionally involved with retarded children.

American Association on Mental Deficiency (1973). *Manual on Terminology and Classification in Mental Retardation,* 1973 Revision, H. Grossman, ed. Baltimore: Garamond/-Pridemark Press. A comprehensive statement on definition, classification and terminology.

American Psychiatric Association (1968). *Diagnostic and Statistical Manual of Mental Disorders,* second edition. Washington: A.P.A.

Cytryn, L. and Lourie, R. (1975). Mental retardation. In *Comprehensive Textbook of Psychiatry,* second ed., A. Freedman et al. eds. Baltimore: William and Wilkins Co. A comprehensive introduction to the subject.

Koch, R. and Dobson, J., eds. (1976). *The Mentally Retarded Child And His Family.* New York: Brunner/Mazel. A good presentation of biological etiological factors, and a multidisciplinary approach to diagnosis and treatment with particular emphasis on education and training.

Menolascino, F., ed. (1970). *Psychiatric Approaches To Mental Retardation.* New York: Basic Books. Overview of the major areas of psychiatric involvement. Diagnostic and treatment issues are highlighted. An extensive bibliography is offered.

Nichtern, S. (1974). *Helping the Retarded Child.* New York: Grosset and Dunlap. A developmental view of retardation with an extensive presentation of the spectrum of interventions.

Robinson, H. and Robinson, N. (1976). *The Mentally Retarded Child,* second edition. New York: McGraw Hill. Good general text. In depth discussion of intelligence, and a good review of psychotherapy with the retarded.

Rutter, M. (1975). Psychiatric disorder and intellectual impairment in childhood. *British Journal of Psychiatry.* 9: 344–348. Highlights the increased incidence of psychiatric disorder and outlines the kinds of difficulties.

Part IV

Psychopathology in a Social Frame

Chapter 25

IMPULSE AND CONDUCT DISORDERS

Norman Straker, M.D.

DEFINITIONS

Impulse Disorders can be defined as those disorders in which there is an inability to control the expression of impulses or their derivatives in thought; rather they are put into action immediately without adequate consideration for legal, moral, ethical, or personal implications or repercussions.

Conduct Disorders can be defined as those conditions in which the main problem lies in socially disapproved behavior. This behavior may take many forms. It can include delinquent acts such as stealing, playing truant, arson, serious mischief involving damage to other people's property, mugging, assault, or murder. It may also include nondelinquent acts such as defiance, lying, acting up in school, or not getting along with other children, as shown by bullying.

Disorders of impulse control, impulsivity, or conduct disorders are commonly encountered in a wide variety of forms and circumstances and are not limited to any specific diagnostic category. In fact, one can see disorders of impulse control in the personality disorders, the psychoses, the borderline conditions, some of the so-called "organic" brain disorders, and in the neuroses as part of an acting-out in a transference situation. In children, impulse control is in the process of being developed and has its own developmental line. Consideration of factors that play a role in the child's development of internal control of his impulses is important to the understanding of the failure of impulse control (conduct disorders) in children, adolescents, and adults.

There are important links in these various behaviors, so that children who manifest conduct disturbances in early school years often go on to become delinquent when they are older, a portent of future serious psychopathology (Robbins 1966).

The psychiatric classification has for some time made a distinction within the overall group of conduct disorders, between socialized delinquency and unsocialized aggressive behavior. This puts particular emphasis on the importance of of the subculture where the child was raised and lives. This idea is that the socialized delinquent is not emotionally disturbed and is relatively well-adjusted within his own group of friends and relatives. Such children typically come from bad neighborhoods. Hence, the group delinquent reaction of childhood or adolescence vs. the unsocialized aggressive reaction of childhood or adolescence. The latter group is defined in DSM II as characterized by overt or covert hostile disobedience, quarrelsomeness, physical and verbal aggressiveness, vengefulness, destructiveness, temper tantrums, solitary stealing, lying and hostile teasing of other children. It is implied that there is no psychiatric disorder in the group delinquent reaction of childhood or adolescence. This raises some questions, particularly about the youngster from this subculture who grows up and becomes a "good citizen" in contrast to a sibling or neighbor who continues the delinquent path.

REVIEW OF LITERATURE

Many factors have been explored and cited as important in the development of impulse disorders or conduct disorders. They fall into three major categories: psychological, biological, and sociological. In addition, there are some factors which clearly overlap. Numerous *psychological factors* have now been reported to be associated with the development of conduct disorders. The large number of these factors can be identified under the heading of *insufficient parenting*. These include broken homes, severe parental psychopathology, child abuse, child neglect, inconsistent punishment, and families with large numbers of children. The parents of delinquents, as compared to nondelinquents, also have a father who is much more likely to have been involved in criminality (Offord 1978). In addition, there is an association for boys between conduct disorders, reading disabilities, and aggressive temperaments.

Bowlby (1951) reviewed the literature up to 1951 and concluded that prolonged deprivation of maternal care for the young child can result in a lack of opportunity for forming an attachment to a mothering person, and thus can lay the groundwork for psychopathy. Although delinquency is often associated with prolonged neglect in early childhood, from retrospective studies a causal connection has not been clarified.

Children who come from large families with at least four to five children are also more likely to have conduct disorders. The exact reasons for this are unclear. However, large families are more likely to live in lower class urban neighborhoods, to be crowded, and to suffer financial difficulties and greater family discord than the average.

One of the more recent associations is between school failure, learning disabilities, and conduct disorder. About one-third of children with antisocial behavior have reading difficulties. The reasons for this are again not clear. Could it be that the same basic problems that led to reading disabilities also lead to conduct disorders? Or do the conduct disorders follow the failure at school because of resentment, depression, and so on? It has also been observed that children who from the outset tend to have a more aggressive temperament, continue to be more unpredictable, impulsive, and assertive (Rutter 1975).

What about *biological causes* for conduct disorders? The exact importance of biological factors is as yet unknown. At this time no biological factor has ever been proven to be a major cause of conduct disorder or delinquency. Hereditary factors have never been established. There was interest for a time in a relationship between body type (mesomorphism) and delinquency but this has not been borne out.

Epilepsy and violent behavior have long been and probably are erroneously equated. Studies of prisoners have concluded that the automatic behavior of temporal lobe epilepsy is a very rare explanation for crimes of epileptic patients. There have been reports of increased aggressive behavior in several rare metabolic disorders, including phenylketonuria, and Spielmeyer/Voyt and San Filipo Syndromes. Those with Down's Syndrome tend to show an increase in aggressive behavior in the third decade which is correlated with lesions confined to the hippocampal cortex. Again, these conditions are very rare and account for very few of those with impulse disorders (Goldstein 1974).

Some drugs, particularly alcohol and other depressants, such as barbiturates, can lessen impulse control. Hallucinogenic drugs and those that cause organic psychosis, such as "Angel Dust," are also reported to result in disturbance of behavior.

Levels of testosterone have also been hypothesized to be associated with aggressive behavior. At present this research is in the preliminary stage and conclusions await further study.

Sociological theories of conduct disorders tend to focus on the importance of being a group member and the peer pressure to commit antisocial acts. Sociologists also point to the importance of oppression and the inability of some individuals of the lower class groups to achieve goals of social status or material goods without resorting to social deviancy (Merton 1957).

There are also two descriptive disorders *whose cause is not clearly psychological or biological.* These are the hyperkinetic syndrome and the emotionally unstable personality.

The hyperkinetic syndrome, covered elsewhere in this book, is a behavioral syndrome which can include impulsivity and aggressive behavior. It has also been labeled minimal brain dysfunction although there is no morphological damage that can be observed in the brain. Cantwell (1978) in a review article reports that the available data indicates an association between hyperkinetic syndrome and antisocial disorders in childhood, adolescence, and adulthood. The reasons for the differential outcomes of hyperkinetic syndrome (i.e., antisocial vs. no antisocial disorder) are unclear.

The emotionally unstable personality is described by Klein (1969) as follows: "These patients are predominantly female adolescents whose mood disorder consists of short periods of tense, empty unhappiness, accompanied by inactivity, withdrawal, depression, irritability and sulking, alternating with impulsiveness, giddiness, low frustration tolerance, rejection of rules, and short-sighted hedonism." Klein treats them with lithium carbonate and reports good results.

INCIDENCE

The incidence of these disorders is not established. Statistics available for the incidence of juvenile delinquency and hyperkinetic syndrome are presented in other chapters.

ETIOLOGY AND DYNAMICS

It would seem most advantageous to briefly review some of the current theoretical constructs that attempt to explain the development of socially acceptable behavior. This is indeed a complicated process and one that is imperfectly understood.

In general, the following factors are believed to be of importance: an intact nervous system, "good enough mothering" or parenting, adequate models for identification, and the opportunity to experience both instinctual gratification and frustration, such that frustration can be tolerated. Excessive stimulation or frustration of both sexual and aggressive impulses undermine the child's developing ability to control his impulses.

The development of impulse control has been looked at by behaviorists as a series of learning experiences. Parents and peers are seen as reinforcing behaviors that would lead to the development of a socially accepted repertoire of behaviors. A smile, a word of praise are thought of as reinforcing. A frown, a harsh word, or punishment are thought to serve to extinguish unwanted behaviors (Barker 1972). However, it is clear that there are many other variables. The relationship that exists between parents (or surrogates) and a child will to a large extent determine whether the praise or punishment will be heeded.

The concept of the superego, introduced by Freud in 1923 in *The Ego and The Id,* was delineated as a set of functions resulting from the identification with and internalization of the conscious and unconscious attitudes of the parents. This set of internal functions is developed out of the needs of the child to retain the love of the parents. The functions of the superego have been divided into two major categories: those that prevent the expression of forbidden instinctual impulses, and those that represent the ideals and values of man. A sense of guilt serves to keep prohibited impulses in check, while the feeling of heightened self-esteem associated with approaching the ideals and values of the parents serves to direct the child's behavior toward standards that are acceptable to the parents.

Beres (1958) points out that disturbed parent-child relationships result in disturbed ego and superego development. In early childhood social compliance is achieved in response to fears of punishment or the dangers of the loss of the love of the parents. The term "sphincter morality," first used by Ferenczi, describes the child's compliance with the parents' demands for control of excretory functions. The child has to modify his instinctual expressions in order to avoid both the loss of love and punishment or criticism by the parent. The child uses the defenses of reaction formation and turning against the self to gain parental love and avoid criticism. These defenses as well as the child's use of the parents' prohibition which the child repeats, at first aloud, then to himself, are the forerunners of the superego.

The internal sense of wrongdoing, i.e., the sense of guilt, results from the passing of the oedipal stage when identifications are internalized with some degree of stability. Then the moral values and prohibitions of the parents are internalized. Beres points out that dissociations of superego function are

358 Clinician's Handbook of Childhood Psychopathology

found to some extent in all persons but are especially marked in those children who have had limited opportunity for satisfactory identification.

These difficulties were especially well illustrated by Aichhorn in "Wayward Youth" (1935). He described the "latent delinquent" as an individual who shows tendencies toward seeking immediate gratification first, and one who considers the satisfaction of instincts more important than gratification from relationships. Right and wrong is subordinated to gratification.

A more subtle defect in impulse control results from what Johnson (1949) termed sanctions for superego lacunae. These can be defined as lacks of superego functioning in certain circumscribed areas of behavior that are the results of the parents either consciously or unconsciously encouraging such behavior. Often the child's behavior may be encouraged unconsciously but the parents may be consciously offended by it and be punitive when it is manifested.

DIAGNOSTIC CONSIDERATIONS

A child's behavior should be evaluated initially from a *developmental* point of view in terms of personality and cognitive development of which age is only an approximate gauge. It would be erroneous for example to assign the diagnosis of conduct disorder to a young child under five if he took another child's toy or told an untruth.

As with any other evaluation, a careful history with emphasis on the pregnancy, delivery, development, and family life is imperative in arriving at a diagnosis. A history of neurological damage at birth through illness or injury or any focal or nonspecific signs of *neurological deficit* should lead to a full neurological evaluation with an EEG. Failures in attaining age-appropriate levels in development should alert the clinician to entertain the possibility of mental retardation. The Gesell Maturational Scales and psychological testing would aid in this diagnosis. Family history of hereditary neurological disease is important to the diagnostic work-up to rule out the onset of an *hereditary neurological disease.* A careful history of the youngster's ability to maintain interest in a learning experience or activity is necessary to rule out the attention deficit so frequently encountered in a child with *hyperkinetic syndrome.* Hyperactivity, learning difficulties, and poor peer relationships, in addition to the impulsive behavior, would lead one in the direction of considering hyperkinetic syndrome.

A history of recent events which might be traumatic for the youngster, such as a birth, death, illness, illness of parent, divorce, school failure, etc., might indicate a *reactive disorder* in response to an overwhelming experience. An inventory of coping mechanisms with particular emphasis on symptom formation could lead to a diagnosis of *neurosis,* or *personality disorder.*

The presentation of significant ego impairment would suggest the possibility of a *borderline condition* or *psychosis.*

A careful consideration of the cultural and peer pressure influences would be important in the diagnosis of the *group delinquent reaction of childhood or adolescence.* Finally, a history and psychiatric interview that reveals hostile disobedience, quarrelsomeness, physical and verbal aggressiveness, vengefulness, persistent temper tantrums, solitary stealing, lying and hostile teasing is diagnostic of an *unsocialized aggressive reaction of childhood or adolescence.*

TREATMENT

The treatment of the heterogeneous group of children and adolescents under this broad category of impulse disorders would depend both upon the diagnosis and the evaluation of family and dynamic factors.

In attempting to come to some understanding of the family and dynamic issues to be addressed as part of treatment planning, special attention should be paid to the following: the developmental level of the child, the quality of the relationship between parents and child, the parents' attitude and behavior regarding discipline, physical abuse or erratic punishment, the quality of parental supervision, a history of the tempermental style of the child, the quality of the early mother-child interaction, a history of prolonged separations during the early years, the type of relationship that existed with caretakers, and the psychopathology of parents and siblings. In addition, the manifest impulsive behavior of the youngster has to be evaluated in terms of its dangerousness to himself or others. All of these factors, as well as the diagnosis, have to be considered in formulating a treatment plan.

Those with neurological deficits or mental retardation would require remedial efforts to address the specific handicaps, as well as special education programs. Anticonvulsants for those with seizure disorders are indicated.

Those diagnosed as having hyperkinetic syndrome or minimal brain dysfunction should receive a trial of stimulants, such as methylphenidate, dextroamphetamine or pemoline. In addition, attention should be paid to remedial efforts to correct learning disabilities. Secondary psychological problems might require individual psychotherapy. The treatment modalities for the reactive behavioral disorders, neuroses, borderline conditions, or psychoses run the gamut from crisis intervention, medication, individual psychotherapy, child analysis, group psychotherapy, and family therapy to hospitalization or residential treatment.

The treatability of those diagnosed as group delinquent reactions of childhood and adolescence or unsocialized aggressive reactions is open to question. Any hope for treatment would depend on some recognition of a problem and some cooperative effort on the part of the individual and family.

DISCUSSION

The heterogeneous group of disorders under the heading of impulse disorders requires an holistic approach. The clinician, researcher, family court judge, or public policy planner should have some awareness that the manifestations of impulse disorders are only the symptoms of a large number of factors interacting with each other. The clinician who is often called upon by the family court, school, social agency or parents to advise in such cases must show a wide background of knowledge. He or she requires a thorough knowledge of the concepts of development, psychodynamic theory, neurology and the cultural contributions to personality formation. The researcher should be broadly based in his or her approach such that important variables are not neglected. The family court judge or public policy planner should be educated as to the complexity of factors involved in each individual case and how the same overt manifestations can be due to different factors, so that simplistic solutions based on global approaches like greater punishment or greater tolerance of impulsive acts, do not emerge.

A more rational approach to the problem for all those

concerned with the welfare of children and future generations involves the earliest possible diagnosis of children who are at risk for impulse disorders so there can be early intervention. A much greater effort should be directed toward educating the public and prospective parents as to the needs of children and good child-rearing practices. Courses on parenting and child-rearing could easily become part of the high school curriculum. Further research is also required to more carefully delineate the various risk factors and how they interact with maturational, developmental, familial, and societal stresses to produce childhood syndromes. Follow-up evaluations of the various psychological, sociological and biological interventions are also required.

SUMMARY

Some of the factors that are important in the child's development of impulse control have been presented. In general, they include an intact nervous system, "good enough mothering," adequate models for identification, and an opportunity to experience both instinctual gratification and frustration such that delay of instinctual gratification can be tolerated.

The concept of psychobiological and psychosocial vulnerabilities to the varying familial, maturational, developmental, and societal stresses seems to be a most useful point of view from which to understand the manifestations of psychopathology as they unfold in children and adolescents. It also provides a framework for the assessment of children at risk and for possible interventions.

BIBLIOGRAPHY

Aichhorn, A. (1935). *Wayward Youth.* New York: Viking Press.

Barker, P. (1972). Emotional problems of childhood and adolescence—antisocial behavior. *British Medical Journal* 3: 34–36.

Beres, D. (1958). Vicissitudes of superego functions and superego precursors in childhood. *Psychoanalytic Study of the Child* 13:324–351.

Bowlby, J. (1951). *Maternal Care and Mental Health.* Geneva: WHO Monograph.

Cantwell, D. (1978). Hyperactivity and antisocial personality. *Journal of the American Academy of Child Psychiatry* 17:252–261.

Freud, S. (1923). The ego and the id. *Standard Edition* 19.

Goldstein, M. (1974). Brain research and violent behavior. *Archives of Neurology* 30:1–35.

Johnson, A. (1949). Sanctions for superego lacunae of adolescents. In *Searchlights on Delinquency,* ed. K. Eissler, pp. 225–245. New York: International Universities Press.

Klein, D., and Davis, J. (1969). *The Diagnosis and Treatment of Psychiatric Disorders.* Baltimore: Williams and Wilkins.

Merton, R. (1957). *Social Theory and Social Structure.* New York: Free Press.

Offord, D., Allen, N., and Abrams, N. (1978). Parental psychiatric illness, broken homes and delinquency. *Journal of the American Academy of Child Psychiatry* 17: 224–238.

Robbins, L. (1966). *Deviant Children Grow Up.* Baltimore: Williams and Wilkins.

Rutter, M. (1975). *Helping Troubled Children.* New York: Plenum Press.

Chapter 26

DELINQUENCY

William Krakauer, M.D.

DEFINITION

Juvenile delinquency is a designation covering a broad range of possible psychiatric diagnoses and behaviors which have in common two things: (1) an age limitation roughly from latency through adolescence, and (2) the quality of the response it evokes in others. In the *Psychiatric Dictionary* Hinsie and Shatzky state that "in psychiatry the term refers to minor offenses against the culture with which the individual is expected to conform. The psychiatric use of the term is not essentially different from its legal use. Delinquency is an offense created by a minor. It includes such acts as truancy, undue pugnacity, vandalism, nomadism, overt sex practices, lying, stealing, incendiarism, etc." Eissler (1949) in the introductory chapter to *Searchlights on Delinquency* defines delinquency in terms of inner conflict.

Delinquency—and this is the first point of our definition—refers to behavior, thoughts and feelings that tend to infringe upon values. In human personalities these values find representation

to a varying degree of intensity, consciousness and awareness . . . The adolescent, however, who seemed to have integrated social demands and devoted himself assiduously to his
studies, but then abruptly throws to the winds his accustomed
way of life and starts to drink or commits a theft, has become
dissocial. He had accepted a representation of a value system
but it was temporarily thrown out of working order by the impact of a strong instinctual demand. The instinctual demand, in
this instance, had to work its way through strongly opposing
forces; he became delinquent not because of the absence of
represented values, but in spite of them. . . .

    The second set of defining factors in the phenomenon of
delinquency concerns aggression. . . . In the delinquencies, aggression is always directed toward the outside. . . . Since they can
manifest themselves socially only in that sphere where human
actions reach reality they are dependent on the structure of that
reality. Therefore the contents of the delinquencies are correlated to the variety of the social realities in which they occur.

This last aspect of Eissler's definition leads to the definition
of Lewis and Balla who became involved in working with
delinquency through a clinic attached to a juvenile court.
Their definition begins from the point of social impact (Lewis
and Balla 1976): "The terms 'delinquent' and 'delinquency'
will be used to designate children and children's behaviors
that have officially come to the attention of the juvenile court.
They will not be used for children or acts which, while similar
in quality to those officially termed delinquent, have never
reached the juvenile court's attention."

REVIEW OF LITERATURE

Essentially the modern literature on delinquency begins with *Wayward Youth* by Aichhorn, first published in German in 1925, and in an American edition in 1935. This was a real beginning, in that it was the pioneering attempt to understand and treat adolescents with antisocial behavior according to psychoanalytic principles. Aichhorn was obviously a charismatic and intuitive figure as therapist and writer, and later as a leader of the psychoanalytic community. He produced an immensely readable, stimulating and inspiring account of his precedent-breaking efforts. Indirectly, he was also responsible for another major book in the field, *Searchlights on Delinquency* (1949), which appeared in honor of Aichhorn's seventieth birthday. The book includes articles by most of the important psychoanalytic writers on delinquency up to that time, including the editor, Kurt Eissler, Szurek, Bender, and Redl, and contains the classical paper by Adelaide Johnson, "Sanctions for Superego Lacunae of Adolescents." Redl is the author of important books on dynamics and treatment of antisocial adolescents: *The Aggressive Child* (1957) which contains two previous books, *Children Who Hate* and *Controls From Within.* His books deal at great length with the phenomenology of the delinquent population with which he has worked, expanding our understanding of the subtle and multifaceted ego disturbances involved in antisocial behavior, and presenting his techniques of treating his patients, both through individual therapeutic contact and by working through their environment. Lewis and Balla (1976), approaching the subject via their experience with a Children's Court population, deal with the diagnostic problems of this population. Although such cases are bound together by a significant dimension of behavior and societal response, from a psychiatric point of view there is a considerable amount of diagnostic diversity and, of particular significance to the authors, the "delinquent" behavior may be an expression of, and a mask for, major and often treatable psychiatric and/or neurological disorders.

INCIDENCE

The 1976 Uniform Crime Reports showed that arrests of males under eighteen constituted 23.7 percent (1,387,424) of the nearly six million males apprehended that year. Females under eighteen were 34 percent (380,622) of the slightly over one million females arrested.

ETIOLOGY AND DYNAMICS

In speaking of juvenile delinquency we are talking about a cluster of behaviors which can occur alongside, or as an expression of, other psychiatric or neurological conditions. These behaviors seem to have certain factors in common regardless of concomitant or underlying disease. They are an expression of alloplastic personality organization, characterized by techniques for discharging aggression outward, rather than dealing with frustrating experiences through inner conflicts and/or symptom formation. The ability to do this presupposes in the delinquent a weakness of the superego which permits antisocial behavior with an absence of, or with minimal, guilt and inhibition. The source and nature of this superego deficit is strikingly delineated by Johnson in her theory that superego lacunae can develop specifically in the context of an unconscious parental wish to have certain of their unconscious drives acted out by their child. Redl also has expanded our knowledge of the subtleties of distortion and pathology in the ego of many delinquents. More recent studies have revealed the importance also of parental deprivation, not only the more generally known effects of affectional deprivation by the mother but also the significance, particularly during the oedipal period (ages four to seven), of paternal deprivation, occurring both with frank absence of the father, and with emotional unavailability of the father even if physically present. However as Lewis and Balla (1976) point out most convincingly, the psychic and psychophysiological aggressive drive energies discharged in delinquency may come not only from neurotic and depressed personalities but also from psychotically disorganized minds or from neurological disorganization. In their study they felt that a significant number of delinquent children manifested subtle evidence of psychomotor epilepsy, narcolepsy and other inborn and/or congenital neurological vulnerabilities. Their experience also indicated to them the importance of parental criminality and parental mental illness (with a significantly higher incidence of diagnosed schizophrenia).

DIAGNOSTIC CONSIDERATIONS

Aichhorn and Eissler describe a delinquent personality disorder characterized by a disturbance in superego development relating to disturbed object relationships in the preoedipal period, leading to the formation of an alloplastic behavior disorder. Thus, in their sense, delinquency is diagnostically on a parallel with neurosis and psychosis. This has not come into common usage. Actually, from a psychiatric point of view the diagnosis of delinquency has been complicated by the introduction of the categories of psychopathic personality and, more recently, sociopath. Although at first glance these terms would seem to have some descriptive relevance, the nihilistic "bad seed" implication that they carry, linking a superficially considered pattern of behaviors to a presumed inborn irrevocable state, seems to put them more into the area of angry, moralistic fantasy than objective scientific evaluation. From a practical point of view, however, the importance of accurate diagnosis may not relate to the question of treatment of the delinquent behavior per se but to other more readily treatable difficulties which may be underlying. Such difficulties range from the psychogenic-developmental (whether preoedipal or oedipal) to the physiologic-organic (such as psychomotor epilepsy, narcolepsy) to the psychoses.

It is interesting in another connection that the narrowing of diagnostic categories to young people who have actually been before the court, suggests a particular psychodynamic subgrouping in relation to the need among many delinquents of this category to provoke a hostile and ultimately punitive response from the world around them.

TREATMENT

First of all, in a general way, treatment of a juvenile delinquent obviously must be directed toward any underlying contributory psychiatric or neurological conditions. It goes without saying that if a delinquent child is found to be reacting to, among other things, the disorganizing internal effect of an epileptic condition, or of a psychosis, etc., then appropriate treatment should be directed to that. With relation to the delinquent personality disorder and its disturbances in ego and superego functioning, Eissler (1949), following Aichhorn, sees treatment essentially along psychoanalytically oriented lines. "If the genetic history of the delinquent is consistently submitted to analysis in terms of Freud's dynamic and structural concepts, then appropriate therapeutic measures can be evolved . . . Such analysis would ascertain what therapeutic procedures are required in order to enable the delinquent's personality structure to continue its growth and integration. It would find the way to release the development of individuality at those points where a series of severe traumata have either stunted the growth process or driven the formative energies into deviate behavior patterns." Eissler speaks also of the need to establish a "tight, fool-proof attachment between the psychoanalyst and the delinquent in the shortest possible time." In the same article he also refers to countertransference problems, particularly in avoiding being provoked to anger; and being able to predict the patient's behavior well enough to forestall relapses into manifest delinquency, if possible. Most authors stress the importance of developing an intense relationship between the patient and therapist, made particularly difficult because of the problem the delinquent personality has in dealing with frustration within a relationship. Johnson and Szurek (1952) emphasized the value of psychotherapeutic work involving not only the delinquent child but the parents as well and, in the case of some very young delinquents, involving only the parents. Redl's work, mainly in a group residential setting, led to the development of techniques not only for understanding and treating various subtleties of ego deficit on an individual basis, but also for group and team collaborative therapies.

DISCUSSION AND SUMMARY

It is now over a half century since Aichhorn first published *Verwahrloste Jugend* in Vienna. Although we have continued to gain in our knowledge of delinquency since then, much remains psychiatrically unknown and legally unresolved. The behaviors we call delinquent are defined in relation to the social matrix they offend, can be caused by varying combinations of psychodynamic, psychosocial and neurological factors, and are best understood through psychoanalytic formulations. They remain the object of social and legal inconsistency; are still widely subject to diagnostic confusion and error; and continue to present the frustrating paradox that the successful treatment techniques developed around our psychoanalytic and medical understanding are still largely unavailable, unapplied, unsought, by those dealing with these behaviors and by those suffering from them.

BIBLIOGRAPHY

Aichhorn, A. (1935). *Wayward Youth.* New York: Viking. A classic book viewing delinquent behavior from a psychoanalytic viewpoint, still stimulating and immensely readable.

Eissler, K. (1949). Some problems of delinquency. In: *Searchlights on Delinquency,* ed. K.R. Eissler, pp. 3–25. New York: International Universities Press. The keynote article in this commemoration volume sets forth Aichhorn's theory and therapeutic technique with great clarity and succinctness. This volume is another cornerstone in psychoanalytic readings on delinquency.

Johnson, A. (1949). Sanctions for superego lacunae of

adolescents. In *Searchlights on Delinquency,* ed. K.R. Eissler, pp. 225–245. New York: International Universities Press. Also in *Childhood Psychopathology,* ed. S.I. Harrison and J.F. McDermott, pp. 522–531. New York: International Universities Press. Another fundamental study where the implications of her insights go far beyond the area of delinquency per se. It demonstrates the connection between repressed parental wishes and a child's acting out.

Johnson, A., and Szurek, S. (1952). The genesis of antisocial acting out in children and adults. *Psychoanalytic Quarterly* 21:323–343. An important early paper emphasizing the need for collaborative treatment of the delinquent child and his parents.

Lewis, D. and Balla, D. (1976). *Delinquency and Psychopathology.* New York: Grune and Stratton. An important, concerned book, which views delinquency as a multi-caused medico-socio-legal entity. Valuable, thought-provoking, with an extensive bibliography.

Redl, F. and Wineman, D. (1957). *The Aggressive Child.* Glencoe, Illinois: The Free Press. Combining two books previously issued separately, *Children Who Hate* and *Controls From Within,* it presents Redl's influential approach to psychodynamics and treatment.

Chapter 27

THE LAW AND CHILD PSYCHIATRY

Jesse M. Hilsen, M.D.

THE COURT SYSTEM AND PSYCHIATRY

In recent years the relationship between psychiatry and the law has become a topic of increased importance. Broadly defined, forensic psychiatry involves the interplay of psychiatry and law. A number of factors account for the increased prominence of legal psychiatry. The seemingly unparalleled increase in violence and the use of psychiatric explanation to understand aberrant behavior, as well as emphasis on rehabilitation of offenders, have all increased the use of forensic psychiatry in courts during the past decade. Furthermore, there has been a greater interest in forensic child psychiatry concepts associated with the common law doctrine of *parens patriae* (where government assumes the obligation to intervene in the lives of all minors who might become community problems). Advocates for social reform have also used psychiatric information and expert testimony to substantiate requests for changes in the law.

FAMILY-JUVENILE COURT SYSTEM

Involvement of governmental agencies with the family unit has varied from the most voluntary types of counseling to the most authoritarian forms of social control. In the not too distant past, legal manifestations of problems arising from family or domestic relationships were handled by separate courts with established jurisdiction over one or more types of family matters. Fragmentation and inadequate resolution were results of this system. In the early 1960s New York State as well as other areas throughout the country chose to relocate most of the family-based legal problems in a new family court system, replacing the bewildering assortment of courts which previously had jurisdiction. It was hoped that a newly reorganized family court system could provide greater understanding of the problems and more consistent, humane, and just treatment for troubled families. The family court, as it is presently constituted in New York State, is essentially the result of a combination of two areas of the law which had separate though related development—juvenile courts and domestic relations courts.

JUVENILE COURTS

The juvenile courts ideologically are older than the domestic relations courts, in that the earliest roots in the English common law concept indicate that a child below the age of seven was incapable of forming the criminal intent necessary to be found legally guilty of a crime. This concept in more recent times has been extended to include children up to fourteen or sixteen years of age. Furthermore, the common law doctrine of *parens patriae* obliges the courts to intervene in the lives of all minors who might become community problems. Juvenile antisocial behavior compelled the workers in this earlier system to recognize that some special forms of treatment were necessary for these youngsters. This recognition led the criminal courts to develop segregated detention and special procedures for children accused of crime. The multiplicity of problems encountered led to the development in the early 1950s of formal psychiatric clinics associated with many juvenile courts. Initially, these court-related psychiatric services were limited to diagnostic studies of visibly disturbed individuals and those who presented histories of emotional and mental disturbances. These clinics also provided personnel to consult with judges and probation officers. The presence of these behavioral scientists in the court system accelerated the development of entirely separate noncriminal, judicial tribunals in the handling of juvenile misconduct. The theory was that a nonpunitive family court type of system with specialized procedures and services provided through the courts would help troubled youngsters to reorient themselves toward a more socially useful and acceptable manner of behavior. In addition to the juvenile court's handling children who violated the laws of the community (juvenile delinquents), it also handled youngsters who could not be controlled by their parents, or whose parents refused to care for them. The latter group of children are currently known as "persons in need of supervision" (PINS). As early as the mid-1930s juvenile court hearings were changed from criminal hearings to noncriminal type hearings.

DOMESTIC RELATIONS COURTS

Prior to the development of a family court type of system in various parts of the country in the 1960s, it was not uncommon for disputes between husbands and wives to be treated in the same legalistic fashion and be comingled with offenders accused of gambling, theft, and robbery. Family members appearing in these various courts frequently had other family members appearing in the juvenile court system. These separate, fragmented, ill-prepared and ill-equipped courts clearly could not deal adequately with the complex problems of families and juveniles. The adversary system of the law has traditionally involved pitting one side against another with the fundamental aim of achieving "justice." Sometimes judicial results were not always related to scientific psychological facts. The development of the family court was an attempt to minimize the adversary aspects of the system and maximize factual and psychological input for the benefit of the involved children and families.

FAMILY COURT SYSTEM

Special family courts were created so that procedures could be developed for aiding youngsters and their families. Since the situation and the needs of each individual and family are unique, the concept of individual justice came to the fore. The guidelines for the family court in this country became "to help rather than punish, to rehabilitate rather than reject." Criminal court terminology was altered. A trial, a defendant, and a prosecutor became known respectively as a hearing, a respondent, and a petitioner.

Since the goal of the court was to help rather than punish, initially procedures were created which removed many of the individual safeguards available in the criminal courts. There was little, except the judge's concept of fairness and justice, to prevent a youngster from being labeled a juvenile delinquent based on incompetent hearsay or gossip. Gradually the concept of a law guardian (legal counsel) developed to provide for the protection of the rights of those parties before the court.

THE FAMILY COURT PROCESS

There are essentially three parts of the family court process. Introduction to the court processes starts at intake where an information clerk does the first screening to determine if the age, geographic area, and other data establish jurisdiction. The cases are then assigned to an intake officer attached to the court whose job it is to see whether the case can be diverted from the court to other appropriate community services. If the individual's or family's case is adjusted—settled and referred to an appropriate community agency—then no further court action is necessary. If a potentially helpful solution cannot be worked out on intake, the individual or family may *petition,* that is, request access to the court for a court hearing. In a petition, one party accuses another party of having committed an unlawful act. The second stage of the court process is *fact-finding.* This is a hearing before a judge to determine whether the respondent (person accused of an act) did the act or acts alleged in the petition—e.g., for a person in need of supervision, to determine whether the respondent is habitually truant, incorrigible, ungovernable, or disobedient and beyond the control of his parents or guardian. If the judge feels that the allegations have been proved beyond a reasonable doubt, he makes a finding of fact indicating that the respondent (accused) was responsible for the act he was accused of committing. This is similar to a criminal court finding in which an adult defendant is found guilty. The last stage in the court process is the *dispositional hearing.* During this hearing all data on the child, his parents, school reports, other social agency data and psychiatric reports, if requested, are to be submitted to the judge together with recommendations for disposition best designed to help the child and also protect the community. This is the stage of family court proceedings in which the psychiatrist has traditionally offered assistance in finding the most appropriate, least offensive disposition.

Currently, the juvenile justice system in New York State and elsewhere in the nation, is in a state of flux. The problems characterizing earlier court systems (fragmented and compartmentalized delivery of service and lack of adequate and detailed information about families and children) are still present despite repeated restructuring. The increased incidence of crime and violence committed by adolescents has most recently resulted in demands for changes in the court system and for treating adolescents as criminals. As the family courts have been swamped by a multitude of the most troubled and deprived individuals, the appeal of simplistic solutions has intensified, although history has shown that solutions to serious problems cannot be achieved by patchwork changes. Joseph Noshpitz, a former president of the American Academy of Child Psychiatry, stated "all of the money, all the good work of any one part of the system will come to naught if there are not the necessary elements present to handle a full range of problems which arise."

THE UNIQUE ROLE OF THE CHILD PSYCHIATRIST AS AN EXPERT WITNESS

At the outset, it should be pointed out that there is a similarity between psychiatry and the law, in that both deal with human behavior and motivation and each attempts to exert some corrective influence. Despite these similarities between psychiatrists and members of the legal profession, there is often an air of suspicion and distrust when the two disciplines interact. Psychiatry stresses the welfare of the individual patient. It views human behavior as determined in great part by unconscious forces. In contrast, the court, while guarding the individual's rights, is primarily concerned with the general welfare of society. To make the individual legally responsible for his acts, the court has established a concept of the individual's free will and choice. Furthermore, the law is dynamic and capable of changing, but it does rely heavily on precedent and tradition. This at times stands in stark contrast to the speculative nature of psychiatric work. These differences are not irreconcilable as long as it is recognized that the court serves as a special kind of social agency where psychosocial methods can be applied toward the amelioration and control of highly destructive antisocial behavior. The court system can operate as a last resort to help distressed families with emotional problems, while also protecting society from disturbed and antisocial behavior. The psychiatrist tries to prevent or ameliorate permanently crippling effects of rigidly administered punishment.

THE ART OF COURTROOM TESTIMONY: METHODS OF MAINTAINING CREDIBILITY IN THE COURTROOM

Many physicians consider testifying an imposition, a waste of time which can be better spent in patient care. It may also represent a minor financial burden or require extra hours catching up on canceled appointments. But often, it is your patient who needs your help in obtaining the justice he deserves. That help is as much a part of total patient care as the other services you provide him.

Being a good witness is an art. The challenge of the art lies in presenting your expert medical opinions to the court with maximal effectiveness and efficiency. Accomplishing this requires adequate preparation and effective presentation.

Pretrial preparation begins the day you are contacted by the patient or lawyer and requested to testify or consult on the case. The psychiatrist or behavioral scientist must attempt to review or learn as many of the material facts of the case as possible. He should also discuss with the lawyer those questions which will be asked and those that should be asked to allow presentation of relevant facts. Where courtroom testimony is involved, it is not uncommon for the consultant to be requested to provide a brief written report for the case folder, as free as possible from technical language. Whenever possible, this report should contain a clinical diagnosis, a dynamic formulation of the case, and provisional recommendations as well as answers to the questions originally formulated by those seeking the consultant's services. After the evaluation, a conference between the consultant and person requesting the consultation (usually the patient's lawyer), plus any other parties whose involvement might be helpful, should be arranged prior to courtroom testimony. It is desirable that you formulate your professional opinions concerning the case prior to this conference. At this meeting you and the patient's lawyer will discuss the most effective ways of presenting your professional views. During this meeting you can be helpful to the lawyer in providing him with unambiguous lay terminology which can be used by him in the court room examination in asking you questions. Similarly, he will give you indications as to how, based on courtroom procedure, he can best question you so that your testimony is presented most effectively. Prior to courtroom appearance, it is essential that you be prepared to support your contentions and thoughts about the case with appropriate medical references. However, because of special rules of law which allow such statements only when specifically asked for by the opposition counsel, you must not quote the names of the specific references. It is advisable to have the medical records and helpful notes available to you during your court room testimony, but presenting your testimony extemporaneously is the most effective method of testifying. Objections, deviations from expected routine, and cross examination are the rule in the courtroom. If you expect these events and are able to maintain your composure during them, your testimony will be most effective. Lastly, prior to testifying, think how your testimony is vulnerable. Ask yourself whether there is anything that can be challenged which you would find difficult to substantiate. You will be more secure in the courtroom situation if your words are well chosen and your statements could be made to a group of co-professionals without embarrassment.

Four major criteria should be fulfilled in effective answers to courtroom questions. (1) Statements should be true, to the best of your knowledge. Once again, choose words carefully and don't overstate your point of view. (2) Avoid answering with data irrelevant to the question. Medical testimony is often confusing to nonmedical people. As a consequence, only include information called for, to avoid confusing your listeners. (3) Be concise and understandable. Most questions on cross examination can be answered concisely in a single sentence. If you are testifying and your answers are consistently confusing or verbose, cross examination may degenerate into your being required to answer with yes or no statements. Thus, more lengthy answers may be disallowed when you need them most. (4) Be unbiased. Although lack of bias may be difficult to achieve in some cases, present the one-sided evidence in as neutral a manner as possible. Do not be hostile toward the opposition. Resist the temptation to be condescending or to openly display resentment of a challenge to your medical opinion. If you are wrong about something, or do not know the answer to a question, admit it. Similarly, avoid jocularity, informality, mannerisms, aloofness, or any other potentially irritating characteristics.

If you follow these four rules, you will almost never be

subjected to a traumatic cross examination. If you do encounter such a situation, it is essential for you to maintain
your composure. Your professional credentials can only be
enhanced by your refusal to become involved in inappropriate conflict. In summary, a good expert witness will be adequately prepared and will effectively present his professional
opinions.

Some operational definitions of medicolegal terms are
contained in the glossary at the end of this chapter.

FREQUENTLY ENCOUNTERED TYPES OF FORENSIC CHILD
PSYCHIATRY CASES

The child psychiatrist is most commonly involved in the
following categories of cases: marital discord and divorce,
custody and visitation, foster care, adoption, child abuse and
neglect, juvenile delinquency, persons in need of supervision, determinations of dangerousness, and commitment
proceedings.

In 1974, the parents of more than 1,000,000 children were
divorced—twice the number of a decade ago. One American
family in six is now being raised by a single parent. Concurrently, we are seeing a significant rise in teenage drug abuse,
alcoholism, suicide, juvenile delinquency and crime, and a
rise in the rate of illegitimate births among adolescents. Although all of these problems are found with greater frequency among the poor and nonwhite, middle class families
of today are approaching the level of social disorganization
that characterized the lower income family of the 1960s. In
addition, with 51% of American mothers with school age
children working outside the home, there has been a shift of
child care to outside individuals and agencies and away from
significant family members. Sometimes the child psychiatrist
can be of help in efforts to keep the family intact, by arrang-

ing for marital counseling or family therapy. Failing this, he can endeavor to minimize the detrimental effects which often occur in broken families.

PROFESSIONAL LIABILITY AND REGULATION

A variety of complex medical and legal issues have arisen related to the patient's rights movement. The movement to protect individual liberty at times may contravene the right of the individual to receive needed and appropriate treatment. The legislation and caselaw decisions which will permit protection of individual rights while safeguarding the receiving and giving of psychiatric treatment are still in the process of being developed. Some significant medicolegal issues will be discussed below.

RIGHT TO TREATMENT

Several New Jersey courts have ruled that patients involuntarily committed are entitled to receive appropriate and effective treatment. If the therapy is unavailable within the state system, then placement of the patient in an out-of-state center to receive therapy, is indicated.

Mental patients denied their right to treatment, who are not dangerous to themselves or society and are "capable of surviving in the community with the help of willing and responsible family or friends," are entitled to their release from psychiatric facilities.

RIGHT TO REFUSE MEDICATION

The courts have also been involved in trying to sort out whether voluntary and involuntary hospital patients have a constitutional right to refuse psychotropic medication. Some courts have prohibited hospital staff from forcibly medicating patients "except where there is a serious threat of . . . extreme violence, personal injury or attempted suicide."

RIGHT TO SPECIAL EDUCATION

Law suits have been initiated which are designed to force states to provide disabled children with free appropriate education geared to their special needs. Various state courts have ordered that special educational services be provided for learning-disabled students.

RIGHT TO PROTECTION FROM HARM

The right to protection from harm while the patient is in an institution was developed and utilized in the Willowbrook case (*N.Y.S. ARC and PARISI* v. *Carey-E.D., N.Y.,* 1975), where the Court entered an opinion that these mentally retarded residents had a constitutional right (Eighth and Fourteenth Amendments) to protection from harm. As a result of this lawsuit, institutional standards and procedures were set up to insure the constitutional right to protection from harm for Willowbrook's residents and members of this class (group). A recent additional step in judicial enforcement of court orders has been for the court to appoint monitoring bodies as ombudsmen empowered to hear complaints, conduct investigations, monitor activities, and make reports and/or recommendations to the court.

ABORTION AND PATIENT RIGHTS

In some states the principle of *parens patriae* has been invoked to authorize abortion for severely retarded pregnant females. In the past sterilization laws have been abused. Legislation on involuntary abortion with procedural standards and safeguards is needed.

POWER TO COMMIT

In *O'Connor* v. *Donaldson,* (422 U.S. 563, 1975), the Supreme Court outlined some of the limits of the power of a state to confine a person for mental illness. In the landmark case of *Wyatt* v. *Stickney* (M.D. Ala., 1972) and the subsequent case of *Wyatt* v. *Hardin* (M.D. Ala., Feb. 1975, July 1975) in Alabama, a federal court for the first time ordered implementation of the constitutional right to treatment for institutionalized patients. The latter case set forth the minimum constitutional requirements (administrative procedures and safeguards) for the employment of aversive conditioning, electroconvulsive therapy, psychosurgery, and other similar treatment modalities which were regarded by the Court as "extraordinary or potentially hazardous modes of treatment."

Recently a federal court declared a Georgia statute, which permitted "voluntary" admission of minors to state mental hospitals on the authority of their parents, unconstitutional because the law failed (from the due process clause of the Fourteenth Amendment) to "provide procedural safeguards to see that even parents do not use the power to indefinitely hospitalize children in an arbitrary manner." The Court maintained that psychiatric diagnosis is too inexact and the possibilities of mistakes too great to overcome the need for procedural protection for the child. Recent court rulings appear to be saying that a parent or guardian cannot waive a minor's due process rights to object to his psychiatric hospitalization.

The Psychiatry and Law Committee of the American Psychiatric Association adopted a draft of principles under which implied consent to emergency admission or retention in a hospital is felt to exist. Implied consent would apply in situations "where it would be reasonable to assume that the person would give consent to emergency admission or retention, if he were competent and able to make a rational decision, or the person is unable to control his behavior which threatens serious harm to himself or others." This definition covers patients who are unconscious and comatose, as well as the actively psychotic patient. This formulation is similar to emerging definitions of "dangerousness." Due process assures the patient the right to a court hearing, with counsel and independent medical opinion, notice of all rights, and periodic medical review every six months.

CONFIDENTIALITY AND PRIVILEGED COMMUNICATION

Medical ethics and therapeutic considerations require that the psychiatrist maintain the confidentiality of the doctor-patient relationship. In the treatment of children and adolescents it is essential to indicate that there is one circumstance under which he will violate their confidential therapeutic relationship—if he determines that the youngster is engaged in or is actively planning an activity which is extremely dangerous to himself or others. Under these conditions, the therapist will be compelled to inform the parents or guardian of the potential forthcoming danger.

Although privileged communication between client and lawyer is an accepted tradition in the courts, the communication between a patient and his psychiatrist remains an unresolved legal issue except for a few states where statutes have been enacted providing for privileged communications in psychiatric treatment. In caselaw, the Supreme Court of

Alaska has recognized that privileged communication between psychotherapist and patient must be recognized by the courts. The Court acknowledged such a privilege, according to four guidelines: (1) whether the nature of the communications involved in the relationship is confidential; (2) whether confidentiality is essential to achieve the goals of the relationship; (3) whether the community believes a relationship ought to be fostered; and (4) whether the harm to the relationship caused by disclosure would be greater than the benefit gained from the correct disposal of the litigation. The Alaska Court validated that the psychotherapist/patient relationship satisfied all four criteria, but restricted this privilege to psychiatrists and licensed psychologists.

LIMITS OF CONFIDENTIALITY

The Professional Services Review Organization, as well as third party payers, may threaten confidentiality of health records by exposing them, not only to professional reviewers, but also to administrators, clerks, technicians and statisticians. Significant efforts are being made to find ways of protecting the confidentiality of medical records. From a legal point of view, written psychiatric records can be subpoenaed for legal purposes and must be made available. As a consequence, one should consider in psychiatric records adequately describing a patient's status, without putting into the record intimate detail concerning the patient's personal fantasies and ideations. There is a clear trend in the direction of government accumulating more and more medical and psychiatric information, ostensibly for purposes of health planning and cost effectiveness programs. The New York State Appellate Court has ruled that the State Department of Mental Hygiene can maintain identifying data and illness infor-

mation concerning outpatients (*Volkman* v. *Miller of N.Y.S.*
May 1976).

COMPETENCY

With the increased concern for the constitutional rights of
the individual, the problem of competency to stand trial has
gained in importance. Pretrial psychiatric evaluations involve
four separate areas: diagnosis, commitability, criminal responsibility, and competency to stand trial. Since 1843, the
rules of criminal responsibility and competency to stand trial
were governed by the *M'Naghten Rule* which stated that a
person is not exempted from criminal responsibility because
his choice of action is determined or affected by pathology.
He is exempted when he lacks moral judgment. This rule was
significantly altered in 1954 by the Durham decision which
opened the question of criminal responsibility and competency to stand trial to the widest possible scope and stated
that the accused is not criminally responsible if an unlawful
act was the product of mental disease or mental defect. At the
time of adoption of the Durham decision, it had not been
foreseen that this would lead to the exculpation of sociopaths
from criminal liability. The M'Naghten and Durham Rules
were further modified in 1961 by the American Law Institute
Model Penal Code: (1) a person is not responsible for criminal conduct if at the time of such conduct as a result of mental
disease or defect, he lacked substantial capacity to appreciate
the criminality (wrongfulness) of his conduct or he did not
have the mental capacity to conform his conduct to the requirements of the law; (2) the terms mental *disease* or *defect*
do not include an abnormality manifested only by repeated
criminal or otherwise antisocial conduct. Under these new
rules, the presence of mental illness does not preclude

competency to stand trial. To be considered competent to stand trial, an individual must possess sufficient mental capacity to comprehend the nature and object of the proceedings and his own position in relation to those proceedings, and to be able to advise counsel rationally in preparation and implementation of his own defense.

MALPRACTICE ISSUES

1. *Release Patient vs. Restrain Patient—the Psychiatrist's Double Bind.* Recent increases in litigation have put new responsibilities on psychiatrists to find alternatives to institutionalization for psychiatric patients (the least restrictive alternative). Psychiatrists may feel that they are in a double bind where they fear releasing or restraining a patient lest they be held legally liable for a poor outcome. The point to be understood by psychiatrists is that the courts have rarely imposed liability on psychiatrists for failure to predict dangerousness. It has been well documented that psychiatrists cannot effectively predict dangerousness. A release decision should be supported in the clinical record by descriptions of the patient which are consistent with the release decision. If a case should go to court, all that would be expected is that a reasonable decision be made based on a thorough review of the patient's case history. Courts recognize the potential for creating a double bind and in order to maintain the least restrictive (open door) policy they do not expect error-free decisions. Even in the Tarasoff case, liability was not based on a failure to predict dangerousness, but rather on a "failure to warn."

2. *Duty to Warn—Tarasoff Case.* The California case of *Tarasoff* v. *Board of Regents of the University of California* (Cal. Sup. Ct. July 1976) established that a psychotherapist who knows

or should know that a patient represents a "serious danger of violence" to a third party must demonstrate "reasonable care to protect the intended victim against such danger," including warning the victim or notifying the police. The American Psychiatric Association and other professional groups have indicated that this duty to warn can destroy the effectiveness and confidentiality of the doctor-patient relationship.

3. *Child Abuse and Neglect Cases.* Failure to make the diagnosis of child abuse and/or neglect in the face of clear-cut clinical evidence may subject the mental health practitioner to a malpractice law suit. Furthermore, current state and federal laws require the reporting to a central registry of all cases of *suspected* child abuse and neglect. Various legal penalties have been prescribed for those health professionals who fail to report a suspected case.

CURRENT TRENDS

Medical, psychiatric, and lay literature in recent years has been replete with attacks upon the specialty of psychiatry. These attacks come from outside as well as within the specialty. Those who are the most nihilistic attack the very roots of psychiatry by denying its authenticity, theories, methods, and values. Reduced governmental resources have resulted in cutbacks of psychiatric training grants, as well as increased demand for accountability by psychiatry. Psychiatric practice is particularly vulnerable to challenge because of its inherent difficulties in providing clear-cut diagnostic categories and establishing the validity of various treatment modalities. The accumulation of data validating criteria for medical necessity of treatment as well as norms for predicting length of treatment represents a future goal for the profession. With this data it is possible for child psychiatry to more effectively work with the legal-political community toward the development of government programs and public policy which will facilitate the more normative growth and development of children and their families.

GLOSSARY

Action: An ordinary proceeding in a court by which one party prosecutes another for the enforcement or protection of a right, the redress or prevention of a wrong, or the punishment of a violation of law.

Arraignment: The calling of the accused by name, reading to him the charge, demanding of him whether he be guilty or not guilty, and the entering of his plea.

Crime: An act forbidden by law, and punishable upon conviction by imprisonment, fine, or other penal discipline; except that offenses and traffic infractions are not crimes. *Felony:* A crime of the more serious degree which is punishable by imprisonment. *Misdemeanor:* Any crime which is not a felony. *Offense:* A violation of law less serious in degree than a crime.

Decedent: A deceased person.

Disorderly conduct: A series of specified activities which tend to disturb the public peace or decorum, scandalize the community, or shock the public sense of morality.

Dispositional hearing: A hearing to determine what disposition should be made on a case.

Fact finding hearing: A hearing to determine whether the allegations in the petition are supported by a fair preponderance of the evidence.

Habeas Corpus: An order directed to one person who is detaining another person commanding the former to produce the latter before a court so that the court may determine whether the person is being wrongfully detained.

Hearsay evidence: Evidence not proceeding from the personal knowledge of the witness, but from the mere repetition of what he has heard others say.

Juvenile delinquent: A person usually less than sixteen years of age who does any act which if done by an adult, would constitute a crime (a felony or misdemeanor).

Person in Need of Supervision: Usually a person less than sixteen years of age who is an habitual truant, or who is incorrigable, ungovernable or habitually disobedient and beyond lawful control of parent or other lawful authority.

Petition: A written application to a court requesting its action upon some matter therein laid before it.

Petitioner: The party who files the petition initiating the case.

Pleading: The answer of the accused to the charge made against him—guilty or not guilty.

Proceeding: Any case or matter in a court of justice which is not an action.

Respondent: The party who answers the charges alleged in any case which is initiated by the filing of a petition.

BIBLIOGRAPHY

Berlin, I., ed. (1975). *Advocacy for Child Mental Health.* New York: Brunner/Mazel. An authoritative overview of the child mental health system with a description of problem areas and medicolegal suggestions for improvement.

Goldstein, J., Freud, A., and Solnit, A. (1973). *Beyond the Best Interests of the Child.* New York: The Free Press. This book by two psychoanalysts and a legal authority represents a collaborative effort to integrate psychoanalytic and legal insights into child placement practices.

Holder, A. (1977). *Legal Issues in Pediatrics and Adolescent Medicine.* New York: John Wiley. Conflicts and controversies concerning current medicolegal issues are vividly described.

Mental Disability Law Reporter. Volume 1 (1976). Volume 2 (1977). A bimonthly publication of the American Bar Association Commission on the mentally disabled. These volumes provide the most current and comprehensive information on medicolegal matters and also contain valuable special articles.

Slovenko, R. (1973). *Psychiatry and Law.* Boston: Little Brown. A comprehensive textbook of legal psychiatry.

Chapter 28

BATTERED CHILD SYNDROME

Desmond Heath, M.B.B.Ch.

DEFINITION

The *battered child syndrome* and its inevitable concomitant, the abusive parent, guardian, institution or society, arise typically from no single psychopathological entity but are the result of complex intrapersonal, interpersonal, societal and/ or environmental influences and entities. The field of child abuse and neglect has generated definitions in legal, pediatric, psychological, psychodynamic, societal, and even philosophical and political terms.

The National Committee for Prevention of Child Abuse defines child abuse to include "nonaccidental physical injury and malnutrition, neglect, sexual abuse and exploitation of children." Kempe and Helfer's definition of the battered child is: "any child who received nonaccidental physical injury (or injuries) as a result of acts (or omissions) on the part of his parents or guardians." Expanding the definition beyond the physical and emotional repercussions in the child to include parents and guardians requires recognizing motives and antecedents in the parents that brought about the incident or pattern of abuse or neglect. Thus the field expands from the physical treatment of the child to include a treatment response to parents. Other definitions further expand the scope. For example, Fontana says this is a "medical-social phenomenon." Gil refers to child abuse as a "dysfunctional social phenomenon."

The manifestations are too diverse for a descriptive approach and the causations too complex for a terse, all-encompassing genetic definition.

REVIEW OF LITERATURE

The nonaccidental physical injury to children, its recognition in the child, and treatment belong primarily to the field of pediatrics, as does failure to thrive in small infants. Other effects of abuse of children, such as disturbances in emotional development and pathological personality patterns with their sequelae especially in parenting patterns, command the interest of child and adult psychiatrists. The early references are to be found in pediatric radiology and pediatrics in general. Historically, however, child abuse in the form of infant abandonment, child labor, or harsh educational practices is as old as man. Civilizations have been rated on their treatment of children, the sick, and the aged. A turning point in the history of child abuse was the case of Mary Ellen, removed from her adoptive parents under the intervention of the Society for the Prevention of Cruelty to Animals. This brought about the founding in 1871 of The Society for the Prevention of Cruelty to Children in New York City. But it was not until Caffey (1946) reported on "multiple fractures in the long bones of infants suffering from chronic subdural hematoma" that the critical breakthrough was made that marked the beginning of this ever widening literature.

Caffey's report represented sufficient hard fact, in x-ray form, to break through a blanket of denial against the painful but inescapable conclusion that these injuries were caused by the caretakers of these children. As the evidence grew, the facts of child abuse were forced upon the medical world and society in general. In 1961 at the symposium on the Problems of Child Abuse held by the American Academy of Child Psychiatry, the appelation "battered child syndrome" was chosen specifically to dramatize before the medical community and the public, via the mass media, the seriousness of the problem. The breakdown of the forces of denial resulted in a wave of publicity and the passage of child protective laws with unprecedented rapidity throughout every state in the nation.

This history is well documented in *The Battered Child* (Helfer and Kempe 1968). This volume is the basic text in the field and marks the end of the breakthrough period in the recognition of child abuse as a major and persistent presence in society. Its sequel, *Helping the Battered Child and His Family,* (Kempe and Helfer 1972), reflects the expansion of energies toward treatment, prevention, and prediction. The scientific approach, represented in these two volumes and in an ever expanding literature in the journals, has been paralleled by a body of work directed at a wider audience. Since this is not an attractive, and in that sense popular, subject but one of broad and painful significance to individuals and society at large, a literature has developed, including newspaper and magazine articles, with the express purpose of bringing into the open what has been over the centuries and remains subject to such strong forces of suppression and denial.

A series of slim booklets on Child Abuse and Neglect presented by the Department of Health, Education and Welfare contain in summary one of the most significant contributions to the understanding of this field: Helfer's *World of Abnormal Rearing* (W.A.R.). He has constructed a theoretical framework which gives cohesion and organization to this otherwise confusing field, and illuminates diagnosis, treatment and prevention. He conceives of a cycle of abuse in which children who experience abnormal rearing grow up to repeat these experiences in raising of their own children. Child abuse and neglect, he points out, are only two of the spin-offs of this cycle. Other spin-offs are criminality and character pathology.

Finally, *The Abusing Family* by Justice and Justice (1976) goes further than a cycle concept (as in the "world of abnormal rearing"), developing a psychosocial systems model and applying a couples group treatment based on transactional analysis concepts. The specific focus is on a "central theoretical concept," which they identify in the abusive family and name "shifting symbiosis."

INCIDENCE

All sources indicate that child abuse is of national importance. It is frequently considered to be of epidemic proportion. In 1977, 39,682 reports of suspected child abuse and maltreatment were received by the New York State register. With an estimated population of 4,386,983 children under the age of fifteen this gives a rate of reporting of 9.05 per 1000. The 1977 New York City rate was 8.50 reports per 1000 children. The state figures show that in 45 percent of the cases in which a determination was made there was some credible evidence of child abuse or maltreatment. Fifty-five percent of the cases were "unfounded."

ETIOLOGY AND DYNAMICS

To elucidate the complex dynamics of child abuse one might view Helfer's W.A.R. diagram (Table 1) through the spectacles of the Justices' "symbiosis" concepts. "Basic in the abuser's attitude toward infants," the Justices quote Steele, "is the conviction, largely unconscious, that children exist in order to satisfy parental needs. Infants who do not satisfy these needs should be punished . . . to make them behave properly . . . It is as though the infant were looked to as a need-satisfying parental object to fill the residual, unsatisfied, infantile needs of the parent." The Justices go on to note that "symbiosis begins as a life sustaining relationship between a mother and child in the earliest stage of development." However "when a child for whatever reason does not grow beyond symbiosis and into a separate identity, the result is a continual quest for someone to meet his unmet needs symbiotically. . . . The person manipulates others into meeting his needs without considering whether they are willing or able to do so." In the first quarter of the W.A.R. cycle (Table 1) the parent wants the pregnancy—avoids birth control or abortion expecting that "the new baby . . . will keep her company or even take care of her or comfort her in her loneliness." The child may be a rewarding baby meeting sufficient of his mother's needs to be cherished. However, at different stages of development or because of colic or other illness the baby becomes a disappointment. The unrealistic expectations of a parent for a child can be conceptualized as a quotient or index. The greater the discrepancy between the parent's mental representation of the child's developmental capacities and the child's actual status, the greater the likelihood of psychopathology in the child. The discrepancy may be an overestimation—expecting the child to be more grown up—or an under-estimation—i.e., infantilizing the child and maintaining a symbiotic relationship. Such a discrepancy during development constitutes a cumulative trauma leading commonly to problems in the economy of self-esteem (feelings of inadequacy with compensatory grandiosity), a dynamic common in abusive parents.

Role reversal and compliance are concepts which aid understanding of the confusing pictures seen in this syndrome. Gil (1970) summarizes Morris and Gould's original concept as follows: "An abusing parent views his victim not as the child he really is, but as his own parent who has failed, hurt and frustrated him. . . . The child in such cases is expected by the parent to meet his (the parent's) complex emotional needs rather than having his needs met by the parent. When the child fails to do so, the frustrated parent attacks, injures and at times destroys the child." Compliance refers to the child's capacity to achieve his parents wishes to comfort and look after them. A child who is very attached becomes over-solicitous and careful not to upset his abusive parent. This adaptation to parental needs rather than to his own childhood developmental needs for space, fantasy, and play, amount to "childhood missed," referred to at the bottom of the W.A.R. cycle diagram (Table 1). Such children have to fend for themselves and do not learn a confident expectation of warmth and nurturance though this is sought later in a symbiotic relationship. Trust is not learned, and isolation becomes part of his overall pattern and of the family unit that he may establish on growing up. Each parent "seeks from the other satisfaction of his needs to be cared for or nurtured. As a result, neither parent's needs are met and each may, at different times, turn to the child, no matter how young, to be the nurturer and decision maker." This shifting symbiosis, as described by the Justices, is the basic dynamic that creates a family system that, rather than "processing" effectively only increases crisis and stress. The pattern is one of relative isolation, inability to use others for help, inability to give help, and feelings of helplessness and incapacity. In the psychosocial model of the Justices, "the child and the stressful behavior . . . are considered the agent that precipitates the abuse. . . . The abuse results from a system of multiple interactions between parent and child, husband and wife, adult and environment, child and environment, and culture and parent. All play a part, but the child is most commonly the immediate source of external stress for the abusing parent. The child's very proximity makes him an easy target for the parent whose frustrations spill over into physical aggression . . . when the child makes unusually great demands or represents an exceptional stress, he is in even greater danger."

DIAGNOSTIC CONSIDERATIONS

The diagnosis of child abuse is a matter primarily for the emergency room physician where the injury with insufficient or inconsistent explanation must be viewed as a possible case of abuse. The first order of pediatric response should be protection of the child, and admission of a child less than five years old is routine. Admission is for more careful evaluation. Intensive questioning tends only to increase the parent's denial since the investigator becomes like the abusers own critical, suspicious, untrusting parent. Where the child or adult psychiatrist enters most profitably into the diagnostic team is in the understanding and illuminating of the resistance that militates against the recognition or diagnosis of child abuse.

Helfer stresses that in the diagnosis of child abuse three

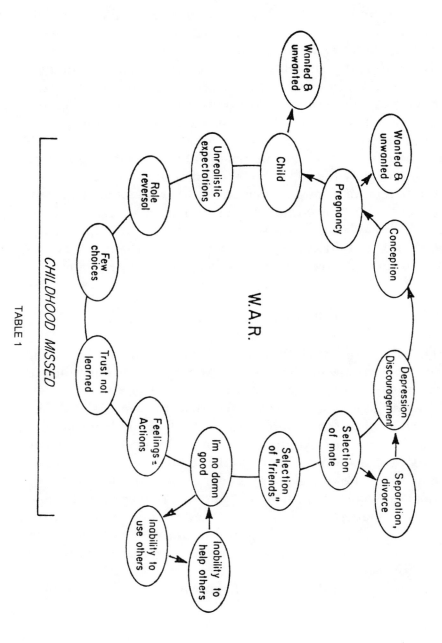

WORLD OF ABNORMAL REARING CYCLE

W.A.R.

Wanted & unwanted

Child

Unrealistic expectations

Role reversal

Few choices

Trust not learned

Feelings = Actions

I'm no damn good

Selection of "friends"

Selection of mate

Depression/Discouragement

Separation, divorce

Conception

Pregnancy

Wanted & unwanted

Inability to use others

Inability to help others

CHILDHOOD MISSED

TABLE 1

elements must be present: the parent, the child, and the crisis. The parent must have the potential to abuse. Steele (1975) notes that "no two abusive parents are exactly alike" but states that they share in some degree in a variety of combinations all of the following characteristics: (1) a special form of immaturity and the associated dependency in its various manifestations; (2) tragically low self-esteem and a sense of incompetence; (3) difficulty in seeking pleasure and finding satisfaction in the adult world; (4) social isolation with its lack of lifelines and reluctance to seek help; (5) significant misrepresentations of the infant, especially as manifested in role reversal; (6) fear of spoiling infants; (7) strong belief in the value of punishment; (8) serious lack of ability to be empathically aware of the infant's condition and needs and to respond appropriately to them.

Helfer's parent-child-crisis formulation emphasizes that the child "is not just *any* child but a very special child. One who is seen differently by his parents; one who fails to respond in the expected manner; or possibly one who is really different (retarded, too smart, hyperactive or has a birth defect)." The crisis, on the other hand, may consist of a minor domestic mishap or a major logistical problem in family management.

TREATMENT

The dictum that diagnosis dictates treatment holds firm in child abuse. The diagnosis is more than the knowledge of the presence of abuse but rather contains a knowledge of how the parents, the child, and the environment fit together to create a malfunctioning system that produces episodes of abuse or patterns of neglect. What is clear is that without a knowledge of this complexity (1) this condition is not recognized and (2) the treatment response tends to be harsh, investigative, and punitive. With a knowledge of the W.A.R. cycle and a family systems view, treatment can proceed. Based on the above, various principles of treatment are evident and many of these principles are often in conflict with each other. For example: protection of the child yet at the same time preservation of the family if possible; providing support in crisis, yet at the same time collecting sufficient data for legal removal of the child from the family should this be necessary. Each quarter of the W.A.R. cycle suggests its own specific treatment response. In the first quarter (Table 1) the overcoming of resistance to family planning, contraception, and abortion. In the second quarter the parents need to lessen the discrepancy between their expectations of their child and his actual capacities. This may be done by decreasing the parents' need to turn to their child for symbiotic need gratification, by offering support and "mothering" from other sources (professionals, hospitals, schools, Parents Anonymous, or other parent group therapies) which meet needs but also foster insight and more effective parenting. Because the repetition of parenting patterns is so powerful and engagement of these isolated and suspicious persons is so precarious, treatment is frustratingly arduous and is often not maintained.

Removal of the child from his parents may be part of the treatment program aimed at returning the child when the home is once more safe. However permanent placement of children is often necessary. On principle, placement with grandparents is unwise for, as Helfer points out, that is where the trouble for the abusing parent began—with his or her own parents. Psychosis in a parent often causes such a biased view of a child and his needs that the risk of psychological damage, abuse and neglect are high. Similarly, drug addiction is often such an encompassing preoccupation that a child's needs are not met. Child protection laws commonly require reporting to state agencies the birth of an infant to a known addict.

Although society's response to child abuse has shifted away from legal reporting, investigative, and punitive measure, toward a supporting, nurturing, medical psychotherapeutic response, the need remains for strong and fully implemented child protection laws.

New York State law, for example, defines abuse, neglect, and maltreatment, requires reporting and empowers certain agencies and persons including physicians to place a child in protective custody even without parental consent. Such legal support for immediate admission is a vital component in the protection of an abused child. Orderly reporting, evaluation, and assumption of custody by the Bureau of Child Welfare is often a very necessary progression toward the placement for treatment of many abused and neglected children whose parents resist intervention.

DISCUSSION

A knowledge of the dynamics is essential to enable the professional to face the possibility that he is dealing with a case of abuse or neglect. This avoids a feeling of helplessness that often leads to denial of the possibility of abuse or a refusal to confront one's suspicions. Because good physicians and nurses need effective procedures by which to deal with their suspicions of abuse, every hospital should have available on call a specialized team which will take over the responsibility of evaluating the situation and sticking with it until proper resolution is achieved. Dealing with the requirements of the law, complexities of bureaucracy in the child protection agency, and fears that reporting will not help matters is often too burdensome for many professionals to face alone. The natural history of this condition is that it goes unrecognized—a child repeatedly injured is taken to a different emergency room for each episode of abuse and receives treatment only for the present injury. The question of abuse is left for the follow-up visit which is characteristically missed. No outreach follow-up is made and the child remains at risk of death or serious morbidity. Although this condition cuts across the boundaries between the medical, social, political, and economic, it seems that pediatricians and child psychiatrists have led the way and will remain the prime movers in the future.

SUMMARY

Child abuse, although as old as man and of epidemic proportions in our society now, has had only a short history in medical literature. Forces of denial and suppression are strong, preventing its recognition. However, medical models, explaining its existence in terms of fateful transmission from generation to generation of abnormal rearing and dysfunctional psychosocial systems, effectively combat these forces of denial and provide a rationale for strong treatment methods.

BIBLIOGRAPHY

Caffey, J. (1946). Multiple fractures in the long bones of children suffering from chronic subdural hematoma. *American Journal of Roentgenology* 56:163–173. A paper of historical importance.

Gil, D. (1970). *Violence Against Children.* Cambridge, Mass.: Harvard University Press.

Helfer, R. (1974). *A Self-Instructional Program on Child Abuse and Neglect.* Chicago: American Academy of Pediatrics. Denver: National Center for the Prevention and Treatment of Child Abuse and Neglect. These three audio tapes together with a manual make easy going of the W.A.R. concept, diagnostic criteria, the diagnostic process, and therapeutic programs.

——— (1975). *Child Abuse and Neglect: The Diagnostic Process and Treatment Programs.* Washington: United States Department of Health, Education and Welfare Publication Number (OHD) 75–69.

——— (In press). *Childhood Comes First.* East Lansing, Mich.: R. Helfer, M.D., Box 1781.

——— and Kempe, C. (1968). *The Battered Child.* Chicago: University of Chicago Press.

Justice, B., and Justice, R. (1976). *The Abusing Family.* New York: Human Science Press.

Kempe, C., and Helfer, R., eds. (1972). *Helping the Battered Child and His Family.* New York: Lippincott.

Steele, B. (1975). *Child Abuse and Neglect: Working with Abusive Parents from a Psychiatric Point of View.* Washington: United States Department of Health, Education and Welfare Publication Number (OHD) 75–70.

Part V

Horizons of Treatment

Chapter 29

FAMILY APPROACHES TO ASSESSMENT

AND TREATMENT

Ann Z. Korelitz, M.S.W.

Ronald R. Rawitt, M.D.

Paul V. Kennedy, M.D.

INTRODUCTION

In other chapters of this book psychopathologies of childhood are discussed primarily in terms of the conflicts within the child, and the way these conflicts affect both the child and his social environment. This viewpoint, however, provides an incomplete picture. In an effort to present a more complete view, we must look at the child in terms of his familial environment. In family therapy, we are interested in the parent-child, child-parent, and parent-parent interactions as the foci of individual problems within the child. It is only by examining the family dynamics that the problems of the child can be fully understood.

The symptomatic child patient who is referred for treatment may manifest intrapsychic suffering, but he is not alone in this dilemma, for his parents and siblings suffer as well. Frequently the parents of such a child involve him in a complex and confusing marital situation in which the child-patient plays a pivotal role. This parental-child relationship allows for many complex interactions that need to be understood in order to help the child.

To understand the relationship of the troubled child and his family it is necessary to conceptualize the family in a systematic manner. Various methods of diagnosis and classification have evolved to help define the problems and choose which method to use in treatment. Such standardization of communication, methods of research, and diagnosis and classification are more important as this field develops and becomes more widespread.

REVIEW OF LITERATURE

The literature of child psychotherapy ranges from the individual intrapsychic approach of Anna Freud to Haley's concept of the child as an integral part of the family system. In family therapy the interaction between family members is stressed and the intrapsychic view is regarded as irrelevant.

From a classical viewpoint, such as that of Anna Freud, the troubled child is viewed as an individual with internalized conflicts. These conflicts are overlaid on a basic constitutional framework consisting of characteristic neurologic, metabolic, and intellectual patterns. With these basic endowments the child must ascend the developmental ladder. This developmental ladder is fraught with difficulties, and in the case of the troubled child there is inevitable fixation, regression, and symptom formation. It is this symptom formation that the outside world, i.e., the parents, respond to in seeking treatment for their child.

According to family therapy theorists such as Nathan Ackerman (1958), child psychiatric symptomatology carries an additional significance in terms of family. Regardless of any particular view of family structure and function, theorists generally agree that the troubled child is part of a dysfunctioning family unit. The three predominant approaches within this theoretical orientation are the intrapsychic viewpoint, the concept of role relationships, and systems theory.

The intrapsychic view of family pathology and treatment is best represented by Grotjahn. In this method of treatment, the patient's family is involved in the therapy to expose the patient's intrapsychic structure. This by necessity limits the family role and focuses therapy on the individual, not the interpersonal.

Ackerman, who is considered the "grandfather" of the modern family therapy movement, maintained an approach which took into account internal mental processes, family interactions, and societal interactions. This synthesis is the key to his approach, from which he derived the concept of role relationships, or societal role. The concept of societal role links intrapsychic life with social participation. In other words, it is the ability of an individual to intrapsychically come to terms with his environment. This concept of social role allows for description of a plurality of transactions where roles are always complementary or reciprocal. Ackerman asserted that homeostatic mechanisms function to maintain these social roles in the face of time and change. In essence, it is the capacity of the family and its individuals to grow, learn, and adapt in a flexible and supportive environment. When a breakdown occurs within these homeostatic mechanisms, pathology formation results.

The systems theory approach to family therapy as advanced by Jackson, Haley, or Satir is concerned with the family as an entity consisting of interactional complexes of elements. In this sense, they see the family system as a whole greater than its individual parts. This axiom is true when the family is viewed as an interrelated, constantly changing system. The individuals in a family system are related through a process of feedback which maintains the function of the family. It is important to examine the relationships between the elements and how they are structured. These theorists see the family as a unit which copes with life in a characteristic manner. If the family structure is designed to deal with subjects in a specific manner, then the outcome will remain constant no matter what the subject is: children, money, sex or any other topic. Jackson, Haley, and Satir have each been concerned with patterns of communication and cognition, power and feelings, in dysfunctional families.

The focus of systems theorists on the variables affecting family interactions and behaviors changes according to the individual theorist's particular realm of interests. Treating families of schizophrenics, Bateson developed a double bind theory of communications. He described a modification or distortion of the learning process due to a combination of genetics and environment. Bateson also used this theory in his work with nonschizophrenic families. Wynne, too, studied schizophrenics and their families. He noted that the schizophrenic individual and his family have problems in role relations; understanding these individual roles and the communicational patterns and pathology are of prime importance.

Minuchin studied repetitive patterns in family interactions, and developed a structural approach to family treatment. He is concerned with family issues of power, alliances, and generational boundaries, allowing for cultural differences.

Bowen theorized that an individual starts life as part of an undifferentiated ego-mass in the family system, and must establish his own identity in order to separate from the family. This is done by a stepwise evolution of the triad of child and parents via a process of detriangulation. Detriangulation permits a greater range of responses than "stay and be angry" or "leave and be guilty."

Framo (1970) suggests that issues of transference and transference-distortion, not only of the individual family members but of the entire family, are critical to an understanding of family systems.

The literature of family therapy is fast growing with much current attention given to the use of paradox and strategic methods of treatment. Of particular interest is the work of Palazzoli-Selvini (1974) and Watzlawick, Weakland, and Fisch (1974).

ETIOLOGY AND DYNAMICS

Each family operates by a series of rules, of which the members may or may not be aware, but which regulate the behavior of all family members. The therapist who can understand these rules can understand the forces which determine the symptomatic behavior of the child who is a member of that family.

Before there were children in the family, and even after, the marital partners in dysfunctional families use each other to fulfill roles designed to deal with conflicts which arose in their own families of origin. Later, children are used for the same purpose. The parents project parts of their own conflicts, derived from unresolved conflicts in their families of origin, onto their perceptions of their children. They then treat their children in accord with these distorted perceptions, and the children internalize and identify with their parents' perceptions of them. The parents may then receive gratification from identifying with the children who are displaying the parents' conflicts. Children collaborate in the process of adopting parental views of themselves out of loyalty, a wish to help the parent, or fear of losing the parent.

Each person in a symptomatic family is carrying out specific roles, not just the identified patient. Indeed, who is selected as the patient will depend upon the roles of the family system. Sometimes particular children are singled out for "parentification." These children are expected to take over the parenting functions in the family while the adults abdicate their executive roles. These children are loyal to the family and often take the role of "healer" or "mediator," or even the "martyred burden-bearer." Other children may take the role of "scapegoat" for the family pathology, helping to bring attention to a troubled family when they involve the legal systems or the helping professions with the family (Boszormenyi-Nagy and Spark 1973).

Within a family, Framo (1970) explains how different children may internalize different aspects of a marital conflict: "One child may identify with the aggressive role, going through life victimizing others; another child may incorporate the victim role and always get into situations which provoke abuse; another child may incorporate both aspects as an intrapsychic conflict; and still another child may block it all out and become silent and withdrawn. . . ."

Certain events, such as the birth of a child, or a child moving out of the home, are normative crises for a family and test its flexibility and resiliency. The more a child is trapped in parental role projections, the less able will he be to accomplish the process of growth and change required by these normative crises. The breakdown of generational boundaries by the process of parentification results in a particular noxious restriction of a child's ability to adapt to his changing life tasks.

Bowen judges the health of family members by their differentiation from the "undifferentiated family ego-mass." He sees the family ego-mass as being built up of interlocking triangular relationships. The triangulated person, frequently a child, embodies both sides of the conflictual relationship of the original dyad.

It is frequently seen in family therapy that the identified patient, the child, manages to divert the focus of the session onto himself if his parents start to argue, become sad, or if they change and begin to get along well. The child in the first situation fears the loss of his parents and so tries to get them to stop arguing by diverting their attention to his symptomatic behavior. In the second situation he protects the parents from confronting their own depression. In the third situation, he feels uneasy with his parents' new-found amicability, not knowing if he can get the same gratification that he used to get for his symptomatic behavior. The efforts of his parents to create triangles is a result of a failure in their dyadic relationship. The child sacrifices himself, continuing his symptomatic behavior in order to keep conflict from being expressed in the marital dyad (Satir 1967).

DIAGNOSTIC CONSIDERATIONS

After twenty years of attempts to classify and establish a "family vocabulary," the field remains so fluid and unfixed as to make diagnosis or classification in the orthodox sense difficult. Attempts have been made to use adaptive and developmental models, with mixed results.

The term "diagnosis," with its reliance on a medical model of illness, may be contraindicated in relation to understanding families (Fisher 1977). This single issue places family therapists in a somewhat defensive position. The questions raised by colleagues center around "How can we treat without a diagnosis? Wouldn't it help to call the father passive-aggressive with intellectual defenses? Wouldn't it help to call the mother an hysterical paranoid and describe the child with enuresis as caught in an oedipal conflict?"

The answers are complicated. Road maps of established diagnostic categories are not useful to the therapist who is trying to understand the family. In fact, they can prove detrimental to this understanding.

The beginning family therapist will do better to approach the initial family session without the burden of diagnostic categories. The therapist should meet the family with as open a view as possible. His reluctance to grasp for prelearned, recognizable terms will save him from confusion. Only after he has become experienced in family session should he resort to his knowledge of individual psychopathology. When he is conversant in "family" he may draw upon "individual." He will then also be ready to use the abundant literature on family diagnosis.

For the clinician whose specialty is child psychiatry, it is particularly important to resist the powerful pull to identify with children (patient) and thus ignore or be unable to see the *family* as the patient. While some families are truly malignant, the vast majority of them, when viewed as interacting, interdependent systems, are simply caught up in the common human struggle. This struggle is handled with varying degrees of success and failure.

Frequently, families come into treatment coalesced around an identified child-patient. He or she is the "sick" one. In fact, it is relatively simple for the therapist to agree with the family that the child's symptoms are indeed the only clear problem. If symptom reversal is the goal, one can approach the problem from a structuralist point of view, and often achieve dramatic results (Minuchin 1974). Enuretics stop wetting, anorexics start eating, pyromaniacs stop setting fires, etc. This approach is useful and often pacifying for the therapist. However, it not to be used casually or without prior understanding and training.

Our preference is for the beginning therapist to listen to the symptom and hear it as a sign that something is wrong in the family. Just as psychosis can be a poignant cry for help, so can the identified patient be viewed as the family member who sounds an alarm. In fact, he or she may eventually be viewed as the strongest or healthiest family member.

A useful guide to the initial interview can be found in *Techniques of Family Psychotherapy* (Bloch 1973) which offers detailed aid. The therapist greets the family and remains standing until the family has seated themselves. Often a first diagnostic clue can be found in the manner that the family arranges themselves. Do the parents sit together? Is the identified patient isolated? Which parent does he sit next to? Is there some confusion in the family over how best to arrange themselves? Who takes charge?

The family therapist should have four simultaneous video-tapes going in his head. (1) What does the family say? (2) What is the meaning of the nonmanifest content? (3) What does the nonverbal behavior mean? (4) Perhaps most relevant: what am I experiencing as I sit here with this family?

The simultaneous quadri-tape begins to spin. Does this family show signs of affective ties? Do they have a capacity to communicate clearly? Do they have humor? How angry or sad are they? Is there a perceptible "contagion of affect" (Ackerman 1958)? Are there boundaries between the generations? Splits between the sexes? Are they intent on scapegoating the "patient"? Are their defenses rigid? Can they abstract? Does the family stick together—is it a gluey stickiness (enmeshed)? Or is it warm and supportive?

All of these criteria are observed and gradually, as the session progresses, the therapist begins to chart a diagnostic map. The therapist understands that the family has a private language to which outsiders are not privy. Some families, like some individual patients, will want to unload and spill everything at the start of treatment. Most will undo or re-tell it all at a later stage. Therefore, the therapist should be cautious in his interpretation of the initial information.

The basic question the therapist keeps asking is "How does it work?" The family therapist should be vigilant in his adherence to this question and not to questions like "How did it happen?" or "Who did what to whom?" Again and again, how does this family system work? Who is sick at whose expense? What function does the symptom play in the survival of the family? All of these psychological questions need to be interspersed with environmental, sociological, and historical ones.

It is possible, in fact, it is necessary for the therapist to make a *family* diagnosis. However, the need to make a diagnosis should not burden the inexperienced family therapist. It is more important that he learn to observe the family and be aware of his own feelings as he attempts to understand. If the family perceives him as accepting and interested, they will help him make the diagnosis. They may even tell him what the problem is ("We've never been able to talk." "We're too serious," or "too sad," "too lazy," etc.). Underneath all of these clues, the family is commonly asking the questions all people ask: Are we savable? Helpable? Do you like us? Are you (the therapist) able to avoid getting swept up in our craziness? Will it ever be better, what will happen if we do change, will you be there to guide us? Are we loveable? . . . Can we trust you?

TREATMENT

The treatment of the whole family attempts to bring about change in the malfunctioning of the system. Change should remove symptoms and improve functioning. The therapist is a key person in effecting this change. Treatment begins with the first contact. The therapist is the active change-agent and the manner in which he listens and responds to the organization and affect of the family has an immediate impact on the development of a therapeutic alliance.

The therapist attempts to relabel the child's problem as a problem for the whole family. The family may resist this interpretation and stop treatment. They may feel judged or guilty. The parents may feel that they are the cause of the problem, or they may see themselves as helping the therapist to "fix" the child. It is not important at an early stage to agree on the function of the family in the treatment. More germane is an agreement that the family and the therapist want things to be different.

After the family agrees to attend sessions (most commonly, once a week, with all members present), they may suspend judgment and passively put themselves in the hands of the therapist. They may depend upon him to effect the "cure." They may resist change as a result of an internal family system shift. If "cure" does not come quickly, the family may begin to miss sessions, come late, resist the therapy.

This second stage of treatment is difficult for the therapist and for the family. The inexperienced therapist may cast about for techniques and magic maneuvers in order to reassure the family and himself that the treatment is working. The family may pressure the therapist. They may challenge him and fall back on their initial conviction that the child is the real "patient." They may ask the therapist to see the child alone.

The therapist may decide that it would be useful to see members of the family individually for some sessions, or alternate parents and siblings, father and son, or grandparents and parents. However, these decisions should be thought out and determined by the therapist, not by the pressure of the family. This is especially difficult for the new family therapist, who often feels besieged by demands of different family members.

DISCUSSION AND SUMMARY

In conclusion, family therapy has come into its own as a modality for understanding and treatment of the psychopathologic manifestations of children in the context of their families.

It is important to acknowledge the necessity for specialized training in family therapy in addition to child psychiatry. It is clear from the information in this chapter that more is involved in family treatment than including the family in a child-focused treatment. Clinical supervision as well as familiarity with the literature is essential.

It remains true in family therapy, just as it does in individual therapy, that the foundation for success is the partnership of patient and therapist. The family must have a need to change and trust in their therapist to help guide them in the struggle. The therapist must be in control of the treatment and be able to assist in the rigorous and exciting struggle for change. The results can then be extraordinarily satisfying for all.

BIBLIOGRAPHY

Ackerman, N. (1958). *The Psychodynamics of Family Life.* New York: Basic Books. Introduction to family concept bridging the intrapsychic and the interpersonal by a family psychiatrist.

Bloch, D. (1973). *Techniques of Family Psychotherapy.* New York: Grune and Stratton. Description of various techniques such as home visit, initial interview, co-therapy, sculpting.

Boszormenyi-Nagy, I., and Spark, G. (1973). *Invisible Loyalties: Reciprocity in Intergenerational Family Therapy.* Hagerstown, Md.: Harper and Row. Formulates a theory of intergenerational relationships; parts of this are heavy going.

Bowen, M. (1978). *Family Therapy in Clinical Practice.* New York: Jason Aronson. A volume collecting most of Bowen's work, published and unpublished.

Fisher, L. (1977). On the classification of families. *Archives of General Psychiatry* 34:24–33. Review article on attempts at classification.

Foley, V. (1974). *An Introduction to Family Therapy.* New York: Grune and Stratton. A comprehensive survey and comparison of theories and theorists of family therapy.

Framo, J. (1970). Symptoms from a family transactional viewpoint. In *Progress in Group and Family Therapy,* eds. C. J. Sager and H. S. Kaplan. New York: Brunner/Mazel. Attempts to relate transactional family dynamics to object relations considerations.

Minuchin, S. (1974). *Families and Family Therapy.* Cambridge, Mass.: Harvard University Press. The structural approach to family case histories.

Palazzoli, M. (1974). *Self-Starvation.* London: Chaucer. New

York: Jason Aronson, 1978. Strategic approach of paradox with anorexic patients.

Satir, V. (1967). *Conjoint Family Therapy.* Palo Alto: Science and Behavior Books. Unique in its clarity and descriptive detail.

Watzlawick, P., Weakland, J., and Fisch, R. (1974). *Change: Principles of Problem Formation and Problem Resolution.* New York: Norton. Strategic approach for a theoretical basis for brief psychotherapy.

Chapter 30

PSYCHOPHARMACOLOGY IN CURRENT PRACTICE

David Schulman, M.D.

The basic therapeutic frame of reference employed throughout the Division of Child Psychiatry, at the Mount Sinai Hospital, continues to be derived from psychoanalysis and can best be described as representing a psychodynamically oriented medical model with emphasis on early developmental considerations. The diagnostic process is a thorough one and consists of taking a careful history, mental status examination, all necessary and indicated laboratory studies, consultation with other specialists as needed (pediatrics, pediatric neurology, speech and hearing, psychology, social service, and education), a psychoeducational assessment, and a family appraisal. This comprehensive work-up is directed toward establishing a diagnostic statement from which a carefully designed treatment plan of choice for both the child and the family are constructed. The treatment plan includes recommendations for (1) psychotherapy for the child and/or family; (2) a synthesis of psychotherapy and psychopharmacology as indicated; (3) other therapeutic modalities including behavioral modification techniques, educational remediation, and other environmental interventions when necessary. This chapter is directed toward a discussion of the pharmacological dimensions of therapy which are increasingly being employed as a major adjunct in treating the acute and chronic symptom disorders of children and adolescents. The combined approach of utilizing psychotherapy and psychopharmacology is most often viewed as a harmonious and synergistic one. (Group for the Advancement of Psychiatry [GAP] 1975). When medication is used appropriately, it fosters the physician's therapeutic relationship with the child by reducing anxiety, diminishing symptoms, and improving behavior. Sometimes medication can have an adverse effect on the course of psychotherapy by reinforcing resistances, encouraging denial and the search for magical solutions. Just as medication may influence psychological phenomena including ideation, affect, and behavior, so must psychotherapy, when viewed as a biological therapy, ultimately influence the underlying chemical and molecular substrate of the brain. In most cases, the combined use of psychotherapy and medication is arrived at on an empirical basis, and whether it is continued, modified, or abandoned, is decided on the basis of clinical experience.

While medication has been important in the treatment of children since Bradley's work in 1934, recent developments in the pharmacological treatment of the psychiatric disorders of childhood and adolescence have been particularly interesting and potentially useful to the clinician. These developments include the use of medication in the treatment of: (1) the psychotic disorders of infancy, childhood, and adolescence; (2) phobic disorders of childhood, including the school phobias, agoraphobia, and some chronic panic states; (3) the attentional deficit disorders including the hyperactive syndromes of childhood and adolescence; (4) stereotyped movement disorders such as the Gilles de la Tourette syndrome; (5) the sleep disorders of childhood; (6) specific developmental disorders including enuresis and encopresis; (7) the nonpsychotic affective disorders of childhood and adolescence; (8) the conduct disorders in the nonpsychotic and central nervous system (CNS) impaired child.

DEFINITION

Psychopharmacotherapy is an adjunctive form of treatment of mental illness, behavioral maladaptation, or other problems of childhood and adolescence which utilizes psychotropic drugs in conjunction with psychotherapy for the purpose of removing, modifying, or attenuating existing symptoms or disturbed patterns of behavior, thereby facilitating normal personality growth and development. Psychopharmacotherapy is directed toward influencing those symptom disorders that are thought to derive from the complex interaction of biopsychosocial factors causing fixations and regression at different stages of development. The earlier the disorder develops, the more undifferentiated and disorganized the child and the more impaired his sense of self, object relatedness, and reality testing. When psychoactive medications are employed, they are used to reduce anxiety, diminish aggressivity and impulsivity, and to improve the child's ability to attend and concentrate. These all facilitate the integration of many ego functions, thereby improving social behavior, peer relationships, readiness to learn and, hopefully, promoting the resumption of the normal developmental process. As far as we know, none of the medications used to date has any specific ability to influence the underlying causes of mental illness. The clinical conditions that affect children have their onset at varying times and ages and the associated symptoms can be influenced by medication. The symptoms at which we aim our medications are referred to as target symptoms. Diagnosis in child psychiatry continues to be hazardous because of the paucity of well controlled studies in early childhood and the difficulty in delineating differentiated syndromes in the young child. (Campbell and Shapiro 1975). Nevertheless, there are benefits to be derived from refining diagnostic entities and identifying target symptoms commonly associated with them. Medications useful in influencing those target symptoms may then be studied. The diagnostic classification which follows is an attempt at identifying those clinical disorders and their target symptoms responsive to medication which occur at various ages and developmental stages. Contributions from GAP (1966) and DSM III* are incorporated within this framework.

PRINCIPLES OF MEDICATION USAGE

After completing the workup and elaborating the diagnoses and other psychotherapeutic parameters, consideration should be given to the issues of motivation, comprehension, and ability of both the child and family to cooperate. If a psychopharmacological approach is to be utilized, outline its purposes and the symptoms of the child's disorder that you plan to influence. The goals might include increasing attention span, reducing hyperactivity, controlling bed-wetting, controlling delusions and hallucinations, and/or enhancing the child's relationship with the physician. Once the physician decides on the diagnosis, target symptoms, and the dynamic issues involved, then he may make the decision to

*Diagnostic and Statistical Manual III, American Psychiatric Association (in press: 1978).

start treatment with one specific medication. If he is going to use the neuroleptics,* he will want to get a complete CBC, urinalysis, liver profile, and have base line blood pressure done. If he is going to use the tricyclics, he will also want a baseline EKG. If he plans to use lithium he will want to rule out cardiovascular or renal disease and get T_3–T_4, BUN and Creatinine levels, in addition to the other lab tests mentioned. When planning to use psychostimulants, an initial base line reading for weight and height should be plotted on a growth chart.

It is always important to inform the child and family of your plans for medication, discussing with them the significant side effects and inviting questions until their fears and doubts are allayed. The actual dose of a medication is determined by the physician's clinical judgment depending on the age and weight of the child and the duration and severity of the emotional illness.

The child psychiatrist who uses medication should know nine or ten agents very well. The nine most important medications in child psychiatry, in my experience, are: chlorpromazine, thioridazine, haloperidol, methylphenidate, dextroamphetamine sulfate, imipramine, diphenhydramine, diazepam, and lithium. Once the physician has chosen the medication he plans to use and has thoroughly familiarized himself with what it can do, cannot do, and the dangers of using it, then he should give consideration to the starting dose. Start at the lowset dose recommended to be certain to avoid unexpected allergic or other unanticipated reactions and side effects. The daily dose may then be increased until

---

*Dorland's Illustrated Medical Dictionary [25th ed. 1974] defines neuroleptic as follows: "denoting a neuropharmacologic agent that has anti-psychotic action affecting principally psychomotor activity, and is generally without hypnotic effects, as a tranquilizer; it may produce extrapyramidal syndrome."

TABLE 1

THE DISORDERS OF CHILDHOOD & ADOLESCENCE RESPONSIVE TO PSYCHOPHARMACOTHERAPY

	Target Symptoms	Medication
A. With Psychoses		
1. Psychoses of Infancy & Early Childhood (0–6 years)		
a. Early infantile autism	Impulsivity, agitation	Phenothiazines (chlorpromazine, trifluoperazine, thioridazine); Lithium (may be useful, needs further evaluation)
b. Interactional psychotic disorders—symbiotic psychoses	Aggressivity, panic states	
c. Other organic brain syndromes with/without mental retardation	Hyperactivity, anxiety, self-destructiveness, self-mutilation	
2. Psychoses of Later Childhood (6–12 years)		
a. Organic brain syndromes—acute & chronic	Agitation, impulsivity, aggressivity, hyperactivity	Phenothiazines
b. Schizophreniform psychoses	Introjected voices and objects, delusions, hallucinations, thinking disorders	Phenothiazines
c. Affective psychoses of preadolescence	Manic psychotic states, delusions of grandeur, elevated mood, psychomotor excitement	Phenothiazines, lithium

continued on next page

Table 1, *continued*

	Target Symptoms	Medication
3. Psychoses of Adolescence (12 years–adulthood)		
a. Acute confusional states—infectious, drug-induced, metabolic, etc.	Disorientation, memory impairment, delusions, hallucinations, panic states	Removal of etiologic agents from body. Phenothiazines, lithium
b. Affective psychoses of adolescence —unipolar and bipolar types	Depression, mood swings, manic states, delusions, flight of ideas	Lithium, phenothiazines, tricyclics, MAO inhibitors
c. Schizophrenic disorders of adolescence—adult type	Delusions, externally perceived auditory hallucinations, thinking disorders	Phenothiazines, butyrophenones, thioxanthenes
B. *With or Without Psychoses* 1. Phobic Disorders of Childhood & Adolescence (6-years–adulthood) a. Separation anxiety disorders		
1. School phobia—often associated with psychoses during adolescence	Clinging to parents, school refusal, somatic complaints, stomach aches, headaches, fear of dying	Diphenhydramine, imipramine, phenothiazines
2. Agoraphobia—often associated with psychoses during adolescence	Fear of leaving the house, traveling	imipramine, phenothiazines

continued on next page

Table 1, continued

2. Attentional Deficit		
a. With/without hyperactivity, MBD and/or learning disability	Short attention span, fidgetiness, impulsivity, psychomotor excitation, low frustration tolerance, easy distractibility	Methylphenidate, dextroamphetamine, pemoline, imipramine, chlorpromazine, thioridazine, psychotherapy
3. Stereotyped Movement Disorders		
a. Motor verbal tic disorder—Gilles de la Tourette (3 years–adulthood)	Multiple involuntary head and body tics, vocal tics, coprolalia	Haloperidol, phenothiazines
C. *Without Psychoses*		
1. Sleep Disorders of Early Childhood & Latency (2–12 years)		
a. Nightmares	Frightening dreams	Diazepam
b. Night terrors (pavor nocturnus)	Difficulty waking, agitation, amnesia	Hydroxyzine
c. Insomnia	Difficulty falling asleep	Diphenhydramine
d. Sleepwalking	Disorder of arousal, amnesia	Chloral hydrate
e. Narcolepsy	Brief irresistible sleep attacks with/without loss of muscle tone (cataplexy)	Methylphenidate, amphetamines
2. Specific Developmental Disorders of Latency (6–12 years)		
a. Enuresis		
1. Familial	Wetting during first hours of sleep	Imipramine
2. Crisis related	Wetting during late hours of sleep and during daytime	Psychotherapy
b. Encopresis	Fecal soiling	Imipramine
c. Mixed type—enuresis and encopresis	Both wetting and fecal soiling	Psychotherapy, imipramine

continued on next page

Table 1, *continued*

	Target Symptoms	Medication
3. Depressive Disorders of Childhood (6 years through adolescence)		
a. Masked depressive reaction Depressive equivalents		
1. Behavioral disorders associated with/without enuresis and/or encopresis	Increased motor activity, physical complaints, sleep difficulties, fears	Psychotherapy, imipramine, diazepam
b. Depressive Reaction—Adult type (6 years—adulthood) associated with affective and vegetative components	Sadness, unhappiness, cannot enjoy very much, suicidal ideation and behavior, vegetative symptoms	Imipramine, amitriptyline, MAO inhibitors, psychotherapy
4. Anxiety Disorders of Childhood and Adolescence (8 years up)		
a. Anxiety neuroses	Intrapsychic conflict, anxiety Hyperventilation, fear, dread, sweating	Psychotherapy No medication
b. Anxious-phobic-depersonalization syndrome	Anxiety, fears, phobias, depersonalization, insomnia, behavior disorder, sleep difficulty	Diazepam imipramine, diphenhydramine
c. Overanxious disorder	Disturbance of emotion with sensitivity, shyness and social withdrawal	Benzodiazepines (diazepam)

the target symptoms are affected or side effects intervene. If one gets the desirable response associated with unwanted side effects, then cut back on the dose to eliminate the side effects and hopefully, maintain the improvement. The failure of response of one medication in a class, does not necessarily mean failure with another. For unknown reasons, children may respond to one tricyclic or phenothiazine and not another. While the total dose can be given at one time during the evening before sleep, because of the bolus effect due to the sudden introduction of high blood levels of drugs, I prefer to give medication in divided doses, perhaps giving one half or two thirds of the dose at night before sleep and the remainder during the day, except for the stimulant medications, which are given during the mornings and early afternoons.

Many child psychiatrists are timid in prescribing medication, often discontinuing the medication too soon. Once a physician prescribes a medication, he should continue giving it until therapeutic dose levels are reached before deciding that it is ineffective. While these medications should not be used carelessly, fear of side effects should not prohibit the physician from treating the distressed child with therapeutic doses.

ANTIPSYCHOTIC MEDICATIONS (Neuroleptics and Lithium)

The antipsychotic medications, which include the neuroleptics and lithium, have wide clinical usefulness in the treatment of the nonpsychotic and psychotic disorders of children and adolescents. Their efficacy lies in controlling the anxiety, impulsivity, and aggressivity associated with these disorders. The neuroleptics consist of a heterogeneous group of clinical compounds which include the phenothiazines, butyrophenones, thioxanthenes, and oxoindoles. Lithium is an ion that exists naturally as a salt and has chemical properties similar to sodium.

The antipsychotic medications do not materially alter the course and outcome of those psychoses that begin in early childhood (0–6 years) (Werry 1978). However, they are useful in managing the associated symptoms of psychomotor excitation, anxiety, panic states, self-destructiveness, and self-mutilation often seen in these children, thereby facilitating adjustment to a hospital setting or residential group. The disorders of later childhood (6–12 years) that are responsive to antipsychotic medications include the schizophreniform psychoses, the organic brain syndromes (with/without mental retardation), the psychoses of preadolescence accompanied by mood disorder, and the movement disorders associated with Gilles de la Tourette syndrome. The neuroleptics have a role in managing the behavioral manifestations of hyperactivity, aggressivity, and impulsiveness seen in many nonpsychotic emotionally disturbed children and in some organically brain damaged children, with or without mental retardation. There is no indication for antipsychotics in those organically brain damaged children who are better adjusted, such as some cerebral palsied children.

The children with schizophreniform type psychoses may present with introjected voices and objects, inappropriate behavior, or changes in eating or sleeping habits. In adolescence, the acute schizophrenic reaction represents the major indication for antipsychotic medication. In this stage, the previously experienced delusions and hallucinations are externally projected and perceived as voices from the outside. These adolescents often present with a marked thinking disorder, somatic and paranoid delusions, and panic states, all characteristic of the adult form of the disease. The earlier the onset of this disorder, the worse the prognosis. The more acute the onset, the more favorable the outcome.

The neuroleptics are useful in the treatment of the drug induced psychotic reactions seen in adolescents, particularly those caused by LSD and amphetamines. Treatment should be designed to facilitate the metabolism and excretion of the ingested noxious agents while using the antipsychotic agents to maintain control of the secondary psychosis. Recently a synthetic agent, phencyclidine (PCP), known as "angel dust," has begun to be used by many adolescents in search of relief from inner tension and anxiety. Early reports indicate that phenothiazines in combination with PCP may cause severe hypotension and even death. These patients should be managed with minor tranquilizers during the acute phase of their illness. Further clinical studies need to be done to clarify the question of the dangers of using phenothiazines with PCP.

The phenothiazines and butyrophenones offer the clinician a choice of agents that can be used to diminish and control the psychotic, organic, and conduct disorders described. All of the neuroleptics have relatively similar antipsychotic potency and the mgm potency of each agent is measured against that of chlorpromazine. The phenothiazines have some advantages over the butyrophenones in the treatment of young children under twelve years, causing less dystonias and akathisias. As a result the butyrophenones have not been approved for usage by the FDA for children under twelve years. In the over twelve group, the butyrophenones are not as sedating and have value for those adolescents who cannot tolerate or do not respond to the phenothiazines.

PHENOTHIAZINES

Chlorpromazine has always been the most reliable anti-psychotic agent in the treatment of children and is particularly valuable in controlling increased psychomotor activity. It may cause a painful sunburn dermatitis in the summer months and make it necessary for the physician to switch to thioridazine which does not cause this side effect. Chlorpromazine causes more sedation than the others, more orthostatic hypotension (with reduction in both the systolic and diastolic blood pressure) and more extrapyramidal side effects. Thioridazine causes less extrapyramidal side effects, less convulsions in seizure-prone children, more retinal toxicity and ejaculatory disturbances in some adolescents. Breast enlargement, lactation, and menstrual irregularities occur with all the phenothiazines. In fifteen years of experience, in treating over 1500 children with phenothiazines at the Elmhurst General Hospital, we have not seen one case of agranulocytosis and no deaths due to psychotropic medication. While leukopenia may occur with all the phenothiazines, the children's blood counts return to normal about three weeks after discontinuing the phenothiazine. Because of our experience, we have discontinued repeating the CBC after the first three months of drug therapy and are guided by the clinical state of the patient. All sore throats and temperature elevations are taken seriously and investigated. Liver function tests are done routinely. We have not seen a case of drug induced hepatitis in years. Weight gain seems to occur with all of the phenothiazines and when it occurs, it is often associated with improvement in the child's clinical condition.

All of the phenothiazines cause extrapyramidal symptoms including Parkinson type reactions, akathisias, dystonias, laryngospasm, oculogyric crises and opisthotonus. Phenothiazines should be gradually reduced over a three to six week period, before being terminated. Abrupt withdrawal can lead to irritability and excitement. Polizos et al. (1973) have reported that approximately 50 percent of those children treated will develop neurological withdrawal emergent symptoms (WES) upon the abrupt cessation of neuroleptics. The most common symptoms consist of involuntary movement of the extremities, trunk, and head. Only a few children have developed oral dyskinesias. Spontaneous remission often occurs if the child can manage without medication. This syndrome may be related to the adult form of tardive dyskinesia. For the acute Parkinsonian reaction, akathisias, or dystonias, diphenhydramine IM or IV is very useful. Once the acute symptoms subside, the patient can be put on oral diphenhydramine or other anti-Parkinsonian agents like Artane. Cogentin is not used for children under twelve. Anti-Parkinsonian agents should not be prescribed prophylactically.

These are powerful and dangerous drugs and should not be used as chemical restraints in controlling youngsters with personality problems, because all of the neuroleptics can cause involuntary movement disorders. When hospitalized, the environment should be rich enough to manage these problems with individual, group, and milieu therapy.

BUTYROPHENONES

Haloperidol is the only significant drug in this group. It is used primarily in adolescents as an antipsychotic agent. The drug is finding increased usefulness in adolescent onset schizophrenia, in institutionalized retarded children who are motorically driven and in youngsters recovering from acute episodes of schizophrenia requiring maintenance medication. In some patients on our wards it seems to have a very powerful antipsychotic effect while in others it is not as effective. Unfortunately, its use is associated with a high incidence of side effects consisting of extrapyramidal symptoms, dystonias, akathisias and dyskinesias. It seems to lower the seizure threshold in vulnerable children. Abrupt withdrawal can produce dyskinesias, so haloperidol should be withdrawn slowly. In addition to its use in psychoses, it is the drug of choice in the treatment of the movement disorders, particularly of Gilles de la Tourette syndrome. Prior to the development of haloperidol, this disorder was difficult to manage at best and often intractable. Tourette's syndrome is a clinical disease that usually begins in early childhood (three to eighteen years) with involuntary, multiple movements of the head and arms which then spread to the trunk. These involuntary movements become associated with a vocal tic and at times with coprolalia. Sometimes the tic takes on the quality of a bark or grunt and very often the child is compelled to utter a stream of obscene words. Haloperidol is often effective in alleviating the muscular and vocal tics. The dosage in adolescents is 2–3 mg/day and in adults, 6–80 mg/day.

LITHIUM ION

Lithium ion is increasingly being used in the treatment of children and adolescents since the first reports of Van Krevelen and Van Voorst in 1959. The reports in the literature are based on uncontrolled studies involving small numbers and diagnostically poorly defined patient samples. While lithium does not appear to be helpful in the treatment of hyperactive children with normal intelligence, it does seem to have potential usefulness in the treatment of manic-depressive illness in adolescence (Campbell, Schulman, and Rapaport 1978).

The acute forms of affective psychoses, particularly of the

manic type and of a cyclical or periodic nature, once thought not to occur in younger children, while still rare, are increasingly being described in the literature as occurring in preadolescent and adolescent youngsters and there are an increasing number of reports of successful treatment with lithium. The advent of lithium as a therapeutic agent has spurred workers in the field to reevaluate theory and to search for clinical entities responsive to this medication. While these reports need further documentation and support through well designed, controlled studies, there is clinical evidence that lithium is useful. I have seen a manic psychotic reaction in an eleven-year-old boy which responded promptly to lithium therapy. His disorder was associated with delusions of grandeur (he thought that he was Picasso), elevation of mood, excitability and overtalkativeness. Retrospectively gathered history suggests that these children have often had a disturbance in earlier childhood; they generally have been appealing, dependent, periodically overtalkative and well-related children. Some have had previous hospitalizations during latency in which they were most often diagnosed as being schizophrenic or hyperactive. Some of the recurring and cyclical psychotic disorders of latency undoubtedly will become the affective disorders of adolescence and early adulthood.

Schizoaffective disorders, which probably represent examples of affective disorders, seem to occur more frequently in adolescents than does the bipolar affective disease, and many cases respond to lithium. Schizophrenic youngsters who have a strong affective component to their disorder and who do not respond to phenothiazines or butyrophenones may be considered as candidates for treatment with lithium.

ANTIDEPRESSANT MEDICATIONS

Progress in the treatment of the depressive disorders of adults has stimulated important work in the field of childhood depression. The early evidence, derived from clinical experience and uncontrolled studies, suggests that the prepubertal depressive disorders of childhood exist in good numbers and appear to be developmentally earlier forms of the adult depressive disease (Puig-Antich et al. 1977). While the existence of depression in childhood is still controversial, there is an increasing experience among child psychiatrists that depression can develop in children (Hersov 1977). Whether or not this depressive disorder might be a form of unipolar depression is a matter of speculation (Winokur et al. 1973). The depressed children in this age group look sad, describe feelings of sadness, and may have suicidal ideation. We are seeing a larger number of children, seven years and up, who have made suicidal attempts. Many of these children have pathological separation anxiety symptoms associated with school phobias. There are some who demonstrate psychotic and endogenous subtypes of the disorder. Many times, children exhibit another type of depressive disorder, a masked type of depression, associated with conduct disturbance, somatization, enuresis, or encopresis. The pharmacological approach toward treating this disorder is helpful and should be employed in association with psychotherapy.

TRICYCLIC ANTIDEPRESSANTS

The tricyclic antidepressants, particularly imipramine, have many uses in the treatment of children. The tricyclics are useful in the treatment of enuresis and/or encopresis (50–75 mg/HS), hyperkinesis (100–150 mg), school phobia (50–150 mg), and childhood depression (1.5–4.5 mg/k/d).

The side effects include autonomic blocking effects, dry mouth, blurring of vision, constipation, and difficulty urinating. Higher doses can cause more serious side effects including cardiotoxic effects and seizures. Some workers (Rapaport 1976) suggest that clinicians do not exceed 100 mg daily except in unusual cases. Because of the serious complications which may occur at higher dosages, some physicians do not use tricyclics for enuresis and prefer the behavioral modification approach of the bell and pad. For the treatment of depression that has existed one to two months, the starting dose of 1 mg/k/d should be given in one dose at night, or in divided doses during the day. The medication is then increased on a four to seven day basis by a 5 mg/k until the child is receiving 4.5 mg/k/d. The FDA has ruled in 1975 that 5 mg/k/d is the maximum allowable dose in children and that EKG monitoring is essential when using imipramine. The tricyclics are far from benign drugs and are responsible for the death of many children through accidental overdosage in the home where children take a parent's medication.

ANTIANXIETY MEDICATIONS

Anxiety manifests itself in a variety of ways at different ages and stages of development. From infancy through the preschool years, anxiety is expressed through feeding disturbances, clinging behavior, multiple and transient fears, temper tantrums and, if prolonged and unrelieved, eventually through regression (White 1977). At school age, the child may be aware of his discomfort and complain of nausea, loss of appetite, or he may experience a variety of sleep difficulties and refuse to go to school. The latency age child complains of stomach aches, loss of appetite, tension states, episodes of hyperventilation, difficulties in his relationship with peers, anxiety over athletic performance in groups, and the onset of learning difficulties. In adolescence, the youngster's anxiety is often experienced around appearance, body image, weight, other bodily complaints, and relationships with peers and parents. The adolescent often tries to ignore, extinguish, control, or explain away his anxiety for fear of revealing his feelings of being different.

When a child's anxiety interferes with his normal functioning and everyday relationships, and he appears to be experiencing obvious discomfort, then attention should be directed toward helping him feel better. If his malfunctioning is severe enough, a good psychiatric diagnostic examination may be useful in identifying the cause and psychotherapeutic intervention may be helpful. Medication is often a useful adjunct to psychotherapy. The scientific literature does not support or oppose the use of antianxiety drugs in children at this time, so the decision is a medical one, based on the patient's perceived needs and the physician's experience and judgment. The physician's ability to tolerate anxiety in his child patient is an important determining factor. Perhaps families choose their physician on the basis of this level of responsivity. In my experience, many children who develop marked anxiety come from families where anxiety is useful in influencing other family members. Anxiety is placebo-sensitive and there are patients who feel better as soon as someone acknowledges their discomfort by prescribing medication. Antianxiety medication should only be used for two to three week intervals when indicated and then the situation reevaluated.

DIPHENMETHANE DERIVATIVES

Hydroxyzine (Atarax, Vistaril) is used in the treatment of mild anxiety and to produce some sedation when indicated. The medication is often used by pediatricians. With the wide range of medications available now, there appears to be little need for the use of hydroxyzine.

Diphenhydramine (Benadryl) is an antihistamine and historically has been one of the most useful medications in treating children with hyperactive behavior problems, sleep disorders, tension states, and childhood psychoses. The drug is well tolerated in children and is used in any condition in which a good sedative or hypnotic effect is desirable. If used for long periods of time, it loses its effectiveness and therefore its value in psychoses is limited. The other major indication for the use of diphenhydramine is in the treatment of medication-induced extrapyramidal symptoms, consisting of dystonias, akathisias, opisthotonus, and oculogyric crises. An effective and rapid way of treating the acute onset of the extrapyramidal symptom disorders is to give the diphenhydramine IM or IV, placing the medication in solution, and delivering enough drug so that symptoms come under control. Diphenhydramine is useful for nighttime sedation in the latency age and adolescent child, but has been displaced by diazepam as the drug of choice in the treatment of insomnia, night terrors, and somnambulism. Occasional dizziness and oversedation can occur so that patients complain in the mornings. Diphenhydramine comes in elixir and capsule form—1 tsp. = 12.5 mg. The dosage range is between 75–500 mg/d and is calculated on the basis of 5 mg./k given in divided doses. For the young child, 1 or 2 tsps. may be a starting dose, and for the older child, start with 25 or 50 mg.

PHENOTHIAZINES

Promethazine (Phenergan) is an antihistamine-type compound which is basically a phenothiazine derivative. Promethazine generally should not be used as a major tranquilizer but is used for its sedative and antihistaminic properties. Its usefulness is essentially the same as that for diphenhydramine, namely for insomnia over the short term, hyperactive behavior disorder, tension states, and sleep disorders. Promethazine comes in tablet and syrup form. Tablets are 12.5, 25 and 50 mg. Syrup is 6.25 mg/5cc or 25 mg/5cc. Oral dose is 12.5–25 mg at bedtime. Paradoxical excitation has been reported in children on a single dose. Promethazine is not recommended in young children because of the risk of paradoxical excitation.

BENZODIAZEPINES

The two benzodiazepines that have usefulness in child psychiatry are chlordiazepoxide and diazepam. Of the two, diazepam is preferred.

Chlordiazepoxide (Librium) was the first drug developed in this group and has been used to reduce anxiety, thereby diminishing hyperactivity and allowing some anxiety-ridden children to return to school. Chlordiazepoxide may make some children excited, hostile, and aggressive. Other side effects include drowsiness, ataxia, increased anxiety, and depression.

Diazepam (Valium) is useful in three major areas: for its effect in childhood sleep disorders, as a sedative-hypnotic and for its anticonvulsant properties. Its prime indication is in the management of sleep disorders, particularly insomnia, pavor nocturnus (night terrors), and somnambulism (sleepwalking). Night terrors occur during arousal from deep sleep (stages III and IV); diazepam decreases the amount of stage

IV non-REM sleep (Anders and Ciaranello 1977). In addition, diazepam increases the seizure threshold and is considered to be an important agent in the treatment of status epilepticus. Diazepam is used as a muscle relaxant. This use has not been proven by controlled study. Diazepam is contraindicated in depressions, psychoses (including schizophrenia), and in the borderline states. It is not recommended for addiction-prone youngsters because of tolerance and physical dependence that occurs. Dosage range is from 2 mg to 20 mg/d for children five to twelve and from 4 to 40 mg for youngsters over twelve years. In status epilepticus, diazepam can be given IV. Medication should be injected slowly (1 mg/minute) until the seizure abates. If given too quickly this medication can cause respiratory arrest.

SUBSTITUTED PROPANEDIOLS

Meprobamate (Miltown, Equanil) has not been shown to be safe, sensible or effective in treating children and therefore, should *not* be used.

BARBITURATES

Barbiturates often cause excitement and increased agitation in disturbed children. The main use of phenobarbital is still as an anticonvulsant. There are other drugs that are better for sedation and sleep than the barbiturates.

CHLORAL HYDRATE

Chloral hydrate (Noctec) is an effective hypnotic agent for children. It comes as a syrup—500 mg (7.5 grains) per 5 ml —and as a capsule—250 mg (3.75 grains) or 500 mg (7.5 grains). The usual dose is 500 mg to 1 gram with a maximum single dose of 1 gram.

PSYCHOSTIMULANT MEDICATIONS

Nowhere in the psychopharmacotherapy of children have child psychiatrists had more success than in the treatment of that heterogeneous group of disorders with varying etiologies that are expressed clinically through the hyperactive child syndrome (Werry 1978). While hyperactivity, impulsivity, irritability, and aggressivity are the major symptoms of this disorder, the child's inability to pay attention is pathognomonic of the disorder. Sometimes it appears that the attentional deficit is selective and that the child can pay attention to those matters that interest him, but not to special demands for his attention, as in the classroom. [For more detailed information on this disorder and its relationship to minimal brain dysfunction and learning disability, see other chapters in this volume.] While individual psychotherapy is of little value during the early stages of hyperactivity and behavioral difficulties associated with this disorder, the child psychiatrist has a role in working out a treatment plan which includes medication, remediation, behavioral modification techniques, and counseling for the parents. Once the child's attention span has improved, then psychotherapy for the child is a consideration.

The medication of choice for this disorder is *methylphenidate,* followed closely by *dextroamphetamine sulfate.* For methylphenidate, start with 5 mg b.i.d. and increase up to a maximum of 60 mg/d. For dextroamphetamine, start with 5 mg/d and increase to a maximum of 40 mg/d. Some children are unusually sensitive and respond to low doses of both medications. The side effects with methylphenidate are insomnia, anorexia, and growth retardation. The insomnia often can be managed by giving the last dose of medication no later than at noontime. Sometimes the anorexia can be managed by

lowering the dose while still maintaining the desired therapeutic effect. Growth retardation for any child does not appear ever to exceed one inch which, however, may be a major
deterrent to using this medication for children who will be
short. Methylphenidate can be used during adolescence for
most children without danger that the drug will be abused,
yet this is clearly a consideration in some cases. Methylphenidate's major effects are apparent during the first twelve
weeks of therapy. Psychostimulant medication and behavioral modification techniques used together offer the optimal
treatment for this disorder. In many cases, children can approach normal levels of functioning with this regimen.

In contrast to methylphenidate (Ritalin) and dextroamphetamine sulfate (Dexedrine), pemoline (Cylert) has a gradual onset of action. With the dosage recommended (37.5 mg
in the A.M., increased by 18.75 mg/d each week), significant
benefits may not be apparent for three to four weeks of
therapy. The drug has a long biological half life and can
easily be given once a day. Pemoline has little potential for
abuse or addiction (DiMascio and Goldberg 1978). The
other medications in treating hyperkinetic disorders are *imipramine* (Tofranil) and *thioridazine* (Mellaril). Imipramine and
thioridazine both work well for about four weeks and then
the patients become resistant and these medications do not
continue to be beneficial.

ANTI-PARKINSONIAN AGENTS FOR CHILDREN

When children are given antipsychotic medication, they
usually do not develop the extrapyramidal symptoms that
typically occur with adults. There are some disturbed children who need high doses of antipsychotic agents and who

do develop extrapyramidal signs and other movement disorders including dystonias. These children may be treated with anti-Parkinsonian agents. The drugs of choice are *trihexylphenidyl HCl* (Artane) and *diphenhydramine* (Benadryl). Doses for trihexylphenidyl HCl are from 1–2 mg twice a day and for diphenhydramine 50 to 500 mg/d. It can be given IV and IM. *Benztropine mesylate* (Cogentin) is *not* recommended for young children, but has usefulness in the older adolescent. The dose is 1 to 2 mg once or twice a day. It can be given IM.

SUMMARY

This chapter presents developmental considerations, onset, diagnoses, and target symptoms of childhood psychiatric syndromes and attempts to relate these to the effectiveness of medication. It includes a review of the current literature, a classification of medications used in child and adolescent psychiatry, principles of drug usage and information on nine of the most valuable drugs used in child psychiatry. Special attention is paid to the use of the neuroleptics, tricyclic antidepressants, psychostimulants, and lithium. Recent information on childhood depression, sleep disorders, school phobia, enuresis, and drug related dyskinesias in children is included.

While the author has been careful to check the recommendations made within this chapter, errors regarding specific medications and dosages are possible. Future developments concerning contraindications, drug interactions and long-term side effects will influence specific recommendations. Each physician is responsible for his own decisions and should check with other sources, including the child's pediatrician and the current literature, before prescribing medica-

TABLE 2

Classification of Psychopharmacological Medication for Children & Adolescents

Medication	Recommended Dosages	Comments
I. Antipsychotic medication		
A. Phenothiazine		
1. Aliphatics Chlorpromazine (Thorazine)	Starting dose: 2–8 mg/k/d in divided doses. For 6 months to 6 years—up to 40 mg/d For 6–12 years—50–300 mg/d Over 12 years—75–1000 mg/d	Dose titrated to the individual needs of each child. Higher dose range for more severe cases. Not recommended for under 6 months.
2. Piperazine		
a. Trifluo- perazine (Stelazine)	Starting dose: 1 mg once or twice daily For 6–12 years—1–15 mg/d Over 12 years—2–40 mg/d	Ratio to CPZ 1–20. 5 mg. Stelazine = 100 mg CPZ. For use in psychotic children only. Not recommended for under 6 years
b. Fluphenazine HCL (Prolixin) (Permitil)	Starting dose: For over 12 years 1–20 mg/d	Ratio to CPZ 1–70. 2 mg. = 140 mg. CPZ. Higher incidence of dyskinesia and dystonia in children and adolescents. Not recommended under 12.
3. Piperidine (Thioridazine) (Mellaril)	Starting dose: 0.5–3 mg/k/d For 2–12 years—30–300 mg/d For over 12 years—75–600 mg/d	Ratio to CPZ 1–1. 100 mg. Thioridazine = 100 mg. CPZ. Not recommended under 2 years.
B. Butyrophenones		
1. Haloperidol (Haldol)	Starting dose: 0.5–1 mg once or twice daily. Over 12 years—1–16 mg/d	Less sedation. Useful in Gilles de la Tourette syndrome. Ratio: 1–50. 1 mg. Haldol = 50 mg. CPZ. Not recommended under 12 years (FDA); need special consent for treatment of Gilles de la Tourette.

continued on next page

Table 2, *continued*

	Starting dose	
C. Thioxanthenes		
1. Thiothixene (Navane)	Starting dose: Over 12 years—6–60 mg/d	Ratio: 1–50. 1 mg Navane = 50 mg. CPZ.
2. Chlorprothixene (Taractan)	Ratio: 1–1. 1 mg Taractan = 1 mg. CPZ. Not recommended under 12 years for either medication.	
D. Lithium ion		
1. Lithium Carbonate (Eskalith)	Starting dose: Under 12 years—150–300 mg/d. Over 12 years—300–1800 mg/d	Blood serum level 0.6–1.2 mEq/1 for over 12 years. Need special consent for younger children.
II. Anti-depressant medication		
A. Tricyclic antidepressants		
1. Iminodibenzyl derivatives		
a. Imipramine (Tofranil)	Starting dose: 1.5 mg/k/d in divided doses or 25 mg HS. Increase 1 mg/k/d for depression until a maximum dose of 4.5 mg/k/d is reached. Increase up to 75 mg. HS for enuresis.	Need EKG monitoring and special permission for doses that exceed 75 mg/d. Useful in treatment of phobias, agoraphobia, school phobia & enuresis. Not recommended under 6 years.
b. Amitryptiline (Elavil)	Starting dose: 1.5 mg/k/d 25 mg/HS. Increase gradually to maximum of 4.5 mg/k/d. Up to 75 mg/HS for enuresis	For over 12 years. Need EKG monitoring for doses over 75 mg. when treating depression.
B. MAO Inhibitors		Not recommended for children at this time.

continued on next page

Table 2, *continued*

Medication	Recommended Dosages	Comments
III. Anti-anxiety medications		
A. Diphenylmethane derivatives		
1. Hydroxyzine (Atarax, Vistaril)	Starting dose: From 1 to 12 years—50–500 mg/d. Over 12 years—75–500 mg/d	No age limit.
2. Diphenhydramine (Benadryl)	Starting dose: From 1 to 12 years—5 mg/k/d to 50–500 mg/d. For over 12 years—75–500 mg/d	Not recommended under 1 year. Elixir 12.5 mg/tsp—3–4 tsps./d. Can be given IM or IV for extrapyramidal symptoms, opisthotonus, oculogyric crises, dyskinesias.
B. Benzodiazepines		
1. Chlordiazepoxide (Librium)	Starting dose: From 6–12 years—10–50 mg/d. Over 12 years—15–75 mg/d in divided doses	Not recommended under 6 years.
2. Diazepam (Valium)	Starting dose: From 6–12 years—2–20 mg/d. Over 12 years—4–40 mg/d in divided doses	Not recommended under 1 year.
3. Dalmane (Flurazepam HCl)	Not recommended under 15 years.	
C. Substituted Propanediols		
1. Meprobamate (Miltown, Equanil)		Not indicated for children

continued on next page

Table 2, continued

D. Chloral Hydrate (Noctec)	For sleep—50 mg/k—1–2 tsp. Maximum 1 gram/single dose.	An effective hypnotic agent. Syrup—500 mg (7.5 grains) per 5 ml. Capsules—250 mg (3.75 grains) or 500 mg (7.5 grains).
E. Barbiturates		Not appropriate for anxiety in children.
IV. Psychostimulant medications		
A. Amphetamines & related CNS stimulants		
1. Dextroamphetamine sulfate (Dexedrine)	Starting dose: 6–12 years—5–20 mg/d. Over 12 years—5–40 mg/d in divided doses.	Not recommended under 3 years.
2. Methylphenidate (Ritalin)	6–12 years 5–40 mg/d Over 12 years—10–60 mg/d in divided doses	Not recommended under 6 years.
3. Pemoline (Cylert)	37.5 mg/d in single early morning doses increased by 18.75 mg/d each week until desired effect obtained or to 112.5 mg/d maximum.	Single morning dose. Not for use under 6 years.

continued on next page

Table 2, continued

V. Anti-Parkinsonian agents for children

A. Diphenhydramine (Benadryl)

Medication	Recommended Dosages	Comments
	Starting dose: 5 mg/k/d in divided doses to 50–500 mg/d.	Can be given IM, IV for control of extrapyramidal symptoms, dystonias, opisthotonus, oculogyric crises.
B. Trihexylphenidyl HCl (Artane)	1–2 mg. twice a day.	No significant side effects.
C. Benztropine mesylate (Cogentin)	1 mg twice a day for acute reactions. 1–2 mg IM, then 1–2 mg twice daily.	Contraindicated in children under 6 years because of side effects.

tion for children. For additional information on the psychotropics used in the treatment of children, see the current
edition of the *Physicians Desk Reference* (PDR).

BIBLIOGRAPHY

Anders, F., and Ciaranello, R. (1977). Psychopharmacology
of childhood disorders. In *Psychopharmacology: From Theory to Practice,* ed. J.D. Barchas, P. A. Berger, R. D. Ciara-
vello, and G. R. Elliott, Chapters 25, 26 and 27. New
York: Oxford University Press.
Campbell, M., Schulman, D., and Rapaport, J. (1978). Position paper on the current status of the use of lithium in
child psychiatry. *Journal of the American Academy of Child
Psychiatry,* in press.
Campbell, M., and Shapiro, T. (1975). Therapy of psychiatric
disorders of childhood. In *Manual of Psychiatric Therapeutics: Practical Psychiatry and Psychopharmacology,* ed. R. I.
Shader. Boston: Little, Brown. An excellent review of
the subject with emphasis on the diagnostic process and
classification. There is a section on treatment modalities,
including treatment of the parents and families.
DiMascio, A., and Goldberg, H. (1978). Psychotropics for
children. *Journal of Practical Therapeutics: Current Prescribing*
1:90–96.
Group for the Advancement of Psychiatry (1966). *Psychopathological Disorders in Childhood: Theoretical Considerations
and a Proposed Classification.* New York: Group for the
Advancement of Psychiatry.
Group for the Advancement of Psychiatry (1975). *Pharmacotherapy and Psychotherapy: Paradoxes, Problems and Progress.*
New York: Brunner/Mazel. A major scientific work that

fosters the idea that psychotherapy and pharmacotherapy are mutually compatible and can enhance one another. Indicates the danger of an irrational bias toward one or the other and suggests areas and strategies for future research.

Hersov, L. (1977). Emotional disorders. In *Child Psychiatry: Modern Approaches,* ed. M. Rutter and H. Hersov, pp. 444–449. London: Blackwell Condon.

Kaplan, C. (1977). Pediatric psychopharmacology. In *The Practitioner's Guide to Psychoactive Drugs,* ed. E. Bassuk and S. Schoonover. New York and London: Plenum. An excellent review of the subject with a special section on Emergencies in Child Psychiatry.

Polizos, P., Engelhardt, D., Hoffman, J., et al. (1973). Neurological consequences of psychotropic drug withdrawal in schizophrenic children. *Journal of Autism and Childhood Schizophrenia* 3:245–253.

Puig-Antich, J., Blau, S., Marx, N., Greenhill, L., and Chambers, W. (1977). Prepubertal major depressive disorder. Paper presented at the American Academy of Child Psychiatry annual conference, Houston, Texas.

Rapaport, J. (1976). Psychopharmacology of childhood depression. In *Progress in Psychiatric Drug Treatment,* vol. 2 ed. D. Klein and R. Gittleman-Klein, pp 493–505. New York: Brunner/Mazel.

Werry, J. (1977). The use of pyschotropic drugs in children. *Journal of the American Academy of Child Psychiatry* 16:446–468. The clinical use, methods of evaluation, safety, and efficacy of psychotropic drugs in children are reviewed. A comprehensive review of the literature of the past five years includes 118 articles.

——— (1978). *Pediatric Psychopharmacology: The Use of Behavior Modifying Drugs in Children,* ed. J. Werry. New York: Brunner/Mazel. A comprehensive presentation of the basic principles of pediatric psychopharmacology and the clinical application of individual drugs. The emphasis of the book is scientific and consists primarily of a series of critical reviews of the state of knowledge in the particular topic covered.

White, J. (1977). *Pediatric Psychopharmacology: A Practical Guide to Clinical Application.* Baltimore: Williams and Wilkins. A monograph designed to be a practical clinical guide to the use of psychoactive drugs in the treatment of children. A comprehensive review which includes sections on the general management of drug overdosage and seizure disorders.

Wiener, J., ed. (1977). *Psychopharmacology in Childhood and Adolescence.* New York: Basic Books. A thorough and useful survey of the field of psychopharmacology in childhood and adolescence. The historical, theoretical, factual, methodological, developmental and ethical background discussion are rich and interesting. The section on the use of specific agents in specific agents in specific syndromes is useful to the clinician.

Winokur, G., et al. (1973). The Iowa 500: familial and clinical findings favor two kinds of depressive illness. *Comprehensive Psychiatry* 14:99–107.

Chapter 31

PREVENTIVE CHILD PSYCHIATRY

Richard K. Hill, M.D.

DEFINITION

Attention has been given in this book to several syndromes which are commonly encountered in children. There are, however, a broad variety of situations which command a great deal of the child psychiatrist's attention. These include the many external events that occur in a child's life, such as divorce of parents or hospitalization, to which the child must adapt. The manner in which therapeutic measures are extended lies in the area of *preventive psychiatry.*

In this chapter we will be concerned with the concept of risk in the life of the child, both innate and developmental, and also with the specific situations which can produce adaptational difficulties.

REVIEW OF LITERATURE

Anthony (1974) uses the concept of the psychologically vulnerable child who is more prone to the development of psychopathology from any negative environmental events than is the less vulnerable child. These children seem to be vulnerable from the beginning of life, indeed probably prenatally, and are born with a low degree of preadaptiveness. Those with an inadequate protective stimulus barrier are also at risk. Moreover, the child with difficulties in controlling response to stimulation or who fails to show a positive response to the environment is similarly considered vulnerable. These qualities or tendencies are considered to be congenital or constitutional in nature.

The concept of primary reaction patterns, as delineated by Thomas, Chess, Birch, and Hertzig (1960), seems directly related to considerations of vulnerability and risk. Constitutional make-up and endocrinological status are considered linked to vulnerability as well.

A child may, of course, be vulnerable for any number of reasons not necessarily related to the above mentioned constitutional types. Thus, a child born with physical abnormalities or congenital impairments of any kind (e.g., a CNS disorder) stands at potential risk.

A child may be at risk at any time during his development, but may be more so at one time than another, particularly at periods of transition to higher modes of functioning. Moreover, early vulnerabilities tend to engender later vulnerabilities. Haggard (1974) discusses the problem of adaptation in relationship to risk, noting that behavior is determined by the developmental stage in relation to the individual in his environmental context. A child's adaptation is thus related temporally to the commonly understood components of drive, ego and reality, and alterations in any components bring about changes in status and are reflected in behavior and adaptation. Stress occurs when these components do not balance properly and the overall effect is related to the duration of the stress.

Since we recognize that the child is a dynamically developing individual and that stresses (environmental disturbances as well as constitutional givens) determine later patterns of emotional growth, personality and adaptive capabilities, it is clear that numerous experiences which a child encounters during his development can act as etiological agents producing psychopathological states. Kliman (1968) has proposed an etiological classification in which the developing child is more vulnerable to risks. These pathogenic experiences include: (1) Overstimulation, particularly as related to psychosexual stages; (2) deprivation experiences including object deprivation (loss or separation from a parent), stimulus deprivation, and superego support deprivation (poor or vacillating impulse control in the parents); (3) parental interference in the solution of normal developmental problems such as exploratory or motoric activities or in mother-child separation; (4) real fear experiences; (5) prolonged anxiety or conflict experiences, beyond the capacity of the child's ego to master; (6) endrocrine abnormality, leading to experiences such as delayed or precocious puberty; (7) interference with development of body image because of congential abnormalities, malformations or acquired physical impairments; (8) interference with cerebral function as in organic mental syndrome.

ETIOLOGY AND DYNAMICS

The risks that a child encounters are multiple and relatively easy to identify as compared to the factors that render him vulnerable to these risks. The fashion in which the child reacts to untoward events is determined by the nature, timing, duration, and intensity of the event as well as the child's own ability to adapt and the developmental stage he is in. It is assumed that more vulnerable children adapt poorly or perhaps pathologically to a given stress situation.

An understanding of the nature of risks and the developmental status and vulnerabilities of children suggest possible avenues of preventive efforts. A discussion of several situations of potential risks follows.

I. Illnesses: *(a)* in the child; *(b)* of a parent or grandparent; *(c)* of a sibling; *(d)* hospitalization of the child; *(e)* fatal illness in the child.

II. Separations: *(a)* death of parent(s), other family members or close friends; *(b)* hospitalization of a parent; *(c)* divorce or separation of parents; *(d)* beginning school; *(e)* working mothers;*(f)* adoption and foster care.

III. Violent events: *(a)* child abuse; *(b)* witness to violence; *(c)* recipient of violence; *(d)* horrifying events.

IV. Special events: *(a)* moving; *(b)* birth of a sibling; *(c)* societal events; *(d)* classroom events—summer camps; *(e)* Overstimulating experiences.

ILLNESSES

A child may experience illnesses in others or in himself. The illness may be acute or chronic, congenital, or acquired. It may result from trauma or the child may experience trauma of a surgical nature. Illnesses can be incapacitating or sharply reduce functioning. Illness may be fatal. It should be recognized that these situations present both significant and specific psychological problems and that they may be approached with the goal of preventing or lessening emotional sequelae.

A child may react to his illness by regression and helplessness or by becoming difficult and obstinate because of defenses against passivity (A. Freud 1952). He may try to hold onto the secondary gains of special care. If he is unaware of the nature of his illness or what can be expected procedurally, he may become anxious with attendant behavioral components. This is particularly true if he does not receive adequate support from parents who themselves are anxious and withholding of information regarding the realities of the situation. If his illness requires any degree of immobilization, he may become restless, anxious, or withdrawn because of intensified aggressive fantasies without the means for normal motor discharge of tension. He may moreover become angry or disappointed with his parents because they were unable to prevent his illness or to alleviate his discomfort. If medication is to be taken, there may be fantasies with regard to its nature or powers. Chronic illness may require a specific unalterable medical regime which is difficult to follow and may become a focal point for conflicts with parents. Furthermore, chronic illness may produce problems in maintaining normal activities or relationships with peers or family; and if the chronic disease is hereditary in nature, the child may blame his parents for giving it to him and the parents may feel guilty that they indeed did.

In chronic illnesses especially, and particularly where physical limitations are a major factor, certain typical maladaptive mechanisms may arise which predispose the child to poor social or school performance: denial of pathology which may be seen along with overcompensatory behavior; a passive withdrawal with strong anaclitic demands on others; a negative, angry attitude towards the world and an increasingly narcissistic stance.

Parental illnesses generally result in a relative lack of attention paid by a parent to the child's physical and emotional needs. The self-involvement of an ill parent renders him less available to the child. This may be interpreted by the child as rejection or chastisement, to which the child commonly reacts with anger. The child may also feel responsible for the illness and consider himself bad. Anger towards parents is difficult for a child to tolerate, especially if there is a wish that the parent might die. The threat of loss of the parent along with the expected retaliation of the parent therefore increases anxiety and tends to underscore guilt and negative feelings that the child may have about himself.

The illness or death of a sibling activates already present rivalries, including death wishes, which are very distressing to the child. Identification with the ill sibling may also occur and perhaps a desire to be ill as well, especially if the child perceives and envies the extra attention the sibling receives and interprets it as greater parental love.

Much has been written concerning the effect of hospitalization on a child (T. Bergman 1965, Calef 1959). The potential for suffering in the child is great not only because his own illness induces physical and emotional stress but because of the anxiety arising from separation from his parents. The relative lack of acceptable parent substitutes also presents difficulties for the child who may be angry about these separations, and also about unfamiliar and painful hospital procedures.

A child may also be frightened by his observations of other children with fatal illnesses or major surgical procedures. He often is unaware of the nature of his own illness and of the nature and usefulness of diagnostic tests and procedures. Also, if he faces surgery, he may view this as a sadistic violation of his body. Even the knowledge that he will receive anesthesia arouses fears that he might not wake up, or worse, wake up in the middle of a procedure helpless and in pain. Another common result of hospitalization is depression which is primarily anaclitic in nature and is particularly pronounced in younger children and in those whose parents cannot or will not spend a good deal of time with them in the hospital.

Illnesses which may prove fatal to the child are clearly distressing to everyone. To a child, the knowledge or suspicion that he will die, and the attendant fear, despair, feelings of isolation and rejection are often compounded by attitudes of hospital personnel and parents because of difficulty in managing their own feelings. Patterns, which range from overindulgence and avoidance of the truth to complete withdrawal from the child, can be seen in hospital staff as well as parents, siblings, and friends.

SEPARATIONS

One of the most critical situations to occur, especially in early childhood, and in which there is nearly always risk, is separation. The work of Spitz (1946) on separation of an infant from his mother and the resulting anaclitic depression is well known. A. Freud (1960) points out some of the results of separation in early childhood during the oedipal phase. She notes that there is regression in ego functioning and instinctual regression as well as libido redistribution. In fact, it is not surprising that there are far-reaching consequences arising from significant separation in the important early mother-child dyad.

The death of a parent is perhaps the most significant separation a child might encounter. The loss, leading to separation anxiety, anger, guilt and depression, along with the feeling of culpability, are compounded by the child's limited intellectual ability to comprehend. This leads to a bereavement which lays the foundation for possible adult emotional illness. H. Deutsch (1937) notes that the loss of a mother predisposes the child toward inadequate affective response in later life. Following the loss of a parent, there may be changes in place of residence, the introduction of new people into the child's life (step-parent and step-siblings), relative lack of parental support and guidance, or possible school problems.

Temporary loss of a parent, as when a parent is hospitalized, can also produce considerable separation anxiety and disruption of normal household functioning, which may engender anger at a parent for not providing adequate care or for perceived rejection. A child can feel left out and may find it difficult in coping with and accepting substitute caretakers as in all cases of illness or death. The child also risks a disturbance in his trust of parents if necessary information regarding the realities of what is transpiring is not shared with him. Chronic repetitive absences serve to compound these difficulties.

Separation and/or divorce of parents can also produce significant difficulties for children. Anger at one or both of the parents for allowing separation to occur is present and may be increased if one parent is particularly blameful of the other for what has occurred. Children frequently feel responsible for their parents not getting along or separating and all too often are directly or indirectly blamed for it, especially when children are used as vehicles for their parents' mutual animosity. The child is even more vulnerable in instances where there has been open hostility between the parents. Even where one parent has been particularly difficult, mentally ill, or abusive, the considerable ambivalence felt by a child concerning that parent presents great difficulty for the child. In the same vein, if a child is barred from visiting a parent, adequate resolution of conflicts, ambivalences, and anxieties cannot be accomplished. It is frequent that children will fantasize about an absent parent and imbue him or her with exaggerated features. It has been noted that parental absence is correlated with delinquency in boys. Ferenczi (1914) has noted that fatherless boys may develop a homosexual problem, tending to fantasize fathers and then seek father substitutes.

Less dramatic types of separations, which can nevertheless be traumatic and present problems for children, are separation from the mother when first entering school and problems arising in the case in which the child has a working mother. The ability of the child to separate from his mother and the ability of the mother to separate herself from the child and adequately manage the transition to a school situation, will determine whether the child can accept a mother substitute, and may set the whole tone of subsequent school performance.

Thus, the ability of a child to routinely accept temporary absence of a mother when she goes to work is similar to entering school except that the separation may occur from early infancy on. This raises serious and controversial questions concerning the possible hazards of being a working mother. Important considerations which bear on this include the extent to which the mother remains available to the child, and the provision of empathic and understanding surrogates who will not be abruptly removed.

Adoption presents its own unique problems which predispose a child to risk, and the child is vulnerable whether he knows of his adoption or not. Considerations here are related to the background of the adopted child, often unwanted or from deprived situations which may have led to poor prenatal and obstetrical care. If adopted at a later age, the child may already have been rendered vulnerable from previous poor life experiences and developmental retardation. Not only the background but the attitudes, desires and needs of the adoptive parent(s) are critical considerations. The adoptive mother does not have the usual preparatory experiences of pregnancy and labor. She may hence feel that the child was never really hers or that he can be reclaimed, or that he will eventually reject her once the truth of his parentage is known. Or, she may be concerned about the possibility of poor heredity and background. She may therefore be quite anxious, may feel that she has to be an exceptional mother, and may make excessive or inappropriate demands on the child. The child with conscious knowledge of his adoption has concerns and fears of his own, including a sense of rejection and unworthiness because of being given up, may be hypercritical of his parents and have a tendency to fantasize and even to seek out his biological parents. He may, moreover, feel vulnerable to the possibility of being given up again to other parents which may increase the usual separation fears that any child encounters. If his parents have not offered the truth about adoption from the beginning, and he later learns of it, it may be traumatic and his sense of basic trust may be damaged. Even optimal handling—that is, learning of his adoptedness slowly and in an age-appropriate fashion—is not fully protective.

Much the same is true of children in foster care, particularly if they are not allowed to communicate with their natural parents, and especially if the child experiences multiple foster homes with perhaps occasional intervals of living with the natural parents. Separation difficulties, anger, anxiety, and depression with their concommitant behavioral manifestations are not uncommon. Poor self-image, excessive dependency or pseudo-independence are also seen. The need to adapt to new homes and new children places additional strains on an already vulnerable child.

VIOLENT EVENTS

The effect on the child whose parents subject him to physical abuse, whether excessive corporal punishment, sudden violent physical attacks, or openly sadistic torture can be, and in most cases is, devastating.

The child's anger at an abusive parent, coupled with his anaclitic needs, produces conflicts which possibly may not be resolvable. Ambivalent feelings concerning a parent are, in many instances, particularly exaggerated. The child comes also to feel that he is basically bad because he is punished and abused and he can be quite overwhelmed by his feelings of wishing that his parent would be similarly abused or die. A sense of rejection, lack of trust, and grossly disturbed object relations usually ensue. Behavioral disturbances may follow, such as withdrawal or markedly aggressive behavior in the home, neighborhood, and school. The child's behavior increases his social isolation and general rejection. Academic progress is thus impeded so that adequate maturation, ego growth and cognitive capacities lag, sometimes drastically.

Child neglect without violent physical abuse tends to produce similar results. Gross neglect, generally at the hands of an incompetent, immature, psychotic, or alcoholic parent can be extremely serious—the more so the younger the child. Manifestations range from failure to thrive and/or death, to malnutrition with its attendant neurological and developmental retardation, to lesser incapacity marked by depression, withdrawal, behavioral disorders, social dysfunction, and academic disabilities as mentioned. The child as a witness to violence or to a horrifying event becomes vulnerable to subsequent dysfunction. The nature and severity of the disability depends on the type of event, its meaning to the child, and his maturational level at the time. Probably most common is the child as witness to his parents physically fighting, involving the fear that he too will be attacked. This may lead to overly strong repression of aggressive impulses. Involved also is the fear that he will lose one or both of his parents, or because of their own inability to control themselves, that they cannot be trusted to help him control his own impulses. Fear on the child's part that he is to blame for the fighting is deleterious to his self image and productive of guilt.

SPECIAL EVENTS

Certain other events in a child's life, depending on the child's level of development and general character, may to one degree or another produce higher risk. Moving or the birth of a sibling are such events. A societal event such as the assassination of President Kennedy can present problems not only from the violence of the event, as in this case, but also from the reactions of parents and society in general to the event. In this category a great many things could be included from systematic genocide, to wars, to neighborhood riots.

Classroom events or summer camp events may also present problems. Often children who already have experienced great social or academic difficulties find themselves in special classes or in special schools where the likelihood of over-stimulating or violent events is greater. Additionally such children can be greatly disturbed by the presence in the class of disturbed or physically stigmatized children. This is frequently experienced as further proof of their own inadequate or damaged state, and is threatening because of the fantasied possibility that they too could become like such children.

Sexually stimulating events take place frequently in class or out of it and sometimes at home as well. These may include primal scene observations, sexual play with other children, and overstimulation or outright sexual abuse of a child by a parent. Some of these events may be traumatic when there is family dysfunction and inadequate opportunity for the child to process his impression of such events.

TREATMENT

Preventive medicine may be subdivided into three components: primary, secondary, and tertiary prevention. Primary prevention involves preventing the occurrence of an illness; secondary, preventing the development of an illness after it occurs; and tertiary, preventing sequelae of the illness. For example, in the case of a child who is about to experience a surgical procedure, primary prevention would consist of emotional preparation of the child for surgery by parents and hospital staff as well as adequate parental support during the entire hospital stay. The aim is to minimize if not eliminate the occurrence of emotional trauma and the development of symptomatology. It must be stated that with proper preparation and support not only can emotional difficulties be minimized but it is possible that the child may even benefit emotionally from the experience through an increased sense of mastery and through ego growth. Secondary prevention involves the treatment of a psychiatric symptom which might, for instance, arise in a child because of a surgical procedure which was unduly stressful or not adequately dealt with in a primary preventive sense. An example would be the occurrence of nightmares or of behavioral problems arising from anxiety (Burton 1974, 1975). Treatment may subsequently be offered by a psychiatrist, nurse, social worker, or a carefully counseled parent. Tertiary prevention, meanwhile, concerns itself with the treatment of long-term psychiatric disturbances arising from the initial symptomatology and its eventual derivatives as well as from new difficulties attributable to the altered behavior of the child.

Recognition of what constitute potential risk situations for children and the initiation of preventive procedures is the responsibility of the community. A great many resources are in fact available, though frequently ill-coordinated. These resources include health care professionals such as pediatricians, internists, and family medicine specialists, as well as surgeons and nurses. These individuals, while frequently engaged in areas involving high risk for children, often do not recognize potential difficulties, however, or having recognized them are at a loss as to how to proceed. In most instances such professionals could themselves take the responsibility for preventive care either directly or by referral to social service workers or social service agencies. Public social service agencies may make available special services to children, as may private nonprofit agencies. Consulting services for special situations such as adoption generally exist, as do special clinics devoted to preventive care and special hospital programs (generally as a part of psychiatric or pediatric departments). Referral of patients to a psychiatrist or child psychiatrist is often helpful especially if the psychiatrist is able to coordinate all elements involved.

Other groups frequently involved in the recognition of risk situations are crisis intervention centers and emergency rooms, police and courts, educational institutions, religious organizations, day care centers, or community action programs. Liaison and consultative services between primary health care providers and such organizations should be established where they do not already exist and should be

regularly utilized. Finally, broad public education is a necessary element in the establishment of an overall and ongoing
preventive care system for children.

SUMMARY

A theoretical background concerning children at risk and
the psychologically vulnerable child has been provided and
a consideration of various types of situations which predispose a child to risk along with certain examples of dynamic
and social considerations has been offered.

Preventative measures in these various circumstances suggest themselves from the considerations mentioned, as well
as from a thorough investigation of the specific case at hand.
General concepts of preventive medicine can well be applied
in any and all of these given situations.

BIBLIOGRAPHY

Anthony, E.J. (1974). Children at psychiatric risk. In *The Child
    and His Family,* vol. 3, ed. E. J. Anthony and C. Kouper-
    nik, pp. 3–11. London: John Wiley.
Bergman, T. (1965). *Children in the Hospital.* New York: Inter-
    national Universities Press.
Burton, L. (1974). *Care of the Child Facing Death.* London:
    Routledge and Kegan Paul.
———— (1975). *The Family Life of Sick Children.* London: Rout-
    ledge and Kegan Paul.
Calef, V. (1959). On the psychological consequences of phys-
    ical disease in childhood. *Journal of the American Psy-
    choanalytic Association* 3:155–162.

Deutsch, H. (1937). Absence of grief. *Psychoanalytic Quarterly* 6:12–22.

Ferenczi, S. (1914). The nosology of male homosexuality. In *Sex in Psychoanalysis.* New York: Basic Books, 1950.

Freud, A. (1952). The role of bodily illness in the mental life of children. *Psychoanalytic Study of the Child* 7:69–82.

———— (1960). Discussion of Dr. John Bowlby's paper. *Psychoanalytic Study of the Child* 16:53–62.

Haggard, E. (1974). A theory of adaptation and the risk of trauma. In *The Child and his Family,* vol. 3, ed. E. J. Anthony and C. Koupernik, pp. 47–61. London: John Wiley.

Kliman, G. (1968). *Psychological Emergencies of Childhood.* New York: Grune and Stratton.

Murphy, L., and Moriarty, A. (1976). *Vulnerability, Coping and Growth from Infancy to Adolescence.* New Haven: Yale University Press.

Spitz, R., and Wolf, K. (1946). Anaclitic depression. *Psychoanalytic Study of the Child* 2:313–342.

Thomas, A., Chess, S., Birch, J., and Hertzig, M. (1960). A longitudinal study of primary reaction patterns in children. *Comprehensive Psychiatry* 1:103–112.

INDEX